LEADERS OF THE WORLD

BIOGRAPHICAL SERIES

General Editor: ROBERT MAXWELL, M.C.

Leonid Ilyich Brezhnev

A SHORT BIOGRAPHY

LEADERS OF THE WORLD

BIOGRAPHICAL SERIES

General Editor: ROBERT MAXWELL, M.C.

LEONID ILYICH BREZHNEV

President of the Presidium of the Supreme Soviet of the USSR, General Secretary of the Communist Party of the Soviet Union

Volumes in preparation

JIMMY CARTER

President of the United States of America

HUA GUO-FENG

Premier and Chairman of the Central Committee of the Chinese Communist Party

KURT WALDHEIM

Secretary-General of the United Nations

Workers of all countries, unite!

Leonid Ilyich Brezhnev

A SHORT BIOGRAPHY

by the Institute of Marxism-Leninism, CPSU Central Committee

Including the new Constitution of the USSR

PERGAMON PRESS

OXFORD · NEW YORK · TORONTO · SYDNEY · PARIS · FRANKFURT

U.K.	Pergamon Press Ltd , Headington Hill Hall, Oxford OX3 0BW, England
U.S.A.	Pergamon Press Inc., Maxwell House, Fairview Park, Elmsford, New York 10523, U.S.A.
CANADA	Pergamon of Canada Ltd., 75 The East Mall, Toronto, Ontario, Canada
AUSTRALIA	Pergamon Press (Aust.) Pty. Ltd., 19a Boundary Street, Rushcutters Bay, N.S.W. 2011, Australia
FRANCE	Pergamon Press SARL, 24 rue des Ecoles, 75240 Paris, Cedex 05, France
FEDERAL REPUBLIC OF GERMANY	Pergamon Press GmbH, 6242 Kronberg-Taunus, Pferdstrasse 1, Federal Republic of Germany

First Edition 1977

British Library Cataloguing in Publication Data

Institut marksizma-leninizma
Leonid Ilyich Brezhnev. -(Leaders of the World. Biographical series).
1. Brezhnev, Leonid Ilyich 2. Statesmen - Russia - Biography
I. Series
947.085'092'4 DK275.B7 77-30493

ISBN 0-08-022266-8
ISBN 0-08-022265-X pbk.

Printed in Great Britain by A. Wheaton & Co. Ltd., Exeter

Contents

List of Illustrations

Президент английской издательской фирмы "Пергамон Пресс" господин Роберт Максвелл обратился ко мне с просьбой написать предисловие к этой книге.

Сам факт, что это издательство решило познакомить своих читателей с биографическим очерком, выпущенным в 1976 году в Москве в связи с моим 70-летием, является для меня не просто по-человечески приятным. В этом факте видится нечто большее: интерес к жизни советского народа, к историческому пути советского государства, к его современным проблемам, к политике Коммунистической партии.

Жизнь каждого человека, особенно если он стремится по мере своих сил участвовать в общественно-политической деятельности, отражает прежде всего общественные идеалы, которым он служит. С молодых лет связав свою судьбу с борьбой за счастье народа, с целями Коммунистической партии Советского Союза, я тем самым, навсегда определил для себя цель и смысл жизни. Миллионы людей в нашей стране могут сказать о себе то же самое и радостно сознавать, что я, говоря словами нашего поэта, - "этой силы - частица".

Думается, что книга, которую предлагает вниманию читателей издательство "Пергамон Пресс", может раскрыть многое из того, что составляло на протяжении последних десятилетий и составляет ныне самое существо жизни моего поколения. Вместе со всей страной мы - молодые рабочие - прошли испытания и трудности в годы первых пятилеток, когда партия призвала нас в кратчайшие сроки превратить нашу страну в передовую промышленную державу. Вместе со всем народом мы - солдаты - защищали и защитили свою Родину и мир от фашизма. Вместе со всей страной мы, будучи уже зрелыми и закаленными в трудностях людьми, восстанавливали разрушенное войной народное хозяйство и вели борьбу против угрозы новой войны.

За шесть десятилетий государство наше прошло путь, равный столетиям. Быть соучастником и свидетелем такого рода свершений - большое счастье для человека.

Сейчас в пору расцвета, зрелости уже вступило первое поколение советских людей, которым не пришлось идти по дорогам войны, переносить тяготы и несчастья военного времени. И мы мечтаем о том, чтобы дети и внуки наши никогда не испытали того, что пришлось пережить нам.

В наше время люди разных стран преисполнены стремления лучше знать и понимать друг друга. И поскольку это глубоко осознанное стремление - один из факторов углубления процесса разрядки международной напряженности, каждый шаг, ведущий к упрочению такого взаимопонимания, благотворен.

Если эта небольшая книга поможет читателям других стран еще лучше понять нашу страну, оценить гуманную и созидательную сущность политики нашей Коммунистической партии, поверить в искренность и самоотверженность благородного стремления советских людей к миру, мне думается, цель, которую преследовало издательство, выпуская эту книгу на английском языке, будет достигнута.

Леонид БРЕЖНЕВ

Москва
8 сентября 1977 года

Leonid Brezhnev: Foreword to this Edition

MR. ROBERT MAXWELL, Chairman of the British publishing house Pergamon Press, has asked me if I would write a Foreword to this book.

That the publishers should have decided to acquaint their readers with the short biography issued in Moscow in connection with my seventieth birthday in 1976 is not just gratifying to me as an individual: there is more to the fact. It reveals an interest in the life of the Soviet people, in the historic road taken by the Soviet state, in its current problems, and in the policy of the Communist Party.

The life of each one of us, particularly if we are determined to play a part in social and political work to the best of our abilities, reflects above all the social ideals which that life serves. Having from first youth linked my fate with the struggle for the people's happiness, with the aims of the Communist Party of the Soviet Union, I defined for myself in so doing my entire life's aim and purpose. Millions in our country can say as much and joyously proclaim themselves, with our poet Mayakovsky, 'a fragment of that strength'.

I believe that this book, brought to the reader's attention by Pergamon Press, can reveal much of what has constituted over the past decades, and still does today, the very substance of my generation's life. Together with the whole country, we as young workers went through the testing hardships of the period of the first five-year plans, when the Party called on us to transform our land, in the shortest imaginable time, into a leading industrial power. Together with the whole people, we as soldiers defended our homeland and the world from fascism. Together with the whole country, we as adults, by now matured and hardened from our trials, restored the war-torn national economy and stood firm against the threat of another war.

In the last six decades our State has traversed a road equal to that of centuries. It is one's good fortune to have been a contributor and a witness to such achievements.

Today the first generation of Soviet people not to have had to undergo the burdens and suffering of war is at full maturity. And we hope that our children and grandchildren will never experience what we had to live through.

In our time, the people of different countries long to know and understand each other better. And in so far as this deeply felt longing is one of the factors of increased *détente*, each step towards cementing such mutual understanding is good.

If this little book helps readers in other countries to understand better our land, to appreciate the human, creative essence of our Party's policy, to trust in the frankness and self-denial behind the noble desire of the Soviet people for peace, then I believe that the Publisher's aim in producing it in English will be achieved.

Moscow
8 September 1977 LEONID BREZHNEV

1

Early Years

The Soviet people are giving effect to the plans outlined by the great Lenin and confidently advancing towards their highest goal—communism. Today, with mature socialism achieved, their creative energy and strengths are unfolding in all their fullness. The Soviet Union is stronger than ever before and its influence on the course of world history more marked. The historic achievements of the Soviet Union's mature socialism have now been given legislative enactment in the new Soviet Constitution which has come as a concentrated result of the sixty years of the Soviet State.

Monumental progress in building communism has been made by the Soviet people under the leadership of the Communist Party, its Central Committee and Politburo headed by the General Secretary of the Communist Party of the Soviet Union's Central Committee, Leonid Ilyich Brezhnev.

This distinguished leader of the Communist Party and the Soviet State, this outstanding personality in the international communist and working-class movement is one of the political leaders brought up and tempered during the years of the Soviet people's dedicated work of consolidating the gains of the Great October Socialist Revolution and building socialism.

The classics of Marxism - Leninism showed the decisive role of the masses in the making of history and the world historic mission of the working class and its political vanguard the Communist Party, and invariably noted the enormous significance of tested proletarian leaders capable of heading the masses in bold revolutionary action, in the great work of building communism. 'Not a single class in history,' wrote Lenin, 'has achieved power without producing its political leaders, its prominent representatives able to organize a movement and lead it.'

The leading role of the Party of the working class and the role and responsibility of its leaders naturally increased with the victory of socialism, when unprecedented scope was given to the planned creative work of the people. The working class and the people as a whole promote to the leadership the most outstanding, knowledgeable, and experienced of their number, those who are capable of getting to the root of social developments and organizing the masses to fulfil the great tasks of building communism.

In just this way, Leonid Brezhnev represents the working class and the entire Soviet people and is a leader of the Lenin type. He has devoted all his life and energy to the service of the working people and has always been bound to them by close and unbreakable ties. Wherever the Communist Party has sent him, he has worked with his usual indomitable drive and perseverance for its great cause. To Communists and to hundreds of millions of people all over the world, his name stands for Leninist adherence to principle, unswerving internationalism, and selfless struggle for peace and social progress.

His versatile, tireless, and productive work is an inspiring example of utter devotion to the socialist homeland, to Lenin's party, and the great cause of communism.

LEONID ILYICH BREZHNEV was born into a working man's family on 19 December 1906 in the town of Dneprodzerzhinsk ('Kamenskoye' until 1936), a major centre of the metallurgical industry in the Ukraine. His father, Ilya Yakovlevich Brezhnev, came from the Kursk Gubernia and worked at an iron and steel plant almost all his life, first as an unskilled labourer and then as a rolling-mill operator. Leonid Brezhnev took his first job at this same factory, where his grandfather, brother, and sister

The Brezhnev family in 1930. Third from left in the front row is Ilya Yakovlevich; at far right is Brezhnev's mother Natalya Denisovna. Behind them, at far left, Leonid Ilyich.

also worked. The Brezhnev family gave the factory many decades of their active life.

It is common knowledge that before the Revolution the son of a working man, if he was to get an education, had to be exceptionally gifted, assiduous, and persevering. These were the qualities that enabled Leonid Brezhnev to enrol in a secondary school which after the Revolution became a school for working men's children. On leaving it at the age of 15 he took a job at the factory, where he continued his education. There, among a large body of workers, he underwent his first real test as the prelude to a busy and eventful life.

Today, the gate which Leonid Ilyich passed through to work no longer exists: the factory, like the town itself, has changed beyond recognition. But the workers still cherish the memory of the glorious

Leonid Brezhnev in 1930.

deeds of those unforgettable years, of the people who worked here at the time.

The workers of Dneprodzerzhinsk have always had high standards of political consciousness and organization. These qualities were assimilated by Brezhnev. 'The way of life at the plant,' he said, 'the thoughts and hopes of working people and their approach to life—all this had a decisive influence in forming my world outlook. What was established then has stayed with me all my life.' Brezhnev remains grateful to the veteran workers who were his teachers and to the town of his childhood, where he spent his adolescence as a Komsomol and his early manhood as a Communist Party member. Speaking to workers of the Likhachev car factory in Moscow on the eve of May Day 1976, Brezhnev spoke with warmth of his days among the work force, of his colleagues of the time who had helped him acquire his first trade and who had introduced him to the complex science of life. 'A never-to-be-forgotten university', said Leonid Ilyich on that occasion.

Brezhnev began his working life at a time when the young Soviet State, having upheld the gains of the Great October Revolution, was making a start on the building of a new society. Those were the formative years of the first generation of builders of socialism who laid the foundations of a powerful socialist industry, who were remodelling the country's agriculture on socialist lines and carrying out a cultural revolution—the generation whose youth belongs to the heroic time of the first five-year plans (*pyatiletki*).

In those years, the Party was engaged on the tremendously important task of bringing the USSR, by means of socialist industrialization, as soon as possible up to the level of the leading industrial world powers. Led by the Party, the working class boldly scaled the summits of industrialization. The basic problems within such a task were resolved in less than fifteen years. By the beginning of the 1940s the Soviet Union had a ramified socialist industry, its gross industrial product and machine-to-worker ratio matching those of the advanced capitalist countries of Europe.

This heroic advance of the Soviet people during the first *pyatiletki* was made in the face of unprecedented difficulties and was an expression of their high consciousness and dedication. This was a period of bitter class battles, a period marked by the unrelenting struggle for socialism, for the general line of the Communist Party and its Central Committee. Trends hostile to Leninism and the savage resistance of world capitalism were overwhelmed in this struggle. Despite all difficulties and privations, the Soviet people worked with enthusiasm and self-sacrifice.

The socialist emulation movement, an efficiency campaign, began all over the country. Records in work were set by Alexei Stakhanov, Pyotr Krivonos, Pasha Angelina, Makar Mazai, Maria and Evdokia Vinogradova, and other heroes of the early five-year plans. 'The staunchness and courage of these people, and their unswerving devotion to the Party's cause, to the cause of socialism,' Brezhnev has said, 'are to this day an inspiring example that lives on in the valorous deeds of the working class of the entire Soviet people, who are building new factories and power stations, developing the expanses of Siberia and the Soviet Far East, bringing forth epoch-making scientific discoveries, and, by their labour, continuing the glorious traditions of the first *pyatiletki*.'

In those years, the upbringing of young people was strongly influenced by the revolutionary enthusiasm and optimism that was inspiring the working class and all other working people to storm the old world and build a new life. Young people were raised and toughened by the Communist Party, under whose leadership the difficulties of the first years of socialist construction were overcome. In his time, Lenin had stressed that ideological conviction hardens in people when they face difficulties, and the gains of the Revolution are thereby more firmly consolidated. This also applied to Leonid Brezhnev when a member of the Young Communist League (Komsomol) and later when a young Party member. At the age of 17, caught up in the fervour of those heroic days, he joined the Komsomol. In 1929 he became a probationary member and in 1931 a full member of the Communist Party. Henceforth his goal in life was to serve with utter devotion the great cause of the Communist Party—the cause of communism.

In 1927 he graduated from a land-improvement technical school in Kursk and then worked as a land surveyor in Byelorussia, the Kursk Gubernia, and the Urals. This grounding served him well, revealing and developing his abilities as an organizer and giving him practical knowledge of agriculture and of the problems of the countryside.

The young land surveyor won the respect of working people, and was elected to the Bisertsky District Soviet of Working Peoples' Deputies, Sverdlovsk Region, where he was appointed head of the district land department and then deputy chairman of the executive committee. His knowledge, energy, and talent for organization were recognized, and he was made assistant chief of the regional land department.

In the late 1920s and early 1930s, when Soviet industrialization began, there was a demand for hundreds of thousands of trained specialists. The Party ran the slogan: 'During the reconstruction everything depends on trained specialists!' This amounted to a call for the creation of a new scientific and technical intelligentsia. Communists with practical experience, with a knowledge of life, were sent by the Party to study at higher technical training establishments.

In 1931 Brezhnev returned to his home town, where he enrolled in the metallurgical institute, at the same time working as a fitter at the Dzerzhinsky factory. He was elected chairman of the trade union committee and then secretary of the institute's Party committee.

In 1933 Brezhnev was appointed head of the workers' evening school which was later reorganized as a technical school. It was no easy

The 1935 graduating class, Dneprodzerzhinsk Institute (Brezhnev at left in front row).

matter for him to combine full-time employment with intensive study. But then Brezhnev had always had an immense capacity for work and an ability to use his time rationally. In 1935 *Znamya Dzerzhinki,* the factory newspaper, ran an article entitled 'He is a Bolshevik'. 'I cannot imagine,' the author wrote, 'where this young man gets his brimming energy and stamina. Up till a month ago he was head of the factory's evening school. The strain on him was enormous. He also studied at our institute. He is our best Party group organizer . . . and his graduation thesis was accounted the best of his year' . . .

'As he goes out into full-time production work, the young engineer shows great promise. And he will live up to it . . . because he is made of the right material.'

When he finished at the institute with honours in 1935, Brezhnev went on to work at the factory as shift leader, in the very workshop where he had started out as fitter. Shortly afterwards he was called up into the army. He did his tour of active duty in the Transbaikal Military District as a cadet of an armoured warfare school to begin with, and later as a political instructor of a tank company, one of the best in the regiment; after this spell of army duty, he returned to his home town.

From November 1936 Brezhnev was head of the Dneprodzerzhinsk Metallurgical Technical School. In 1937 he was elected deputy chairman of the Dneprodzerzhinsk City Soviet's executive council. In that post, his energy, his creative approach to work, and his concern for people—their needs and their requirements—earned him the profound respect of the townsfolk. A year later he was appointed to Party work: first he was a department head, and then in February 1939 he was elected propaganda secretary of the Dnepropetrovsk Regional Committee of the Communist Party of the Ukraine.

Together with the other officials of the committee, Brezhnev ran extensive campaigns among the Communists and all working people for the successful implementation of the tasks set by the Party, giving much of his time to Communists, workers in town and countryside, and young people, educating them in the spirit of Marxism - Leninism, proletarian internationalism, and wholehearted loyalty to the socialist homeland.

The international situation was explosive in those years; the atmosphere was charged with the threat of imperialist aggression. With the Soviet Union encircled by hostile capitalist states, the Party took steps to increase the country's defence capability and enlarge the defence industry.

In 1940 the Dnepropetrovsk Regional Committee was instructed by the CPSU Central Committee to switch some of the region's factories over to armaments. The post of regional committee secretary for the defence industry was created by the Dnepropetrovsk committee to direct this new branch of industry. It called for someone who was not only a competent and technically trained specialist, but also a talented organizer capable of inspiring people to work hard. The choice fell on Leonid Brezhnev.

In the tense situation caused by the outbreak of the Second World War and the ever-growing threat of imminent military attack on the Soviet Union, the question of running industry, particularly its defence branches, became of paramount importance to the Communist Party.

Brezhnev as a student, Armoured Warfare School, Transbaikal Military District, 1936.

The 18th All-Union Party Conference, held in February 1941, reviewed the tasks of Communist Party branches in industry and transport, recommending them to step up the preparedness of these leading sectors of the economy. The conference gave the closest attention to the defence industry, mapping out a wide-ranging programme for its development. The CPSU Central Committee and the Soviet Government gave effect to a series of organizational measures which considerably increased the Soviet Union's military and economic potential on the eve of war.

The Dnepropetrovsk Regional Party Committee likewise contributed to the joint efforts of the Communist Party and the people. Documents from the period, including reports of the committee for the first six months of 1941, have been preserved. Between the lines we glimpse the unremitting work done by the people of Dnepropetrovsk in helping to strengthen their country's defence and in organizing the production of armaments.

As the regional committee's secretary for the defence industry, Brezhnev put his knowledge and skills to furthering this key branch of the economy. When necessary, the regional committee sought aid from the CPSU Central Committee, the Government, and the appropriate people's commissariats (ministries). One example is a telegram dated 7 May 1941, which informed the Minister for Aircraft Industry that the dispatch of technical documentation and special machine tools to one of the Dnepropetrovsk defence factories had been delayed. The telegram ended with the words: 'REQUEST IMMEDIATE ASSISTANCE TO ENSURE VITAL EQUIPMENT, TOOLS, AND MATERIALS FOR THE FACTORY. L. I. BREZHNEV, SECRETARY FOR DEFENCE INDUSTRY, DNEPROPETROVSK REGIONAL COMMITTEE, COMMUNIST PARTY, UKRAINE.' Assistance soon came.

Many difficulties were met with in developing and enlarging the defence industry, but all obstacles gave way before Bolshevik determination backed by the enthusiasm and patriotism of the people. The munitions factories gained strength quickly. Some factories which had been manufacturing exclusively civilian goods switched to the production of armaments and military equipment in record time, and began supplying them in steadily growing quantities.

2

War Service 1941 - 1945

ON 22 June 1941 Nazi Germany launched her treacherous invasion of the Soviet Union. Responding to the call of the Party, the Soviet people rose as one to fight the fascist invaders to the death. This was a stern test for the socialist Soviet Union. Socialism's great gains were in deadly danger. To avert that menace, Party and people had to make a colossal effort and show unprecedented firmness, with indomitable courage and valour at the front and self-sacrificing work at home.

In the spirit of Lenin's injunctions on the defence of the socialist homeland, the Communist Party set about turning the country into a single fighting unit. The Central Committee and the Government drew up and launched a far-ranging programme to put the country on a war footing and mobilize the people to defeat the enemy. This programme was formulated in a directive of 29 June 1941 from the Council of People's Commissars and the Central Committee to Party and government bodies in the front-line regions.

The objectives were:

— To defend every inch of Soviet territory in a relentless struggle with the enemy and fight for our Soviet homeland to the last drop of blood; to put everything into the sole aim of defeating the fascist invaders.

- To strengthen the armed forces to the utmost and organize comprehensive assistance to troops in the field.
- To subordinate all the work of the people to the needs of the front, gear the economy to war requirements, and raise output for the front to its maximum.
- To start a people's struggle in territory seized by the enemy, create intolerable conditions for the Nazi troops in that territory, and weaken their rear as much as possible.
- To devote all ideological and political work to the task of mobilizing the spiritual strength of the people for victory.

The job of the Soviet armed forces was to weaken the enemy in defensive battles, drive him out of Soviet territory, and help the peoples of Europe shake off fascist tyranny. The Party's slogan 'Everything for the front, everything for victory!' set the pattern of life during the war. This slogan became the battle-cry of the Soviet people.

The Communist Party's titanic work yielded tangible results during the very first months of the war. The single fighting unit was achieved. Faith in victory inspired the troops at the front, the partisans and underground fighters in enemy-held territory, the workers in the rear. Communists were everywhere in the forefront, inspiring and leading the people by their own example both in work and in battle.

It was vital in those days to strengthen the Party's leadership of the armed forces, to enhance the role of political organs and Party branches in the army and navy. Parallel with the general mobilization, the Party Committees, on instructions from the Central Committee, selected and sent to the front those Communists and Komsomol members who in the military sense were the best trained. More than a million Communists and upwards of two million Komsomol members reinforced the Soviet army and navy during the first six months of war.

By decision of the Central Committee, many prominent Party officials —Central Committee members and alternate members—were sent to the armed forces. Nearly one-third of the CPSU Central Committee, and many secretaries of the central committees of the Republican communist parties and the territorial and regional committees, joined the troops in the field. One of them was Leonid Brezhnev.

Before leaving for the front, Brezhnev, like the regional committee's other ranking officials, did much during the first and most difficult weeks of the war to place the region's economy on a war footing and mobilize as many of its resources as possible to meet military requirements and, when the enemy approached the Dnieper, to evacuate industrial concerns to the east. He took a particularly active part in everything to do with mobilization and in mustering units of volunteers in the Dnepropetrovsk Region. There, general mobilization went off according to plan. Five divisions, a 100,000-strong volunteer corps, and battalions of assault troops were formed in the course of a single month.

A participant in the events of those years, recalling the formation of the 255th Division, wrote that Brezhnev 'and other leaders of the regional committee made sure that the newly formed division and other units defending the town were properly armed. . . . Our troops were of a special kind, for the most part from Dnepropetrovsk proletarian families, Komsomol students from Dnepropetrovsk University and other institutions, Party officials, and factory engineers. Among us were factory managers, university lecturers, and others with high positions, but all joined the ranks as privates. True, these were soldiers of a special kind: known as political fighters, they all were members either of the Party or the Komsomol, and they considered it their prime duty to be the first into the attack, thus setting an example to the rest. They were the flower and mainstay of our forces. Many of them to my knowledge were sent by Brezhnev to defend the town. He had known them personally before the war, and they knew and respected him as a Communist and a Party leader in the true sense of the word.'

As soon as war broke out, Brezhnev insistently sought higher Party authority to join the troops in the field. This came through in July. A note on the list of regional committee officials issued with weapons states: 'Comrade Brezhnev is now serving in the armed forces.' This document is dated 14 July 1941. From that time onwards Brezhnev served in the army to the end of hostilities, doing his duty honourably as a Communist and soldier right through the war.

Many glorious episodes in the annals of the war are associated with Brezhnev. As deputy chief of the Southern Front's political department and then as chief of the political department of the 18th Army and of the 4th Ukrainian Front, he took an active part in planning and carrying

As deputy chief of the Southern Front's political department, addressing soldiers before battle, 1942.

through many of the Soviet Army's major operations in the Caucasus, Black Sea region, Crimea, and the Ukraine, and subsequently in liberation campaigns outside the USSR. He was known in the army as an experienced political worker and a man of great spirit and courage.

From the very outbreak of war the Communist Party took steps to intensify Party and political work in the services. The entire thrust of military councils, political organs, Party branches in the armed forces, and the Military Commissars as an institution, went against the fascist invaders, gearing Party and political activity to the war situation, instilling in Soviet troops a spirit of utter devotion to the socialist homeland and hatred for its enemies, towards sharpening order and discipline in the armed forces, and increasing the fighting capacity of the troops.

Acting on instructions from the Central Committee, the Chief Political Administration of the Soviet Army, functioning as a division of the Central Committee and the political departments of the several fronts, issued directives to services' political organs and Party branches on questions of Party and political work. One such directive, from the Southern Front's political propaganda department dated 4 July 1941, states: 'Political organs will mobilize personnel for selfless and heroic struggle to destroy the enemy who has invaded our country, and foster readiness to defend our towns and villages, every inch of our land, to the last drop of blood. Decisive in this battle with German fascism are discipline, organization, and the summoning of total moral and physical strength of personnel to defeat the enemy.'

During the initial and most bitter period of the war, Brezhnev, as deputy chief of the Southern Front's political department, concentrated all his energy on organizing Party and political work in the fighting units. The political organs and Party branches in his charge stimulated the morale, political consciousness, fortitude, and courage of the troops in the heavy fighting.

A.D. Kutsenko, a retired major who served in the 18th Army, relates: 'I remember the first grim months of the war. . . . Soviet troops gave of their utmost, displaying heroism on a large scale. There was a growing stream of applications in all units to join Lenin's Party. I am proud that in that time of trial my Party card was handed to me by Comrade Leonid Ilyich Brezhnev.

'It was a long road from those firing-lines to our great victory, a road marked by thousands of battles and losses. But we believed implicitly that that day would come, with a faith given us by the Communists, by political workers such as Brezhnev. Officers and men respected him for his self-control, composure, and ability to read the most complex military situation, to sense the mood of the soldiers, boost their morale for ever-greater valour.'

In hard-fought defensive battles the troops of the Southern Front bled

Handing a soldier his Party card, 1942.

the enemy's finest divisions, disrupting his strategic plans for a blitzkrieg. The Front's political organs and the Army Party branches did their share in fulfilling the military objectives. In November 1941 the Southern Front launched a counter-offensive in the vicinity of Rostov, pinning down large enemy forces during the crucial days of the great battle near Moscow. Throughout this period Brezhnev as deputy chief of the Front's political department was with the troops operating in the main line of the advance.

Thanks to the all-embracing political work maintained by the Party among the troops, the morale of the Soviet officers and men remained high despite the incredible difficulties of the initial period of the war and the men and their commanders were confident of their ability to stem the Nazi aggressors' advance, turn the tide, destroy the enemy and liberate their homeland. Political officers and the Communists among the troops always set an example of staunchness and courage on the battlefield.

In March 1942 Brezhnev was awarded his first Order of the Red Banner in recognition of his exemplary performance during the fighting in the sector allotted to the Southern Front in the course of the Baravenkovo-Lozov operation. The citation read, 'He is deputy chief of the Front's political department, in which capacity he has displayed considerable skill as organizer, putting every ounce of his energy into the work . . .

'Comrade Brezhnev has often visited the troops at their battle stations, mobilizing the rank and file, political workers and commanders to defeat the enemy. Comrade Brezhnev is a fearless political worker.'

The struggle for the Caucasus came simultaneously with the historic battle of Stalingrad in the summer of 1942. The enemy threw in twenty-six picked divisions, eight of them aimed at the Black Sea coast. The German High Command planned to seize the oil-rich Caucasus and the wheat-growing areas of the Don and the Kuban for their resources in prosecuting the war.

At enormous cost, the Germans reached the foothills of the Caucasus and the coast of the Black Sea. In September 1942 they broke through to Novorossiisk, where one of the war's most savage battles was fought.

The city of Novorossiisk was an impregnable fortress blocking the way to the Nazi invaders. Although Soviet troops had to abandon a large part of the city, in the vicinity of the cement factories they set up a line of fire that brought the offensive to a standstill. The enemy was never to use the port of Novorossiisk and not a single Nazi warship entered it. The city became one of the decisive battlefields in the struggle for the Caucasus.

The battle for Novorossiisk has gone down in the history of the war as a shining example of the Soviet people's inflexible will to victory, their valour in battle, and total devotion to the Communist Party and the socialist homeland. The Nazi defeat at Novorossiisk set in motion the collapse of the enemy's powerful defensive fortifications, the so-called 'Blue Line', and was a large factor in the expulsion of the enemy from the Taman Peninsula and the subsequent offensive to free the Crimea.

As on all other fronts, the Party was the heart and fighting brain in the battle for Novorossiisk. Everywhere, whether in the ranks of the troops or the people's volunteers, whether among partisan units or in factories, its loyal and devoted sons gave examples of unshakable ideological conviction, organization, and discipline.

The military political instructors spoke for the Party to soldiers and sailors. In the 18th Task Army, commanded by K. N. Leselidze (member of the Military Council S. E. Kolonin, Chief-of-Staff N.O. Pavlovsky), the instructors as from April 1943 were headed by Brezhnev as chief of the political department.

The North Caucasian Front, of which the 18th Army was a part, and units of the Black Sea Fleet fought bitter battles against the enemy forces outnumbering them. The working people of the North Caucasus and Transcaucasus, the partisan units, and the underground fighters all helped the military units defending the Caucasus to inflict crushing counter-blows on the enemy.

Troops of the 18th Army fought with exemplary courage for Novorossiisk. Eternal glory was won by the heroes of the legendary 'Little Land', a small bridgehead on the western shore of Tsemesskaya Bay captured on 4 February 1943 by a task force under T. L. Kunikov. The bloody fighting on this tiny patch of land less than 30 kilometres square lasted for 225 days. At first, the enemy's superiority in men and armaments was ten to one. There were days when in some sectors the Nazis mounted up to twenty attacks, firing between 8000 and 10,000 shells and flying as many as 2500 combat missions. The small bridgehead came under hurricane fire from dozens of artillery and mortar battalions. It pinned down large enemy numbers, keeping them constantly on the alert and eventually playing an important part in annihilating the enemy grouping around Novorossiisk.

On the Little Land, men dug in side by side, ready to fight to the end. It was the political instructors, Communists, and Komsomol members who did most to raise and sustain the morale of the troops. There were Party and Komsomol branches in all units. Their day-to-day work among the men was skilfully guided by the 18th Army's political department headed by Brezhnev as colonel. Over half the department was constantly with the troops on the Little Land.

Brezhnev regularly visited the bridgehead, usually when the situation there was ominous and the fighting at its height. The defenders invariably welcomed him. He was always smart in appearance and cheerful, with a warm, friendly smile for everyone. By his words and deeds, personal bravery, unflinching presence of mind, deep ideological conviction, and steadfast commitment to communist principles, he inspired

As chief of the political department, 18th Army, Brezhnev (far right) with officers on the 'Little Land', 1943.

the men to surpass their own bravery.

The only way to reach the bridgehead was by sea, and every trip was fraught with danger. Hardly a single launch or motorboat got there and back unscathed. Many ships were damaged or sunk by artillery fire, torpedoes, or night bombers. During one such journey, Brezhnev was on a fishing boat proceeding from Gelenjik to the bridgehead near Myskhako when the vessel struck a mine. The shock wave of the explosion swept him overboard to be rescued by the crew.

During this bitter fighting, Brezhnev shared all the sorrows, joys, hardships, and perils of those holding the bridgehead. His optimism, dynamic energy, and vitality braced them like a tonic, giving them fresh confidence. They knew him by sight and often heard his calm voice amid the roar of battle.

Before one of the attacks, he said to the troops: 'A Soviet man may be killed, but never conquered.'

When visiting the units he was always alert to the conditions under which men and officers were living, and made sure they had everything they needed. On his instructions, the Army's political department repeatedly inspected the supply units, keeping an eye on their work and helping them deal with any shortcomings.

'I particularly remember those days in April, when the enemy had been ordered to smash the bridgehead's defenders at all costs and drive them into the sea,' said Brezhnev on the occasion when the hero-city of Novorossiisk was decorated with the Order of Lenin and the Gold Star Medal. 'I remember 17 April 1943. On that day the Nazis hurled enormous masses of aircraft, artillery and several infantry divisions against our troops on the Little Land. The earth burnt; metal melted; and concrete shattered. The heroes of Little Land beat back this furious onslaught for eight successive days and nights. The Nazis' countless attacks disintegrated before our men's iron determination. After those battles, the Nazis called the defenders of the Little Land "triple Communists".'

At all phases of the struggle for the Caucasus, Brezhnev was active in planning and carrying out the defensive and offensive operations. He was among the initiators of the bold plan for a commando operation in September 1943, using 18th Army units by land and the Black Sea Fleet by sea with the objective of liberating Novorossiisk from the Nazis. The operation was minutely planned and discussed by the Army Command, naval chiefs, and leading political workers.

All Party and political work in the units was focused on preparing the men for the commando operation. A directive signed personally by Brezhnev stressed that 'commanders, their political deputies and Party and Komsomol branches must firmly bear in mind that the success of this operation will in many respects depend on the quality and scale of Party and political work'. The directive called on political instructors to display the maximum energy, initiative, and efficiency, and set examples of courage and valour to the troops.

Brezhnev toured the units and followed the training of the commandos. He appointed as instructors veterans of the battles for Odessa, Sevastopol, and Kerch, and battle-hardened men and officers from the Little Land. They were withdrawn from the firing-line and trained new troops in the art of commando warfare.

Personnel meetings were held in all Party and Komsomol branches in the companies on the day before the operation. Political instructors were appointed to units of the first wave of the task force. They were to be first ashore from the launches under enemy fire, first to carry the flag, and first into the attack. Many came forward for this honour.

During the operation the political instructors in the spearhead units kept the troops' spirit up to fighting pitch. The commandos overwhelmed enemy resistance and grafted ahead, fighting magnificently.

The political organs and Party branches in the Army and the commando units revealed political maturity, efficiency, and the ability to lead men under difficult conditions. At the height of the fighting, Brezhnev noted that Party and political work behind the operation was 'making itself felt in the fighting today in the swiftness and tenacity of the offensive actions of the commandos'.

Just before and during the days of the assault, thousands of troops applied for membership of the Party. Brezhnev personally visited regiment after regiment and handed Party cards to the commandos. It is particularly interesting to note that the number of applications for Party membership increased as the tension of the military situation grew. On 1 September 1943 the 18th Army had 14,206 Communists in 331 primary and 603 company Party branches. In a single month, from 1 to 30 September, more than 1800 men were admitted to membership. Each of them was in the foremost ranks of the embattled units.

On 16 September 1943, units of the North Caucasian Front and the Black Sea Fleet drove out the last of the enemy troops from Novorossiisk.

The work of the 18th Army's political department was highly praised by the Military Council, and many of the staff—including their chief, Colonel Brezhnev—were decorated with battle orders.

The Soviet Army foiled the German High Command's strategic plans for the conquest of the Caucasus. In the battles for that area the Nazis lost 400,000 officers and men and a large quantity of equipment and armaments. 'The heroism of our soldiers,' Brezhnev said in his speech in Novorossiisk, 'proved as insurmountable as the peaks of the Caucasian Mountains.' The troops defending the Caucasus prevented the Nazi invaders from transferring large forces from the Caucasus to Stalingrad.

Following the defeat of the Nazi troops at Novorossiisk, the 18th Army crushed the enemy resistance at the western spurs of the main Caucasian range, advanced along the shore of the Black Sea, drove the enemy out of Anapa, and joined in the liberation of the Taman Peninsula.

The battle of Kerch, in which the 18th Army took part, makes a glorious page in the history of the war. At the town's approaches, the enemy had built deeply echeloned defences well covered by air and sea. The sea approaches were heavily mined.

Preparations for the battle of Kerch began while the liberation of the Taman Peninsula was still in progress. Brezhnev drew the attention of political instructors and of Communists among the men to the need for making the utmost use of the Novorossiisk experience. He formed the political department's personnel into special groups and assigned them to the different units. On his instructions, seminars were held in all units to study the lessons of Party and political work done during the commando operations.

Before the task force groups began their landing, Brezhnev toured each of them, inspecting their preparedness and talking to the men. Knowing that he had taken part in the Novorossiisk commando operation, the men paid special attention to his advice.

The Kerch Peninsula was liberated from the Nazis after heavy and prolonged fighting. The culminating phase of the Kerch operation went through without the 18th Army, which had been transferred to the 1st Ukrainian Front; but its experience of training troops for combat and giving them political instruction was put to good use by other units.

The victories at Kursk and on the Dnieper enabled the Soviet Army to launch a successful offensive west of the Dnieper in the Ukraine. The enemy's aim of consolidating his position along the Dnieper was thwarted by a powerful assault mounted by Soviet troops and partisans. The attempts by the enemy command to strike a counter-blow from the vicinity of Zhitomir towards Kiev ended in failure. General Headquarters watched the plan and actions of the enemy closely and took the appropriate steps to block them. The Zhitomir - Kiev sector was seen as particularly dangerous, and the finest units were transferred to that area. Among them, the 18th Army was moved to Kiev to reinforce units of the 1st Ukrainian Front under General N. F. Vatutin, with orders to cover the main sector of that front—the Kiev - Zhitomir highway—and then mount a counter-offensive.

The 1st Ukrainian Front Command, the commands of the different armies, the political organs, and Party branches all went about preparing the troops thoroughly to resume the offensive. The 18th Army's political department also threw itself into this work.

On 11 December 1943 it reported to Front Command the inadequate provision of food and winter uniforms to units, and breaks in the supply of ammunition and provisions. A request was made for the necessary assistance.

A week later Brezhnev reported to the Front's political department that there had been gratifying improvements in supplies to the 18th Army. 'During the last few days,' he wrote, 'we have received a large quantity of felt boots, sheepskin coats, padded jackets, sweaters and warm trousers. These have been issued to the troops at the advance firing-lines. The food situation is improved. We have received fats and tinned food and have arranged for grain to be milled and bread to be baked. Hot meals are being issued twice daily.' The report ended: 'Morale in the Army is good. The privates, NCOs, and officers have one idea—to carry out as well as possible their battle assignment in the forthcoming offensive. The political organs and the Party and Komsomol branches are doing everything to ensure the successful fulfilment of Command's combat mission.'

Brezhnev was tireless in his concern for the health and morale of the troops. Thus a directive addressed by him to all personnel of the 18th Army political department three days before the new offensive: 'Make sure to safeguard the health and strength of the troops. Regular hot meals for the men must be standard procedure. There must be the strictest control to make sure that men and officers receive everything issued for them by the State. Anyone sloppy or uncaring in this respect is to be severely dealt with. Special care must be given to the work of medical units. The political departments of the formations must assign personnel responsible for the evacuation of wounded from the battlefield and for timely medical attention to them.'

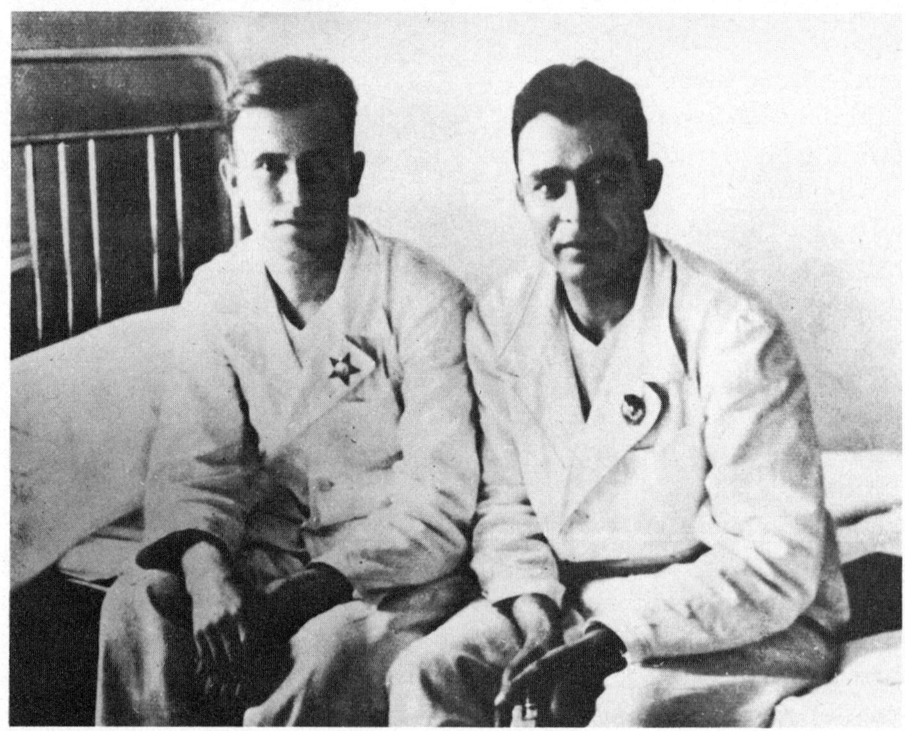

In hospital, 1943.

In December 1943 the Soviet forces resumed their offensive west of the Dnieper. The 1st Ukrainian Front, which operated in one of the main sectors, inflicted a major defeat on the Nazis. The western regions of the Ukraine were liberated and the way cleared for the liberation of Poland. The 18th Army, which was on the left flank, reached the foothills of the Carpathians. The 4th Ukrainian Front, to which the 18th Army was assigned in August 1944, was formed for the advance in the Carpathians, which required special training, equipment, and arms.

The army pushed its victorious offensive along the entire length of the extended Soviet-German front so as to expel all the fascist invaders from the Soviet Union. The heroic efforts of the troops in sectors where the 18th Army operated all went into the great struggle of the Soviet people and their armed forces for total victory over Nazi Germany.

As it advanced westward, the Soviet army liberated several European peoples from fascist enslavement. The troops were anxious to discharge their internationalist duty with dignity and honour, and they entered the territory of these foreign countries as liberators, friends, and brothers.

This new phase of the war, the phase of European liberation, of military operations outside the Soviet Union, brought the political leadership of the armed forces new tasks and made higher demands on Party and political work as a whole.

During this great campaign Brezhnev, as chief of Army and Front political departments, took part in liberating Czechoslovakia, Poland, and Hungary. As chief of the political department of the 18th Army and then of the 4th Ukrainian Front, he was tireless and skilful in directing the work of the political organs and Party and Komsomol branches towards the fulfilment of the new military and political tasks facing the armed forces in their European campaign. Political organs, army Communists, and all Soviet troops made it their concern to explain the noble aims of the Soviet army to the populations of the countries that were liberated.

When Soviet troops approached Czechoslovak soil at the foothills of the Carpathians, they were accompanied by the Czechoslovak Corps commanded by General Ludvik Svoboda. Soviet troops and their Czech comrades were hurrying to the assistance of the anti-fascist uprising in Slovakia. At a friendly meeting between Soviet and Czechoslovak troops, Brezhnev said: 'Dear Czech friends and comrades-in-arms, rest assured that Soviet troops will spare neither effort nor life itself to defeat the enemy. Czechoslovakia will be free. Though much remains to be done, victory is in sight.'

Recalling those stirring and anxious days, Ludvik Svoboda, by now President of Czechoslovakia, said: 'At the end of August 1944, when a popular anti-fascist rising broke out in Slovakia, the Red Army Command decided to help it at once and for this purpose to effect a breakthrough across the Carpathians. We Czechoslovaks were attached to the Soviet 38th Army under Colonel-General Moskalenko with the task of storming the German fortifications in the Dukla Pass, beyond which our homeland lay. As the battle unfolded we were transferred to the Soviet 1st Guards Army under Colonel-General Grechko, which was fighting in the same area. . . . The 18th Army, whose command was soon taken over by Lieutenant-General Gastilovich, whom I had known since the battles for Belaya Tserkov, advanced to the south of us to help the Slovak patriots. Among the top command personnel of that Army I also knew the chief of its political department, Colonel Brezhnev, who was later promoted to Major-General.* All the commanders were gifted, battle-hardened officers. They sincerely wanted to help the people of my country and we respected them deeply for this.'

We know something of the operations of the 18th Army and the work of its political organs and Party branches from documents of that period, including the tersely laconic but highly significant reports from the Army's political department chief. One such report states: 'On 18 September, in the face of enemy resistance and overcoming the natural barriers in the forest-clad mountain locality, our troops reached the Czechoslovak frontier. . . . There are no roads over the terrain where the fighting is. Personnel are displaying supreme courage, great physical endurance, and excellent preparedness. Our soldiers are skilfully infiltrating in small groups deep into the enemy's defences, outflanking and destroying his resistance strongholds. The enemy is suffering heavy losses in men and supplies.'

Another report tells us: 'During the last ten days, from 1 to 10 October, our troops on the left wing of the Army have continued their offensive and reached Czechoslovak territory. The enemy has stiffened his resistance considerably, committing defences prepared in advance. Our soldiers are coping with steep slopes, mined sectors of roads, and blown-up bridges. They are having to carry their own ammunition and arms. Despite gruelling battles and exhausting marches through the mountains, morale is high.'

The people of Czechoslovakia enthusiastically welcomed and helped the Soviet troops, as witness a third report of 14 October 1944: 'As soon as our troops entered villages, the streets were lined with all the surviving inhabitants who brought all sorts of food for the soldiers and showed the most generous hospitality. During the fighting, on their own initiative, many inhabitants of the frontier villages carried away our wounded soldiers and officers in carts, despite being under enemy fire; some of these volunteers suffered wounds, but carried on their rescue work.'

During the liberation campaign, the 18th Army commander General

---

*L. I. Brezhnev was promoted to the rank of Major-General on 2 November 1944.

Gastilovich recalls, Brezhnev spent most of his time with the troops in the Army's battle formations. He intimately knew their needs and mental preoccupations, and did all in his power to rectify any shortcomings. Army Command was aware of the high morale. Whenever the battle situation looked unfavourable, Brezhnev took personal command. Such, for example, was the case south-west of the town of Kosice, at the Slanske Mountains, where the Nazis were resisting savagely. Using artillery and armour, they mounted one counter-attack after another. When the Soviet troops found themselves in a difficult position, Brezhnev went to the firing-lines and led the troops into attack. This was the beginning of a broad offensive that ended with Soviet forces breaking through the Slanske Mountains.

This breakthrough ensured the liberation of Kosice, but it was only won by heavy fighting and at the cost of huge effort and sacrifice. On 20 January 1945, the second day after Soviet troops entered the town, Brezhnev reported to the 4th Ukrainian Front Command: 'Owing to the large number of wounded, the Army gravely lacks bandages. Our stock of them is now exhausted.'

The political instructors appealed to the populace to collect bandages for the Soviet army. The townsfolk brought bedsheets, towels, and tablecloths to the army hospitals. The Soviet Command wanted to pay for these, but the offer was unanimously refused, the people saying 'We do not grudge our rescuers anything.'

There were many heroic and truly dramatic incidents when, in May 1945, the Soviet army destroyed Scherner's large group of German forces as it tried to put down the uprising in Prague and then retreat westward. One cannot read unmoved such documents as the following, written by one of the instructors of the 18th Army's political department: 'I was handed a directive . . . from Leonid Ilyich Brezhnev, ordering all the instructors of the Army's political department to be with the troops and lead them in pursuit of the enemy who was attempting to break through to the west. I returned to the front line, making my way along the trenches. The troops were asleep. It was quiet: a silence I had not known for one single hour in the four years of the war. I looked closely into the tired, haggard faces of the sleeping soldiers and a lump came to my throat as I wondered which of these dear comrades would be missing tomorrow. Who would we be burying? To whose mother or wife would I be writing a short, terrible letter? Then I checked my submachine-gun, dozed for a while, and at dawn the division went into action again. The Nazis retreated, but, as they did so, they pounded us with artillery and mortars, counter-attacking here and there with tanks and self-propelled guns, putting up a desperate counter-fire and then again retreating in a westerly direction. We pursued them for three days without sleep or rest. Our Czech brothers were advancing with us. . . .'

On 2 November 1976, in accepting Czechoslovakia's highest awards, a second Gold Star of Hero of the Czechoslovak Socialist Republic and the Order of Klement Gottwald, Brezhnev looked back to the wartime roads that Soviet troops travelled in 1945 alongside the men of the Czechoslovak Corps commanded by Ludvik Svoboda, back to the people's rising in Slovakia, the fighting for Prague, and the happy days of Czechoslovakia's liberation from the Nazis.

While with the battle formations of the advancing troops, General Brezhnev, as a true and worthy son of the Party, studied and taught the Leninist style of work to the Communists. He constantly saw to it that the personnel of the political organs were with the fighting units, helping their commanders, sharing joy and grief in the struggle of the troops against the hated enemy, and setting examples of staunchness and courage. When the salvoes proclaimed the end of the heaviest and most bloody war ever fought by our country and the victory parade was held in Moscow's Red Square, Brezhnev was rightly among the marchers as commissar of a token regiment of the 4th Ukrainian Front.

In his speech on 7 September 1974, when the hero city of Novorossiisk was presented with the Order of Lenin and the Gold Star Medal, Brezhnev said: 'If a person chances to take part directly in any outstanding event of his time, any event which forms a vital landmark in world history, it remains forever in his memory. For the older generation of our Party, such events were the Great October Socialist Revolution and the Civil War. For us, for my generation, it was the war against Hitler, the Great Patriotic War. Superhuman exertion and complete forgetfulness of self—such was the state of all of us who were in that greatest of all wars in history. And it could not have been otherwise, because we defended and upheld our most treasured possession—our Soviet socialist homeland. And we are happy to have won this great victory over the enemy and to have made our contribution to this victory.'

During the war the Soviet people demonstrated their enormous spiritual strength, their unbounded devotion to their country, and the great

Victory Parade, Moscow 1945. Brezhnev was political chief of the 4th Ukrainian Front.

vitality of the ideals of Marxism - Leninism. Socialist ideology won a brilliant victory over bourgeois - fascist ideology.

'The Nazis', Brezhnev has said, 'had an abundance of supplies and everything needed for battle. Yet we won, because we and the soldiers whom we led knew precisely why we were attacking those enemy fortifications that belched fire and death.' German Nazism and Japanese militarism were waging a predatory, unjust war. The Soviet people were defending their revolutionary gains and socialist homeland in an anti-fascist, just war. Such knowledge increased their strength tenfold, sowing seeds of matchless fortitude and heroism on a large scale.

The Communist Party, Soviet society's guiding and directing force, motivated and organized the victories of the Soviet people and their gallant armed forces. It roused the people to a just patriotic war, inspired them to the performance of great feats, combining their efforts both at the front and behind it and directing them towards the common goal of defeating the enemy. 'In this war,' Brezhnev said, 'the sons and daughters of the united Soviet Union not only upheld their socialist gains with honour but also saved world civilization from fascist barbarity, thereby giving powerful support to the liberation struggle of the nations.' The Party's prestige grew immeasurably during the war, its ranks closed yet more firmly, and its unity with the people became more durable than ever before.

The victory won in the war against Hitler was a victory of the heroic Soviet working class, the kolkhoz peasantry, of the intelligentsia, of the entire multi-national Soviet people. It was a victory of the Soviet armed forces, formed by the October Revolution, brought up by the Leninist Community Party, and indissolubly linked with the people. Victory stemmed from the close unity of the working people behind the firing lines and the troops in the field who were upholding the gains of socialism.

'The Soviet people's great feat in the years of the war', Brezhnev said on the 30th Victory anniversary, 'is inseparable from the many-sided and purposeful activity of the Communist Party. Its Central Committee was the headquarters which exercised the supreme political and strategic leadership of the military operations. It was the Party which organized and united tens of millions of men and women, directing their energies, their will and their activity towards the single goal of victory. The war provided ample confirmation that the Party and the people are united and that there is no force that can shake this invincible unity.'

3

Restoring Industry

The salvoes of victory died down — that victory which had cost the Soviet people so dear.

'There has been nothing like the losses and destruction inflicted on us by the war,' Brezhnev said. 'The war brought the people grief which to this day wrings the hearts of millions of mothers, widows, and orphans. For a man, no loss is more painful than the death of relatives, comrades, and friends. No sight is more heart-rending than that of destroyed fruits of labour into which he had put his strength, talent, and love for his country. No smell is more bitter than that of ashes. The Soviet soldier returning to his beloved homeland, now freed, saw it rent by fire and metal and lying in piles of rubble.'

Twenty million Soviet people laid down their lives at the front line, in hostilities of enemy-occupied territory, and under fascist enslavement. Ruins and ashes were all that remained of 1710 cities and townships and 70,000 villages. Twenty-five million people had been left homeless, thousands of factories, mines, and power stations blown up. The Soviet Union had lost one-third of its national wealth. In no war had any country known such losses and destruction.

Now the Communist Party of the Soviet Union was to lead the people in a great new achievement—in making good with all speed the effects of war and in restoring and further developing the economy. It assigned its finest cadres to carry out this vital economic and political task.

In August 1946, after serving as head of the political department of the Carpathian Military District, Leonid Brezhnev was elected first secretary of the Zaporozhye committee of the Communist Party of the Ukraine on the recommendation of the CPSU Central Committee. The situation was extremely difficult in this region when he took up the post. On 13 October 1946 the newspaper *Bolshevik Zaporozhya* carried an article signed by Brezhnev on the third anniversary of the city's liberation from the Nazis. 'A terrible sight met the eyes of troops of the Red Army when they liberated the city . . .' he wrote. 'There were piles of ruins where before the war there had been the blast-furnaces of the Zaporozhye steel plant, the workshops of the aluminium and ferro-alloy factories, the Lenin Dnieper Hydropower Station, the Kommunar plant, the motor-works, and many other factories. The losses inflicted by the German invasion on the economy and the population of the Zaporozhye Region ran to nearly 19 billion roubles.'

Enormous organizational work among the people, political foresight, and skilful and efficient leadership were needed for the situation to be correctly assessed, the main lines for the work of restoration laid down, and efforts and means concentrated on the key projects. Bolshevik purposefulness, unbounded faith in the creative strength of the people, unbending willpower, perseverance, and a tremendous capacity for work had to be available to surmount the difficulties caused by war disruption and ensure success.

Brezhnev was first secretary of the Zaporozhye Regional Committee for a fairly short period, but much was done in that time. Under his leadership the regional Party organization focused its attention on achieving a radical improvement of internal Party and Party and political work, on thoroughly invigorating the primary branches, and on enhancing the vanguard role of the Communists in all sectors of economic and cultural construction.

As Brezhnev noted time and again, one of the essential prerequisites in the difficult work of restoring the economy of city, region, and leading industrial enterprises was strict observance of Lenin's rule: concentrate maximum effort and material and technical resources in the decisive sectors at the crucial moment. This well-tried Leninist principle was vigorously applied in the drive to restore the Zaporozhye industrial complex.

Brezhnev won immense prestige among Communists and all working people by his talent as a political leader, his knowledge of people, his skill in assigning cadres, and in settling difficult production problems. They knew him as a trained metallurgist who had been secretary of the Party committee of the major industrial Dnepropetrovsk region before the war. Many remembered how, in the grim year of 1941, he took a direct part in the evacuation of the most important factories of the Dnieper area. What difficulties had had to be overcome in that affair, the people of Zaporozhye knew from personal experience.

In speeches to Party activists and in talks with Party officials, Brezhnev emphasized that in organizational and political work the thrust had to go where the construction battle was being won or lost, namely to the production sectors and work teams. Tactfully but firmly, he corrected those Party officials who did not give due attention to Party, political, and educational work among the people, interfering instead with the work of economic executives in the belief that the most important thing was to obtain cement and other building materials by every possible means.

'There is no doubt that cement is needed,' he said in a speech at the time. 'You can't mix concrete without it. But it is much more important that the man laying concrete in a buttress of a dam, a hundred feet up with the thermometer far below zero, should know why that concrete must be laid and tamped. . . . That is why Party organizations must concentrate on educating the people. Then the cement and everything else will more quickly be there—I speak quite literally—and the work will proceed much more smoothly.'

The regional committee and the Party organizations it controlled paid particularly close attention to problems critical to the entire reconstruction work. These were key problems of the economy, of internal Party life, and of the ideology, culture, education, and everyday life of the people. In studying these problems, all options were considered and it was decided what had to be done by the Party organs and the Communists to carry out the various tasks and, more importantly, what specific steps had to be taken. Drawing on the creative experience of the masses and on the collective opinion of the Communists, the regional

Visiting a reconstruction site at Zaporozhye, 1947.

committee could find a way out from even the worst situations.

Brezhnev insisted that cadres pay close attention to the opinions of the working people, accept criticism in a Party spirit, learn from it, and make severe demands on themselves and others.

'For the sake of the work it is essential to spot every loop-hole, to check the work of the Communists and all economic executives,' he told a district Party conference at the Dnieper project. 'And that goes for yourself too. At the end of the day, look at what you have done during it. Ask yourself: Have I done my work properly? And find the courage to tell yourself frankly that you could have done more.'

In those years there was a shortage of many things: housing, bread, manpower, machinery, building materials, working overalls, newspapers, and radios. Brezhnev created an atmosphere of confidence in success under the most difficult conditions. His colleagues at the time noted how his self-control, attentiveness to people, and ability to analyse any question calmly would act like a tonic on those around him, helping them to cope with seemingly insuperable difficulties.

Once, an expensive tower-crane toppled over and was broken while a blast-furnace was being built. Various commissions arrived to investigate the accident. Some insisted on court proceedings against the crane operator. Brezhnev visited the site, got to know the circumstances of the accident, and spoke out strongly against the mood of tension and recrimination. He suggested instead looking for the quick and logical way out of the situation. This was found. The builders replaced the crane with a system of derricks, assembly of the blast-furnace continued, deadlines were kept.

At plenums and at meetings of activists, Brezhnev constantly reiterated that the secretary of a Party organization was, above all, a political leader, and that every Communist was a political fighter. On one occasion, after a speech by the secretary of a district Party committee, Brezhnev said: 'You talk eloquently about tractors and bullocks, but when you come to political work, things aren't so good. This won't do . . . What's needed is political analysis, but this is what you don't offer. Without politically analysing the situation, we can't draw correct conclusions, and hence can't take a single step forward.'

Restoring the industrial complex in Zaporozhye and promoting all branches of the region's economy and culture was made possible by achieving the following pre-conditions: (1) a heightened responsibility among Communists—notably the leaders—for the work entrusted to them; (2) thorough-going improvement of internal Party work; and (3) activation of the primary branches of Party groups as the leading force of production collectives.

On the labour front for the first five-year plan period after the war, one of the main industrial rehabilitation projects in the south was to rebuild the Zaporozhye steel plant. This giant factory, which had taken ten years to build before the war, had to be entirely restored inside five years, the first section becoming operational within a matter of months.

Many felt it would be simpler and cheaper to blow up the remains of the buildings, clear them away completely, and then rebuild the factory from nothing. Such, in particular, was the recommendation of foreign specialists. After their visit to Zaporozhye they unanimously declared that it was impossible to restore the destroyed factory and that anybody attempting such a thing would spend more money on this than on building a new factory. However, the country was urgently in need of

Addressing a meeting to mark a blast-furnac

coming operational, Zaporozhye, 1947.

the thin, cold-rolled steel sheets which it was the responsibility of the first section of the Zaporozhye steel plant to produce, and the Soviet people upset all the forecasts and prognostications of foreign experts.

In April 1947 the Central Committee passed a resolution on the work of the Party committee at the Zaporozhye project, which set the task of radically improving Party and political work in ensuring the speediest possible construction.

The whole country helped to restore the Zaporozhye plant. The most skilled builders and assembly men arrived from other republics. Factories in Moscow, Leningrad, the Urals, and Siberia helped this top-priority project on the Dnieper. The people of Zaporozhye paid back the concern of Party and Government and the assistance which came their way from other republics with their dedicated work under the regional Party organization.

At a meeting of the project's foremost workers it was stated: 'This key year must find not just 365 days but 365 nights as well for work on the priority project.' This was adopted as the motto of the whole undertaking. Work on scheduled installations was on a three-shift basis. Many sector and department heads were seldom away from the site. The office of the Party regional committee's first secretary (also the room where he slept and rested) was in the building of what had originally been the power station. Brezhnev moved into it when the first installations were about to start up. The heads of local Party organizations besieged him there day and night with pressing problems.

Brezhnev missed no chance of acquainting himself more closely with people and their needs and moods. He looked into the work and requirements of the different teams. In their turn the workers often went to him on different matters and always got good advice and support for initiatives that were of value.

At the Zaporozhye steel plant Brezhnev was seen frequently with leading experts, economic executives, and ranking officials of all-union ministries. He toured the workshops and the building sites with them. Urgent matters of construction and production were decided on the spot. Brezhnev warmly encouraged any suggestions to improve the work and insisted that foremost workers should be emulated and, where possible, their methods adopted.

The Soviet nation closely followed the rebuilding of the giant metallurgical plant. *Pravda* sent a special correspondent to the project. All central and republican newspapers were represented at the site. Brezhnev told a press conference: 'I want you to plan your work so that you can accompany us on our tours . . . early every morning. Interesting problems often come up and useful conversations result, and you, as people writing about the project and its heroes, need to hear it all. It will give you a better insight into the important things of the moment.'

Finally, at the end of June 1947, by the tireless attention of the Central Committee and the Soviet Government, by fraternal aid from people throughout the country, by the huge effort made by the regional Party organization under Brezhnev and the thousands of Communist-led workers, a great victory on the labour front was realized: the power station and one blast-furnace at the Zaporozhye steel plant became operational. By the end of the fourth five-year plan period this factory, the pride of the Soviet metallurgical industry, had been completely restored and was producing more pig-iron, steel, and rolled stock than before the war.

Nearly 2000 builders, assembly men, metallurgists, and others who had helped in restoring the Sergo Ordzhonikidze Zaporozhye steel plant received orders and medals. Leonid Brezhnev was awarded the Order of Lenin.

The Zaporozhye Regional Party Committee also gave unstinting attention to the Lenin Hydropower Station on the Dnieper, one of the first industrialization projects in the Soviet Union and blown up by the fascist barbarians during the war. As with other projects, restoration, particularly in the initial period, was beset with formidable difficulties: machinery, tools, and transportation were scarce, and the workers lived in makeshift quarters. But the builders, among whom were people from all the Soviet republics, thought of nothing save how to restore the station as quickly as possible. The huge work force was headed by a district Party committee set up at the project on the initiative of the regional Party committee. The builders displayed true heroism, taking all obstacles in their stride to complete the project.

The power station's first turbine became operational far ahead of schedule, in early March 1947. The project's second section was likewise completed in record time. New turbines gave the station a larger capacity than before the war. The power thus generated went to the Donets Basin, the Krivoi Rog Basin, and the Dnieper area, where with heroic dedication and enthusiasm hundreds of thousands were restoring mines, metallurgical and engineering plants, and other factories.

In November 1947, by decision of the Central Committee, Brezhnev was sent to the Dnepropetrovsk region—one of the Ukraine's largest industrial and agricultural regions—where he was elected first secretary of the regional committee of the Communist Party of the Ukraine. He put all his experience, energy, and knowledge into getting that ore-rich, metal-producing region back on its feet.

The war had wreaked enormous destruction in the Dnepropetrovsk region. Thus, of 16 blast-furnaces, 13 lay in ruins and the rest had been seriously damaged; of 36 open-hearth furnaces, 29 had been razed to the ground; of 56 rolling mills, 35 had been put out of commission entirely. Enormous damage had been inflicted on the region's agriculture.

The difficulties were made even worse by mistakes on the part of the region's former heads. Economic questions had been decided away from the Party's organizational and political work, which was under-valued, and there had been cases of a misguided attitude to criticism, attempts at armchair leadership, and of negligence in the training and selection of cadres leading to breakdowns in economic and cultural construction. All these mistakes and shortcomings were brought to light and severely criticized by the CPSU Central Committee and the high Party organs in the Ukraine.

With Brezhnev's appointment to the leadership of the regional committee, the Leninist style of work was vigorously and consistently injected into the activities of the regional Party organization and all the Party organs, and an atmosphere of high demand, precision, efficiency, and respect and trust for Party cadres was created. Members of the regional and district Party committees began to show more initiative and independence in their work. 'The point is,' said Brezhnev at a regional Party conference in February 1948, 'Party work must be combined correctly with economic leadership. This is an art. And this art in Party work must be learned.' He returned to the idea again and again. 'It must be understood,' he said, 'that anyone who underrates the significance of the Party's work among the masses doesn't in effect understand anything about Party work at all.'

He attached the utmost importance to strengthening links with the people so that everyone, wherever he worked, should know what the Party and the country were engaged on and on what tasks the regional Party organization was engaged. He insisted that all leading officials should get about among the working people more and speak to them in public. On this point he said: 'What sort of leader, what sort of Bolshevik, is a man who cannot address an audience passionately, tell it what the Party Central Committee wants, what our Party will fight for . . . who cannot inspire an audience?'

The success of the economic rehabilitation and the fulfilment of the post-war five-year plans was decided by cadres. But during the first years after the war the problem of cadres was extremely acute, particularly in the republics and regions that had been occupied by the fascists. Thousands of Party and government officials had laid down their lives defending their country at the front, in partisan detachments, and with the underground. Many of the new cadres lacked experience and knowledge. For that reason, one of the first decisions passed by the Party Central Committee after the war concerned the training and re-training of leading Party and government officials.

The Dnepropetrovsk Party Regional Committee gave unremitting attention to the selection, placing and training of cadres. 'The leadership problem', Brezhnev said, 'is all about cadres.' The Party regional committee bureau more than once reviewed the cadre situation, and the political training and ability of Communists given leading posts. Brezhnev consistently spoke for a considerate, attentive attitude to people. He strove to bring out a person's finest qualities and abilities and give him confidence in himself. 'Frequently we don't know our own capabilities. People are different: you're giving an assignment to one man and, without waiting for you to finish, he waves his hand saying: "Oh, no!" and refuses it. Then you convince him. And you find that he gets more done than was asked of him. "I just never realized I could do it", he says.'

'Did people going into battle know they would become heroes?'

While showing day-to-day concern for cadres and for their ideological, political, and professional growth, Brezhnev did not spare careless and dishonest workers who, to use his words, had 'holes in their hearts', nor those ranking officials who had become apathetic and had let themselves 'gather dust'. He counselled a bolder approach to the encouragement of capable, energetic people who had won their spurs during the war and the peace-time construction, and who were not daunted by difficulties.

Here, as during his work in Zaporozhye, Brezhnev pressed for a genuinely Party attitude to criticism and for an ability to learn useful lessons from it. At a regional Party conference in February 1948 the Communists levelled withering but just criticism at some of the region's top officials. In his concluding remarks Brezhnev said that the critical observations of delegates had 'caused some embarrassment to this or that official, to this or that leader of our regional Party organization. I must say that in many cases I assumed that this criticism was levelled at me and took it to heart myself; but we must learn for ourselves the lessons of such criticism. In us Bolsheviks, this dissatisfaction, this inner anxiety should in its turn generate initiative and energy in work, a striving to put right shortcomings as quickly as possible. . . . This is the conclusion I draw for myself personally.'

The regional Party committee put its house in order and improved its guidance of Party committees in the towns and districts with determination and Bolshevik perseverance. It gave them day-to-day help, at the same time enhancing the role of primary Party branches in industry in every possible way, making sure that they used to the full their right to check the work of the managements. This improvement in Party workstyle benefited economic construction throughout the region.

In the Dnepropetrovsk region, industry fulfilled the 1948 plan ahead of schedule, increasing its output by 50 per cent over the preceding year. The region's metallurgists made good the debt incurred to the country as a result of unsatisfactory work in the past. The pre-war level of metallurgical plant utilization was surpassed. The Krivoi Rog and Nikopol mines were restored. The Dnepropetrovsk region was the first in the Ukraine to fulfil the state grain procurement plan for 1948, delivering thousands of tons of high-quality grain over and above the plan.

The regional Party committee devoted much of its attention to ensuring technical progress and to increasing creative co-operation between laboratory and work-bench.

At its meetings, which were attended by secretaries of Party committees, factory managers, directors of research institutes, leading scientists, and innovators in production, the regional Party committee regularly discussed ways and means of speeding up technical progress, promoting co-operation between science and production, introducing modern machinery and technologies, and restoring factories on a new technical level. 'Party organizations and economic executives,' noted Brezhnev at one of these meetings, 'must display more enterprise in introducing new machinery in all branches of industry and in improving technology and mechanizing labour-consuming processes.'

The secretary of the regional Party committee was giving close attention to improving the performance of the colleges, schools, and other educational establishments. Brezhnev said at the time that major scientists working in a variety of fields were on the staff of the colleges and universities, and they represented the cream of Soviet science. It was therefore important to create the best possible conditions for them to work in, both for teaching and research. It was particularly important to strengthen the links between these college scientists and industry, and to draw students into research activities.

The regional Party committee was untiring in its efforts to improve life and living conditions for the people of Dnepropetrovsk and of the region as a whole.

The Dnepropetrovsk region successfully completed the fourth five-year plan of economic rehabilitation and developing under the leadership of the regional Party organization. Many industrial enterprises, including the mammoth Dzerzhinsky and Petrovsky iron and steel plants, considerably exceeded their pre-war output level. The Krivoi Rog and Nikopol mines began to produce sufficient ore for the country's southern and central metallurgical industries. The wounds inflicted on agriculture by the war were largely healed by the end of that five-year period. More land was under cultivation than before the war. Much self-sacrificing work and creative energy was put into all this by the Communists of the Dnepropetrovsk region.

'I have worked for many years in the Ukraine,' Brezhnev said. 'I fought on her soil during the war and, like all Russian people, I am well aware of the wonderful qualities of the Ukrainian people for whom I have a sincere and filial affection.'

4

In Moldavia and Kazakhstan

In July 1950 the CPSU Central Committee assigned Brezhnev to the Moldavian Republic, where he was elected first secretary of the Central Committee of the Communist Party of Moldavia. In that office (1950 - 2) he made a large contribution towards the development of industry, the socialist reorganization of agriculture, and the promotion of culture in the Republic. All who met and worked with him and under his leadership have abiding respect and gratitude for his selfless work.

For the young Soviet Moldavia, the early 1950s were a noteworthy phase of development, a period of important social and economic changes. The kolkhozes and state farms in Moldavia west of the Dniester were still only infants. Lights burned late into the night in the Central Committee building of the Communist Party of Moldavia: how to strengthen the newly formed kolkhozes and state farms organizationally and economically was hotly debated and closely examined, and Communists were selected for work in the country-side. 'This was a difficult period calling for intensive efforts,' Brezhnev recalls, 'but one cannot but speak well of it, because the foundations for the present successes

Brezhnev with kolkhoz workers in Moldavia, 1950 (from a film shown recently on Soviet television).

were laid in those years.'

Brezhnev often toured the kolkhozes and state farms; he knew their managers extremely well and was familiar with the state of affairs on each farm. The collective farmers were always aware of his concern and attention. He liked to talk with them, and was deeply appreciative of their hard work. Because the peasants had only recently joined kolkhozes, his friendly advice and warm words reassured them that they had chosen correctly.

A plan to develop comprehensively the young republic's agriculture and to use its natural wealth and labour resources more fully and rationally was drawn up under Brezhnev's leadership. As he pointed out at a plenum of the Central Committee of the Communist Party of Moldavia in January 1951: 'This year we must organize and give effect to a new phase in our drive to strengthen the kolkhozes organizationally and economically, to boost efficiency in agriculture, and improve the work of the machine and tractor stations. This is the aim towards which we must direct all Party organizations, all Communists and Komsomol members, and mobilize the kolkhoz farmers and agriculturalists.'

Brezhnev headed this drive. Small co-operatives were amalgamated, the area under sugar-beet, tobacco, and essential oils was substantially enlarged, and special attention was paid to the cultivation of grapes and other traditional Moldavian fruit crops.

The year 1951 saw a turning point in the republic's agriculture. Compared with 1949 it produced almost 500 per cent more grapes, nearly 300 per cent more sugar-beet, and over 50 per cent more tobacco. Within a single year the average grape harvest increased by almost a third. The kolkhozes grew much stronger economically and their cash incomes exceeded the 1950 level by more than 25 per cent. The rouble income of one in every four kolkhozes reached seven figures. This advance in agriculture led to a considerable enlargement of Moldavia's food and canning industries.

On Brezhnev's initiative, the republic's Party organization analysed the options open and, on the basis of what had been achieved, made well-considered and substantial recommendations for the further development of Moldavia's agriculture and food industry. These recommendations were reviewed by the Council of Ministers of the USSR; and early in 1952, using them as guidelines, it passed a decision on measures to promote Moldavia's agriculture and food industry.

At a meeting of the republic's Party activists in early 1952, Brezhnev delivered a report in which he minutely analysed the state of Moldavia's economy and defined the immediate tasks of its Party, government, and economic organs. He made the point that success would depend largely 'on the level of internal Party work, on the efficiency of the Bolshevik leadership of state and economic activity, and on the capability and efficiency of the Party organization as a whole.' In the economy, he said, enduring success could be achieved only by improving Party and political work.

He kept the promotion of the republic's industry always in view. Construction was started on the Dubossary hydropower station project, a silk mill, new sugar refineries, canning plants, and wine distilleries. The foundation was laid for industries new to the republic such as mechanical engineering, electrical engineering, and tool-making.

The ruins left by war had not yet been entirely cleared in Kishinev, the republic's capital, but new green streets began to appear, parks were laid out, and modernization proceeded apace. Brezhnev personally studied every new design, frequently convening meetings of architects and builders in his office. He insisted that the latest techniques and the seismic conditions in the republic should be studied when buildings were being designed and put up. Almost every day, on his early morning way to work, he stopped off at the city's main building projects to see what progress had been made.

Kishinev began its first-ever tall apartment houses. Within a short space of time the Moldavian capital had become one of the loveliest cities in the Soviet Union.

The Central Committee of the Moldavian Party attached paramount importance to the communist education of the people. At a Central Committee plenum in August 1952 devoted to ideological work, Brezhnev said that it should not be forgotten that 'as working people of a socialist state, the working class and the kolkhoz peasantry of Moldavia are still young. They have not yet been through the good school of socialist training.' And in truth, some segments of Moldavia's population residing west of the Dniester were still influenced by the customs and traditions of the old society, by survivals of bourgeois - nationalist views. The Central Committee of the republic's Party put its organizations and all Communists to the task of achieving a fundamental improvement of ideological education as a whole, including the Marxist - Leninist education of leading officials. 'Everything new, advanced, and progressive that appears in life and furthers the socialist economy,' Brezhnev said, 'can be identified and developed much faster when cadres have a high level of ideological education.'

In the family of Soviet peoples, the Moldavians, with the Communist Party at their head, were able to take enormous strides in rehabilitating and promoting their republic's economy and culture. A solid foundation was laid for the subsequent swift growth of its economy and development of its culture. 'A land on the crossroads of all misfortunes' was how people spoke of Moldavia in the past. A land where only one in ten of the population could write his own name, where practically everything down to scythes and kerosene lamps had to be imported, it developed into a flourishing socialist republic with a modern industry, a productive agriculture, and a developed socialist culture.

Headed by Brezhnev, the republic's Party organized socialist construction in Soviet Moldavia. All major questions of the economy, science, technology, political propaganda and agitation, education and upbringing, the development of literature and art, and the building of a large network of cultural institutions were decided under the direction of the Central Committee of the Communist Party of Moldavia and its first secretary. 'I should like to recall with affection,' Brezhnev said in a speech commemorating Soviet Moldavia's 50th anniversary, 'the tireless work of the large contingent of Communists sent by our Party's Central Committee to the Moldavian Republic in the post-war years. Their part in the building of socialist Moldavia will not be forgotten.'

His work as first secretary in Moldavia did much to mould Brezhnev into an outstanding Party leader and organizer of the masses and gave him considerable experience. His colossal energy, charm, commitment to Party principles, and ability to see the best in people brought him deserved prestige.

'Bolshevik purposefulness, organization, efficiency, and perseverance,' he said to Party officials in the republic, 'are the qualities that all of us must have as leaders in order to justify with success the great trust placed in us by the Party and the people. We must develop and instil these qualities in leaders at all levels.'

He attached supreme importance to improving the forms and methods of Party work and to developing internal Party democracy, criticism, and self-criticism. In September 1952 he wrote an article for *Bolshevik* under the heading 'Criticism and self-criticism: a tested method of training cadres'. 'Criticism and self-criticism,' he wrote, 'is the mainspring of our Party's enormous strength and invincibility. It underlies the Party's entire life and work and is an indispensable condition for correct leadership at all levels of Party, government, economic, cultural, and scientific work.'

This article attracted considerable attention among Party workers. In it Brezhnev drew upon the experience of the Moldavian Party organization to show that an improvement of all internal Party work and increased activity by the Communists were essential to raising the standards of Party leadership and to training cadres. He noted that the Moldavian Party's Central Committee was making sure that the principles of internal Party democracy were strictly observed in every Party branch, that collective leadership was always present in Party work, and that Party meetings, plenums, and conferences were conducted in a businesslike manner. In conclusion he wrote: 'Bolshevik cadres must soberly assess the results of their work, avoid being flattered by them and sinking into complacency, must work with greater energy, and be more successful in fulfilling the tasks confronting them. Maximum promotion of criticism and self-criticism is the prime condition of our steady advance towards communism.'

The propositions elaborated by Brezhnev in this article were consistently applied in the Moldavian Party organization.

At the 19th Congress of the CPSU in October 1952 Brezhnev was elected a member of the Central Committee, and at a Central Committee plenum he was elected an alternate member of the Presidium and a secretary of the Central Committee. In March 1953 he was appointed chief of the political administration of the Navy and deputy chief of the central political administration of the Soviet Army and Navy.

A vigorous drive for cereals was started in the Soviet Union in the 1950s. Special attention was given by the Party to promoting the grain economy as the basis for all agricultural production. The main factor then in increasing grain output was the development of virgin and disused land in Kazakhstan, Siberia, the Volga area, the North Caucasus, and elsewhere.

In his time Lenin had drawn attention to the economic expediency and vital necessity of utilizing these vast areas of virgin and disused land. Acting on this advice, the Party began the development of virgin land in the eastern regions. The largest areas were in Kazakhstan. It was there that Brezhnev was sent by the Central Committee. In February 1954 he was elected second secretary and in August 1955 first secretary

With *tselinniki* on the virgin lands of Kazakhstan.

of the Kazakhstan Party's Central Committee.

The history of the Soviet Union has always been made by working people: by those who built the Dnieper Hydropower Station, the Magnitogorsk Metallurgical Plant, the Turkestan - Siberia Railway, and the Karakum Canal; by those who converted the Hungry Steppe into a flowering oasis, and who are today building the Kama Auto Works, developing the oil resources of the Tyumen area, and building the Baikal - Amur Railway. In the same way, the virgin land pioneers occupy a worthy place among the heroes of Soviet achievement. This development project is one of the most vivid chapters in the labour chronicle of the Soviet Union.

A new word, *tselinnik,* has entered the Russian language and the languages of the other Soviet peoples, perpetuating in the nation's memory the labour of those who took part in the virgin land development. There can be no higher honour. At a meeting in Alma-Ata to mark the 20th anniversary of the scheme, Brezhnev noted that the true significance of historical events and of major political decisions is usually seen not at once but with the passage of time. By then intentions can be compared with results, the actual impact of these events and decisions on various aspects of life can be assessed, and what is basic comes into bolder relief. In the case of the virgin land project, the basic fact was that the Party set a vitally important, urgent task and that the Communists and the people successfully carried it out.

Success did not come easily. 'Veteran virgin-landers,' Brezhnev has said, 'well remember that time—the piercing wind across the steppe, the storms and frosts, tents pitched in the snow, the first furrows in the fields and the first streets of new communities, days packed with work, nights often sleepless. A score of years have passed since then. . . . But we shall not forget how we won the first hectares and the first tons of grain from the virgin land. One does not forget something one has put one's heart and soul into.'

The people who worked with Brezhnev in those years are unanimous that he did indeed put his heart and soul into this nationally important project. In resolving the difficult major problems that arose during the massive development of virgin land, Brezhnev did indeed display Bolshevik perseverance, purposefulness, efficiency, and the ability to assess the situation and so organize the work as to combine the efforts of the thousands who came from all parts of the Soviet Union. This was tremendously important, especially when the basic difficulties of organizing in uninhabited areas had to be overcome.

Brezhnev was often at the farms and could put names to faces with many managers, Party branch secretaries, state farm workers, and production innovators. He sized up for himself the situation and the difficulties experienced by the new settlers and took the right decisions at the right time, thereby helping all virgin-land state farms. It should be remembered that many of the problems were not local but general in character.

Before the project started, Brezhnev found himself engaged in theoretical controversy with certain experts who maintained that if some of the hay meadows and pastures in Kazakhstan's virgin-land region were ploughed up, the output of animal products would fall. Practical experience was to prove these experts wrong. In addition to wheat, the republic produced increasing quantities of meat and other animal products.

The drive for large-scale grain production involved not only putting more land to cereal crops, but also markedly increasing crop capacity.

The development of virgin land transformed the life of the Kazakh steppes and fundamentally changed the republic's image. Hundreds of state farms and kolkhozes were set up in Kazakhstan as large, highly mechanized grain-producing units. New workers' townships and centres of culture appeared. Towns and industrial enterprises sprang up on uninhabited steppeland, and canals, power transmission lines, railways, and motor roads were built.

This massive virgin-land scheme embodied Lenin's concept that to promote productive forces to the utmost and raise living standards, land must be used with the highest efficiency. In 1972, when many regions of the Soviet Union were hit by an unprecedented drought, Kazakhstan—which had favourable weather—produced over a billion poods* of grain. 'Though valuable in itself,' Brezhnev said, 'this yield of grain perhaps weighed far more for reaching the country at a difficult time.'

The conversion of Kazakhstan's virgin lands into a major granary for the country went down in the annals of Soviet history as an epic achievement, to which Brezhnev made an outstanding contribution. The project was a tangible expression of Lenin's policy of friendship and mutual assistance between the Soviet peoples. The project became a school of internationalist education in the true sense of the word, a school in which people of all nationalities in the USSR joined the wide experience of tillers of the soil to labour skills and the will to win.

As Brezhnev said on the 20th anniversary of the project: 'The virgin lands gave many people their start in life. Many tractor drivers, combine-harvester operators, and builders have become state farm managers, leading specialists, and Party and government officials. But when we say that the virgin lands have got people ahead, we do not judge their growth only by their work records. There is another kind of growth which in human terms is just as significant and noble. I have in mind cultural progress, increased skills, and moral maturity.'

---

*One pood = 16 kilos.

The area owes its present wealth to the heroic days when the project was started and when Kazakhstan's Party organization was headed by Leonid Brezhnev. Speaking in Alma-Ata on the 50th anniversary of the Kazakh Republic and its Communist Party, he said: 'My link with the republic's Party organization dates back to my work here, in Kazakhstan, during the years we ploughed virgin land. I always recall those days with heartfelt warmth and gratitude. They gave me the opportunity to get to know one of our most remarkable republics and its interesting, courageous, energetic people more closely.'

Brezhnev put much effort into promoting the republic's industrial development, chiefly ferrous and non-ferrous metallurgy and electrical energy. In the latter half of the 1950s Kazakhstan was producing more than half of the Soviet Union's copper, lead, and zinc. Its power output was several times greater than the whole of tsarist Russia had commanded. Karaganda, Balkhash, Temir-Tau, Ust-Kamenogorsk, and other industrial centres grew rapidly. The Kazakhstan Central Committee and Brezhnev personally gave unceasing attention to improving the overall administration of industry, modernizing techniques, putting new scientific and technological achievements to work, furthering specialization and co-operation in industry, and passing on new experience. In August 1955 a plenum of the republic's Central Committee was devoted to these questions.

In his report to this plenum, Brezhnev defined the tasks of Party organization in enlarging the republic's industrial potential and showed the ways and means of accelerating scientific and technological progress, critical to the successful growth and improvement of all branches of industry. 'The drive for further technical advancement in our country, for the systematic growth of labour productivity,' he said, 'has been, and remains, the foundation of our economic policy.' The Soviet Union, he noted, had a huge fleet of machine-tools and all conceivable kinds of machinery. The task was to make much better use of equipment, to perfect technologies, and to improve the organization of labour. He emphasized that a conscious attitude to work among the people was decisive. 'Who settles the fate of our plans? People. Thus the main thing is to appeal to the people, to the masses.'

The years during which Brezhnev worked in Kazakhstan saw an enormous increase in the tempo of the republic's economic and cultural development. A new approach to how Kazakhstan's inexhaustible natural wealth was to be exploited for the country as a whole was found by the Party. A particularly large role was given the republic in the efforts to increase the output of grain and animal products. 'The successes in Kazakhstan's economic and cultural development,' Brezhnev said in January 1956 at the 8th Congress of the Kazakhstan Party, 'speak for the Soviet system's enormous potentialities, the great strength of the alliance between the working class and the peasants, and the unbreakable friendship and co-operation among all Soviet peoples.'

Today, Soviet Kazakhstan has a highly developed economy, large-scale industry and agriculture, and an advanced science and culture. This is the result of the selfless labour of the working class, kolkhoz peasantry, and the intelligentsia of Kazakhstan, of all the peoples of the Soviet Union, and it reflects the fruitful activities of the republic's Party organization.

5

General Secretary

AT the 20th Congress of the CPSU, Brezhnev was re-elected to the CPSU Central Committee at a plenum of which in February 1956 he was again elected an alternate member of the Presidium and a secretary of the Party Central Committee. In 1958 he was also elected deputy chairman of the Bureau of the CPSU Central Committee for the Russian Federation. In June 1957 he was elected a full member of the Presidium of the CPSU Central Committee, the highest organ of the Communist Party between plenums of the Central Committee. (In 1966 the Presidium reverted to the name 'Politburo' it had under Lenin.)

The Central Committee assigned Brezhnev to the development of heavy industry and capital construction, the supply of the armed forces with up-to-date equipment, and the promotion of space exploration. He coped successfully with this work, putting his tireless energies to building up heavy industry, the basis of economic progress, and to increasing the country's defence potential.

Brezhnev's office resembled headquarters where major questions of space exploration were decided, and where conferences were held with leading scientists, designers, and specialists in various spheres of technology. He was frequently to be seen at rocket-making plants.

At a hydro-electric power site on the Volga, 1958.

In October 1957 the Soviet Union launched the first ever man-made sputnik, and this Russian word entered the vocabulary of all nations. The launching of the Soviet sputnik was a world sensation.

As a result of the restoration of its war-ravaged economy, its further economic progress, the building of hundreds of large modern factories and scores of research complexes, and the enormous advantages of its planned socialist economy, the Soviet Union reached new heights of economic, scientific, and technological advancement.

A particularly striking achievement was history's first piloted space flight by Yuri Gagarin in April 1961, a triumph of human intelligence, collective will, and dedicated work. Thousands of people—scientists, engineers, designers, technicians, and workers—threw themselves wholeheartedly into the Soviet space programme, building powerful carrier-rockets and space ships, and demonstrating a remarkable fusion of science, labour, knowledge, and talent. Brezhnev's name was linked from the first to Soviet space achievements.

Speaking of space exploration, he stressed that the Soviet Union was not only laying the foundation for mankind's future gigantic achievements, the fruits of which would benefit coming generations, but was already winning direct practical gains for the population of the world, for the Soviet people, and for building communism. He noted on many occasions that space exploration must serve progress, peace, and the happiness of all the peoples in the world, that it should not be an instrument of destruction and war.

The whole of Brezhnev's life and work have been devoted to the interests of the Soviet people and the cause of peace and social progress. His election to the office of President of the Presidium of the Supreme Soviet of the USSR in May 1960 testified to the nation's recognition of his services and of the great prestige he enjoyed. During the four years he was President of the Presidium of the USSR Supreme Soviet, the country's highest legislature passed a series of laws including those raising state pensions, increasing the wages and salaries of those in education, the health service, the municipal economy, the retail trade and catering industry, and other enactments marked by concern for the welfare of Soviet men and women. In those years Brezhnev did a lot to improve the state apparatus, develop Soviet socialist democracy further, to consolidate the rule of law and advance the realization of Leninist foreign policy.

He attached, and still attaches, the utmost importance to improving the work of the Soviets of People's Deputies, which most fully embody the democratic character of the Soviet State. He constantly draws their attention to the need for regular reports to the electorate, publicity, increased popular participation in the administration of public affairs, criticism of shortcomings, and measures to stamp out bureaucracy.

'Whatever post a Soviet deputy holds,' he said at a public election meeting in the Bauman district of Moscow in June 1970, 'he considers it his duty to be guided by the Party's policy in all his actions, to make every effort to implement its programme, and to adhere to its positions firmly. He is well aware it is this, above all, that the electors give him their votes for. Party policy expresses the basic, vital interests of the

With cosmonaut Yuri Gagarin, 1961.

people, and for a deputy nothing can be allowed to come before these interests.'

As President of the Presidium of the USSR Supreme Soviet, Brezhnev contributed actively to implementing a foreign policy aimed at strengthening peace, fostering social progress, and creating a favourable international atmosphere for building socialism and communism in the Soviet Union and in all other countries of the socialist bloc.

On the road from district Soviet deputy to President of the Supreme Soviet, he acquired deep and all-round knowledge of the work of organs of people's power. His name is coupled with the framing and enactment of laws specifying the content of the work of the Soviets and extending the rights of deputies and enhancing their role at all levels of state and public life. To this day, he is active in the work of the USSR Supreme Soviet as President of the Presidium.

The plenum of the CPSU Central Committee in October 1964 holds an historic place in the life of the Communist Party and the Soviet Union. Everything called for a new approach to socio-economic problems: the socialist economy, which had reached mammoth dimensions by that time—the more complex economic links—the growing scientific and technological revolution—the tremendously enriched spiritual world of the Soviet citizen. In order to ensure success in building communism, it was necessary to remove the subjectivism which was in evidence at the time and was hindering Soviet society's progress. All these questions were deliberated at the October plenum.

The plenum once again proved convincingly the CPSU's monolithic unity, its stand on Leninist principles, and its political maturity. It demonstrated the fidelity of the Party and its Central Committee to Marxism - Leninism and expressed the unswerving determination of Communists to adhere to and develop steadfastly the Leninist standards of Party life and the principles of Party leadership, notably that of collective leadership, and boldly and resolutely to set aside every impediment to the creative work of Party and people.

The October 1964 plenum elected Brezhnev First Secretary of the Central Committee of the CPSU. In that high office his talent as Party leader, organizer of the masses, and outstanding political personality of the Leninist type unfolded more strikingly than ever. His profound experience of life and deep knowledge of the theory and practice of building communism enabled him to contribute immensely to working out and implementing the CPSU's Leninist general line, whose validity and correctness has been borne out by the entire course of social development, to the Party's further development of Marxist-Leninist theory in a creative way, to the establishment of Leninist standards of Party and state life. He focused his attention on the main task areas of Party and state. These were to increase the Soviet Union's economic potential, to raise the living standard of the people, to enhance the USSR's defence capability, to strengthen the world socialist community, to unite the entire international communist and working-class movement, and to secure the peace and security of nations.

The Marxist - Leninist theory of socialism as the first phase of the communist socio-economic system has been further developed in documents of the Communist Party and in the speeches of Brezhnev. These define the ways and means of building the material and technical basis of communism, promoting the evolution of socialist into communist social relations, and moulding the new man. In them, key features of the socialist way of life and the objective laws of building communism are comprehensively set out, as are the principles guiding the improvement of economic management and the administration of all public affairs at the present stage.

In characterizing mature socialism, Brezhnev has revealed the dialectics of the development of productive forces and relations of production, the genuinely collectivist character of relations between people, the essence of socialist humanism, the sources of the vigorous social activity of the masses consciously building communism, and their growing sense of responsibility for the affairs of their collective and society.

Brezhnev has fully and eloquently demonstrated in his speeches the socialist economic system's fundamental advantages over the capitalist, and how to use these advantages for the benefit of the people. He has dealt with questions such as the most rational utilization of investments, labour resources, scientific and technological achievements, the socialist principle of distribution according to work, the extension of public consumption funds, the improvement of planning and economic management, the promotion of Soviet democracy, and the education of Soviet people in the spirit of a communist attitude to work.

The titanic work of the Party, the Central Committee, and its Politburo headed by Brezhnev is based on profound analyses of socio-historical practice and is imbued with a Marxist - Leninist approach to economic, social, political, and ideological matters. The Communist Party naturally gives prominence to the country's economic development, for this is the main sphere of society's work, on the success of which its advance towards communism largely depends.

More than half a century's experience of socialist economic management shows that economic leadership has been the most complex task facing the Party after the victory of the socialist revolution. Scientific and technological changes carried through to production, strengthened co-operation among all branches of mature socialist society's economy, and competition between the two world systems of socialism and capitalism—in short, both the internal and the external factors of Soviet development have gone to make the priority that the Party gives to economic policy.

Moreover, the increased scale of socially useful production and new processes in the country's socio-economic life needed the greatest possible improvement of economic management. In view of this, on the initiative of the Politburo and of Brezhnev himself as General Secretary of the Central Committee, the Party worked out a unified and thoroughly scientific approach to the running of mature socialist society and an economic policy that matched present-day requirements; it defined methods of perfecting the economic machinery and the forms of organizing and managing production.

In the mid-1960s the Communist Party outlined its agrarian policy as the first step in fashioning this economic policy and the corresponding methods of economic management, and in improving production organization and management. The important measures to increase agricultural production were dictated by the need for a planned and balanced development of all branches of the economy and for a steady rise in the national standard of living. Furthermore, the Party duly noted that there had been glaring errors and shortcomings in the management of agriculture. At a plenum of the Central Committee in March 1965, Brezhnev delivered a report 'On urgent measures for the further development of Soviet agriculture', in which he emphasized: *'We understand that the promotion of agriculture is vital to us for the successful building of communism. In order to carry out this national task we must give agriculture a solid economic foundation.'*

The significance of this report and of the decisions passed at the March 1965 plenum is that the Party defined the fundamental principles of its agrarian policy at the new stage and laid down detailed guidelines to ensure the steady growth of agricultural output. A new system of planning production and of farm produce procurement was the main limb of this policy. Hard-and-fast procurement plans for several years and financially viable purchasing prices were established. Provision was made for higher payment for products delivered over and above the plan. A guaranteed minimum return was introduced for kolkhoz farmers.

In giving effect to the decisions of the March 1965 plenum, the Party consistently and perseveringly improved the agricultural management system. Greater emphasis was put on economic incentives in the promotion of agricultural production, investments were substantially increased, and agriculture's material and technical resources enlarged.

The role was enhanced of scientific institutions and of scientists and experts in the application of scientific and technical achievements to agriculture. The kolkhozes and state farms were further strengthened organizationally and economically. All this helped not only to improve economic relations in the countryside but also to resolve important social and political problems. Favourable conditions were created for doing away with class distinctions, eliminating qualitative differences as between town and countryside and as between mental and physical work, and for bringing into harmony personal, collective, and national interests.

The Soviet people enthusiastically welcomed the March plenum's decisions. Output of farm machinery and chemical fertilizers increased, more assistance was given to the countryside by the towns, and the efficiency of farm labour grew markedly. The decisions had a beneficial impact in that they stimulated the growth of the kolkhoz and state-farm economy and gave a powerful impetus to strengthen further Soviet society's socio-political and ideological unity.

The Communist Party looked again at such key factors in the intensification of agriculture as comprehensive mechanization, electrification, and the improvement and artificial fertilizing of land. It saw these factors as indispensable to the growth of productive forces of agriculture and the efficient utilisation of land and the enhancement of its fertility. An extensive long-term programme of land improvement was started on Brezhnev's initiative. Modern irrigation and drainage systems of high engineering calibre were built in almost all the regions of the Soviet Union, and millions of hectares of irrigated and drained land were brought under the plough.

The non-Black Earth zone of European Russia is now getting close attention as an area of considerable potential for boosting agricultural production. This extensive area in the heart of the European USSR is to become a zone of efficient crop and animal husbandry, contributing significantly to the country's overall food production.

This comprehensive programme for the steady growth of agriculture laid down at the March 1965 plenum and further developed in decisions of subsequent plenums and of the 23rd, 24th, and 25th Party Congresses, is part and parcel of the CPSU's general line. It is being put into effect. Brezhnev's large personal contribution to the framing and enforcing of the present agrarian policy is highly appreciated by Party and people.

Mature socialism required a new approach to the development of industry as the main sphere of material production. In September 1965 a plenum of the Central Committee considered the question of improving the management of industry, perfecting planning, and giving more weight to economic incentives in industrial production. Measures were instituted to make the methods of industrial planning and management compatible with the current tasks of building communism at a vastly increased order of magnitude in production, investment, and plant assets, and with economic links now so much wider and more complex. Sights were set on raising efficiency in production, achieving the maximum top-quality industrial output with the lowest outlay, applying scientific and technical advances as soon as possible, and strengthening in every way the system of economic incentives for work.

The plenum found that it was necessary to place a heavier accent on economic methods of managing industry, to fundamentally improve planning, to give enterprises more say in settling current economic problems, and delegate greater responsibility to collectives and to each individual for the results of their work and give them larger material incentives. All-Union and Union-republican ministries were set up to improve the management of the branches of industry in question and to speed scientific and technological progress.

In order to carry out the decisions of this plenum, the Central Committee and its Politburo, headed by Brezhnev, directed the efforts of Party and people towards the maximum enlargement of the Soviet Union's economic and defence potential and an upswing in labour productivity on the basis of scientific and technological progress. Taking as its point of departure the need for all elements of economic management to conform to the present phase of Soviet society's development, the Central Committee started its purposeful work of improving economic management methods.

In keeping with Lenin's course, the Party creatively resolves the economic and socio-political tasks of building communism. The 23rd Congress of the CPSU (March - April 1966) was an important landmark on this road. Key questions of Marxist - Leninist theory and the Party's practical work were further elaborated, the results of the country's development were exhaustively analysed, and the main targets of the eighth five-year plan were determined in the Central Committee report delivered by Brezhnev, as were the next tasks in realizing the Party's Leninist foreign policy.

In the context of the Party's development, the period between the 22nd and 23rd Congresses saw a further strengthening of Party membership and the enhancement of its leading role in Soviet society. Leninist principles and standards of Party life were firmly established.

From the standpoint of the USSR's internal development, this was a period when, under the leadership of the Party, the Soviet people reached new summits in economic, scientific, technical, and cultural progress. Socialist democracy continued to extend and make itself fast in the different spheres of social life. The alliance between the working class and the kolkhoz peasantry, the friendship among Soviet peoples, the ideological and political unity of the people and their cohesion around the Party—these political foundations of the socialist system were consolidated.

As to the Soviet Union's international position, the period between the Congresses brought steady growth of the international prestige and influence of the USSR and the entire socialist community, and new victories of the countries and peoples fighting colonial tyranny for independence and social progress. Fresh life came to the working-class struggle in capitalist countries. The international communist and working-class movement made further headway. Capitalism's general crisis deepened along with the aggravation of all its contradictions.

The report to the 23rd Congress dealt with the basic features of the new phase of Soviet society's development and validated the Party's course towards making more use of the socialist system's advantages and potential towards further raising national living standards and perfecting socialist democracy.

The 23rd Congress reviewed the entire range of economic and social problems and set the target of a better-integrated development of the national economy. 'There was a time,' Brezhnev said, 'when to achieve rapid development of heavy industry we had deliberately to restrict our requirements. Now we have mighty productive forces which enable us to speed up the growth of those branches of social production which directly satisfy the material, cultural, and other needs of the people. This Party line finds expression in the five-year plan measures to narrow the gap between the rates of producing the means of production and consumer goods, between the growth rates of agriculture and industry.'

The targets of the eighth five-year plan reflected the unity between the development of socialism's material and technical basis and its social relations. The directives for the plan approved by Congress called for the utilization of all of mature socialism's potentialities to achieve a more dynamic growth of the country's economy. The Party saw this as the key to fulfilling new social tasks and raising national living standards and the cultural level.

Congress noted the beneficial impact of the decisions of the March 1965 plenum on the development of agriculture and voted for a series of measures designed to create conditions that would increase agricultural production.

In this area the thrust went into stage-by-stage intensification of agriculture through mechanization, electrification, the use of chemical fertilizers, large-scale land improvement, and irrigation. Considerably larger budgets went to investment in agriculture. The production of farm machinery was increased and more electricity was channelled to the kolkhozes and state farms. 'It is the duty of Party, government, and agricultural organs, of all workers in agriculture,' Brezhnev said, 'to make the fullest use of each hectare of land, of each rouble invested, each machine and each ton of fertilizer, and to do this skilfully and economically.'

As formulated by the 23rd Congress, the eighth five-year plan was to achieve the fullest possible use of scientific and technical achievements, the industrial development of all social production and an increase in its efficiency and labour productivity for the further substantial growth of industry, high and stable rates of agricultural development, a marked rise in living standards and the fuller satisfaction of the material and cultural requirements of all Soviet people.

The decisions adopted by Congress were aimed at further strengthening the Soviet Union, fostering the utmost development of socialist democracy, improving Soviet legislation, and exercising stricter supervision over the enforcement of the law. As the Central Committee's report emphasized: 'The substance of socialist democracy lies in good socialist organization of all society for the sake of every individual and in socialist discipline of every individual for the sake of all society.'

The 23rd Party Congress re-elected Brezhnev to the Central Committee, and the next plenum elected him General Secretary of the Central Committee and a member of the Politburo.

The beneficial influence of the conclusions and generalizations drawn by the Party, its Central Committee, and General Secretary was felt during the period of the eighth five-year plan. The directives of the 23rd Congress were met for all key socio-economic indicators. Economic management and centralized state planning were improved and more effective use began to be made of economic incentives for output. Significant qualitative changes took place in the national economy, accelerating the rise of living standards and bringing economic and social aspects of life into closer connection with each other.

New forms of managing industry were evolved. Large production complexes, comprising factories engaged on similar or related work and also research and design organizations, were set up in Moscow and Leningrad and later in other regions. These developments were impelled by objective causes—chiefly the need to concentrate production and to convert science into a direct productive force. Each of these complexes, in which production and science were intermingled, was given every facility to specialize and to consolidate production links. These complexes were an entirely new phenomenon in the structure of the Soviet economy.

The growth of production and labour productivity during the eighth five-year plan made it possible to exceed significantly the planned increases in the people's living standards and cultural level. Party and government implemented a series of measures to promote the national material welfare. Minimum wages were raised, the tariff rates of many categories of workers went up, benefits were extended, and higher wages and salaries were fixed for working people in the Soviet Far East, East Siberia, and the European North. Holidays were lengthened for many categories of factory and office workers. Workers on kolkhoz farms were given a guaranteed wage matching that of state-farm workers, and pensions were increased for them, for disabled persons, and for a section of women textile workers. Factory, office, and professional workers went onto a five-day working week. Large-scale housing construction was started.

During the eighth five-year plan the Soviet people, led by the Party, its Central Committee, and the Politburo, achieved noteworthy successes in building the material and technical basis of communism, promoting socialist social relations, educating the new man, and improving the socialist way of life. Tangible signs of mature socialism showed clearly in the country's socio-economic and political development.

In his report 'Fifty years of great victories of socialism' delivered on 3 November 1967 at a joint session of the Central Committee and the USSR and RSFSR Supreme Soviets, summing up the half-century of triumphant progress by the Communist Party and the Soviet people and defining the immediate tasks of communist construction, Brezhnev put forward and substantiated the proposition that a mature socialist society had been built in the USSR and that the task now was to make fuller use of the emerging possibilities for the successful building of communism.

Every phase in the life of Soviet society sets the Party new tasks and requires of it a profound Marxist - Leninist analysis of reality, the determining of a theoretically sound course for internal and foreign policy, and consistent efforts to bring it about in life itself. Under mature socialism, when all aspects of Soviet society's life develop simultaneously and dynamically, considerably greater demands are made on the scientific leadership of economic and social processes.

The CPSU is making successful headway in building communism precisely because it is guided by Marxist - Leninist science, creatively developing it to meet new conditions and using the collective experience of the people. The Soviet Union is advancing along an unblazed trail, but this does not mean that it has to grope its way blindly. The Soviet people's road to the summits of communism is lit by revolutionary theory—the source of whose life-asserting strength lies in socialist reality—in the practical activity of the masses. By making scientific generalization from revolutionary practice, theory determines the prospects for social advancement and illumines the road to the great goal.

Loyalty to Marxism-Leninism, with its powerful life-asserting creative spirit, is an essential condition and indeed the guarantee of success in building communism, in the struggle to champion the interests of the working class and of all working people.

6

Two Congresses of the 1970s

IN 1970 the people of the Soviet Union and other socialist countries, Communists, and working people the world over marked the centenary of the birth of VLADIMIR ILYICH LENIN. This anniversary was celebrated in 126 countries. Brezhnev addressed a joint session of the CPSU Central Committee and the USSR and RSFSR Supreme Soviets, delivering a report 'The cause of Lenin lives on and triumphs.' He pointed to Lenin's greatness as a thinker and revolutionary, as the brilliant continuer of the teaching and work of Marx and Engels, founder of the Communist Party of the Soviet Union, and leader of the greatest socialist revolution in history, of the world's first socialist state, and of the international working class.

The entire contemporary era, unique revolutionary accomplishments, and the fundamental transformation of the face of world society are associated with Leninism. In Lenin's teaching the international working class acquired a powerful theoretical weapon and a minutely elaborated programme of revolutionary action. With the Communist

Party at their head, the Soviet people are advancing along the course set by Lenin. 'In carrying out the programme charted by the Party,' Brezhnev stated, 'Soviet people, by their tireless work and heroic efforts, are blazing the path which will sooner or later be followed by the working people of all countries. Every success and every victory won by us bring nearer the hour when all mankind will break the social and moral chains of the past and enter a new world—the world of communism.'

A considerable contribution was made to the theory and practice of scientific communism by the 24th Party Congress (March - April 1971). The Central Committee report and other congress documents embodied the continuity of the Party's Leninist policy, its foresight and realism, its ability to fix priorities in the drive for communism, and—accurately assessing the situation—to work out a scientific political course and consistently fulfil the adopted programme.

The Congress summed up the results of extensive Party theoretical and practical work during the eighth five-year plan and thoroughly analysed and generalized the experience that had accumulated. It was stressed at the Congress that, since the victory of socialism in the USSR, Soviet society had been developing dynamically and at a swift tempo. Mature socialism was bringing striking changes in all spheres of social life. The self-sacrificing efforts of the Soviet people had resulted in the establishment of a fully developed socialist society in the USSR. The Soviet economy made a new big step forward. In 1971 the daily social product of the Soviet economy was ten times larger than at the close of the 1930s. Socialist social relations had moved on to a higher level. There had been a noteworthy rise in national prosperity, education, and culture. Impressive advances were made by Soviet science. Co-operation between the working class, the peasantry, and the intelligentsia had tightened its bonds and reached a new height. A new type of individual had emerged, active in all affairs of state and in all spheres of public life. Nations were flourishing and drawing closer together, strengthening still further their friendship and fraternal cooperation on the basis of proletarian internationalism.

In its report to the 24th Congress, the Central Committee characterized the mature socialist society in detail and defined the immediate tasks of building communism. The continuity of Party policy was seen in the fact that this congress enlarged upon the propositions put forward at the preceding one, at the same time noting that its own propositions and conclusions applied not only to the ninth five-year plan period but also to a longer term. The prime goal of the Party's economic policy was to ensure a steady rise in the Soviet people's living standards and cultural level. This was becoming an increasingly pressing need of economic development itself and one of the basic pre-conditions for the swift growth of production. Mature socialist society has a unique facility for making fuller use of the advantages and potentialities of the socialist system, its intrinsic forms and methods of economic management, and the latest achievements of science and technology.

The Central Committee report set out how to tackle the basic questions of economic policy in a mature socialist society. A switch to mainly intensive development of social production was the priority. This called for greater efficiency in all branches of the economy, continued application of scientific and technical achievements in the national economy, better use of manpower, production assets and investments, better-quality output, the enhancement of the role of material and moral incentives for work, the correct combination of these incentives, and an improvement of the entire system of economic management.

Brezhnev formulated a new and historically important task, namely, that of integrating the achievements of the scientific and technological revolution with the advantages of the socialist economic system. He drew attention to the existing possibilities for doing this, and also pointed out that in socialist society at its mature stage a vital need arises to improve production efficiency by accelerating scientific and technical progress and further raising labour productivity.

The 24th Congress continued and deepened the elaboration of the principles underlying the Party's agrarian policy. Brezhnev defined the key elements of that policy: to create economic conditions for the more rapid growth of agriculture; to extend capital construction and the building of a powerful and comprehensive mechanized base for agriculture and livestock breeding: to intensify agricultural production; to promote agricultural science; to train specialists and machine operators; and to continue the policy of setting up inter-kolkhoz and state-kolkhoz associations and also agro-industrial complexes.

The Central Committee report and other documents of the 24th Congress reviewed social policy in the context of economic development. Brezhnev closely analysed the social structure of Soviet society, a society that had reached the stage of developed socialism and was advancing towards social homogeneity and the elimination of class distinctions. All classes and social groups were drawing closer together and the Soviet people's social unity was being consolidated under the banner of Marxism - Leninism, which expressed the socialist interests and communist ideals of the working class.

Having discharged its historical mission, the state of the dictatorship of the proletariat had gradually evolved into a socialist state of the whole people. However, the latter remains a class organization. The position objectively held by the working class in production relations and its revolutionary spirit, discipline, organization, and collectivism determine its leading role in socialist society. The unbreakable alliance of workers and kolkhoz peasantry and their unity with the people's intelligentsia is a living fact and token of the Soviet people's further progress. The Party is, as always, doing everything to continue strengthening that alliance. Its policy is to foster the union of the working class, the kolkhoz peasantry, and the intelligentsia, thus promoting the gradual eradication of the essential distinctions between town and countryside.

The Central Committee report generalized what had been accomplished and bore out the conclusion that a new historical community, the Soviet people, had emerged during the years of socialist construction in the USSR. New and harmonious relations between classes, social groups, nations, and nationalities—relations with friendship and co-operation as the hallmarks—had appeared in the course of their joint work during the building of socialism and the battles in its defence. The Soviet people had been welded together by Marxist - Leninist ideology and the lofty aim of building a communist society.

Socialism is the most humane and most democratic social system known to history. Speaking of the full development of the individual as the central task facing the Party in communist construction, Brezhnev emphasized the importance of helping the broad masses to develop a communist world outlook and a new communist attitude to work. The Party educates the Soviet people in the spirit of the lofty ideals of communism. This is the noble aim of its ideological work among the people and of the activities on the part of state and public organizations. The all-round development of socialist democracy and the attainment of a higher cultural level and living standards via improved social production are essential to the success of the communist education of Soviet citizens. Man, concern for national welfare, satisfying the people's requirements, and building on their capabilities are central to the CPSU's work and policy.

In his closing speech at the 24th Congress, Brezhnev spelled out the policy line, the programme charted by the Congress for all spheres of social life.

Economic policy was directed to improving the life of the Soviet people. Without losing sight of the development of heavy industry, among it the defence branches, the Party made a substantial rise in general living standards the central aim of all economic work.

Social policy was for closer unity in Soviet society; for greater unity between classes and social groups and between all the nations and nationalities of the Soviet Union; and for the consistent development of socialist democracy and the involvement of ever-growing numbers of people in the administration of public and state affairs. Further, this policy sought a higher level of communist consciousness in all working people, the utmost promotion of science and culture, the spiritual florescence of the Soviet citizen, and the consolidation of the moral and political atmosphere in which people breathed easily, worked efficiently, and lived with a sense of security.

Party construction policy was for improved methods of Party leadership of society, strict observance of the Leninist standards of Party life, further closing of the Party ranks, and maximum efforts to bond the Party's links with the working class and with the entire Soviet people.

Foreign policy was for peace and international security, closer fraternity among socialist countries, and stronger alliance with anti-imperialist forces fighting for their liberation throughout the world.

At the Central Committee plenum held after the 24th Congress, Brezhnev was unanimously re-elected General Secretary.

A nationwide drive to bring about the decisions adopted by the 24th Congress and fulfil ahead of schedule the assignments for the ninth five-year plan was begun under the Party's leadership.

The Central Committee plenums held in December 1971 after the 24th Congress and the speeches delivered to them by Brezhnev played a huge and inspiring organizational role in mobilizing Communists and all the people to carry out the directives of the Party. In these speeches Brezhnev specified and enlarged on the current key problems of the CPSU's economic and social policy and of Party and state construction. He stressed the need for raising efficiency in social production, noting that it was necessary to make more intensive use of all resources, perfect the entire economic machinery, achieve a further improvement in economic management, and promote the creative initiative of the people in all areas of social life.

A powerful upswing of political and labour activity was triggered by the preparations for the 50th anniversary of the USSR—a great festival of friendship and brotherhood among the peoples of the Soviet Union. By their selfless work the multi-national Soviet people showed their whole-hearted approval of the Communist Party's policies and their monolithic unity around its Leninist Central Committee.

At a joint session of the Party Central Committee and the USSR and RSFSR Supreme Soviets in December 1972, Brezhnev delivered a report 'The fiftieth anniversary of the Union of Soviet Socialist Republics', in which he exhaustively analysed the Communist Party's work in implementing Leninist national policy and showed the historic significance of the formation of the USSR.

The Soviet people, he said, are a close-knit family of comrades united by a common ideology and the great aim of building communism. The development of nations and national relations in the USSR rests on the economic relations of mature socialism, on an integral economic complex shaped in the course of socialist construction, and on the common economic interests and aims of all Soviet nations and nationalities.

The political foundation on which nations flourish and draw together has been still further strengthened by the fact that the Soviet Union has become a state of the whole people and by the fact that the Party consistently abides by Lenin's precept that this state must be strengthened and developed. The spiritual unity of the nations and nationalities of the USSR is cemented by Soviet multi-national culture, which is socialist in content, i.e. in the basic direction of development, diversified in national forms, and internationalist in spirit and character. It may be termed an amalgam of the cultural values created by all the peoples of the Soviet Union.

Many other important aspects of multi-national state development and of Party national policy were dwelt on by the report. Brezhnev stressed that in the aspects in which it has been inherited from the pre-revolutionary past, the national question had been fully resolved in the Soviet Union. But even in mature socialist society, national relations 'continue to be a constantly developing reality, which keeps posing new tasks and problems.' For this reason the Party gives them its unflagging attention, settling the related questions in the interests of all the nations and nationalities and in the interests of building communism in the USSR.

The Party strengthens friendship among peoples in every possible way and educates Soviet citizens in the spirit of socialist patriotism and proletarian internationalism and in the spirit of pride for the Soviet Union as a whole. This is a lofty sense of community pride in the achievements of all the peoples of the USSR in the drive for socialist transformations, in the struggle for the triumph of the ideals of Marxism - Leninism, and for communism itself. It is a sense that heightens further as the working people of the USSR advance along the road towards creating communism and as the multi-form links uniting all Soviet peoples grow stronger.

The 50th anniversary of the multi-national Soviet Union vividly demonstrated the indestructible alliance of the working class, the kolkhoz peasantry, and the people's intelligentsia; and the socio-political and internationalist unity of the peoples of the USSR and their common will to move to new successes in building communism under the leadership of the Communist Party.

The strengthening of Soviet society's socio-political unity, the robust growth and the drawing together on every side of all the nations and nationalities of the USSR, and the consolidation of the Soviet people as a new historical community, all stem naturally from social development and from the many-sided work of the Party, its Central Committee, the Politburo, and Brezhnev himself. The Party shows unflagging concern for the people's education in the spirit of socialist patriotism and proletarian internationalism. This is borne out by decisions of its Congresses, by such Central Committee resolutions as those on the work of the Tashkent City Party organization, the Lvov Regional Party organization and the Tbilisi City Party committee, and by many of Brezhnev's speeches. These documents set out guidelines for internationalist education, and have been approved and supported by the entire Party and all working people.

Developments have shown the correctness of the policy chosen by the 24th Party Congress. Headed by the Communist Party, the people of the Soviet Union have scored further major achievements in economic, scientific, and cultural development. As in preceding years, the Party's

With Young Pioneers in Kiev, 1973.

work during the period of the ninth five-year plan was marked by a creative approach to the fulfilment of the difficult tasks posed by life and by ability to rally the people round itself and inspire them to heroic feats in the name of communism. The dedicated work of the Soviet people and the wise leadership of the Communist Party ensured the steady growth of the Soviet Union's economic potential, the strengthening of its security, and the fulfilment of the basic socio-economic assignments of the ninth five-year plan. The ninth five-year plan was unequalled for the absolute increment in the Soviet Union's economic potential and the breadth of the completed social programme.

As the 24th Congress foresaw, industrial output increased by 43 per cent during the ninth five-year plan, while basic production assets increased by 50 per cent, that is by more than 100 per cent on the 1965 level. This means that within ten years an amount was added to the economic potential equal to that which had taken nearly half a century to build up.

The ninth five-year plan witnessed a considerable growth of the country's productive forces, the further improvement of social relations, a rise in national living standards, and the extension of socialist democracy.

The 25th Party Congress (February - March 1976) was another milestone on the Soviet people's road to communism. Delivered by General Secretary Brezhnev, the 'Report of the Central Committee of the CPSU and the immediate tasks of the Party in internal and foreign policy' added to the treasure-chest of scientific communism and became a policy document of the Party. The report contained an in-depth and comprehensive analysis of the major processes of our time, of the revolutionary and transforming work of the Party and the Soviet people, of the entire course of the world revolutionary process. It also outlined key objectives of the Party's Leninist domestic and foreign policies at the present stage. In the report a strictly realistic assessment of successes achieved and potentialities available is found alongside a clear and precise determination of long-term tasks and programme guidelines. The report is filled with a spirit of revolutionary optimism, practical mindedness, and a class/Party approach to weighing the complex phenomena of social life, the urgent tasks of building communism, and the struggle for peace and the freedom of nations.

Lenin's words about the oneness of Marxist theory and policy providing a guideline 'not only in the sense of explaining the past but also in the sense of a bold forecast of the future and of bold practical action for its achievement' are entirely applicable to the documents of the 25th Congress.

The CPSU has always been guided by Lenin's injunction on the need for a clear-cut theoretical assessment of social development, for a knowledge of its underlying laws, and above all for an analysis of 'what might be called the stages of the economic maturity of communism'. This Leninist approach to the fundamental problems of building communism is eloquently borne out by the Central Committee's report.

In this report Brezhnev filled out the characterization of developed socialism given by him at the 24th Congress and summed up the results of the ninth five-year plan, during which the intensive and self-sacrificing work of the Soviet people was crowned with outstanding achievements in all areas of building communism. The Central Committee's report, the entire Congress proceedings, and the decisions adopted by it prove that under the leadership of the Party the Soviet Union is advancing consistently and confidently along the road charted by Lenin, and that the advantages of the existing socialism are ever more clear.

Brezhnev spoke of new prospects for building communism, formulated the Party's present economic strategy, and set out the guidelines of economic development and the tasks involved in enhancing the welfare of the people during the period of the tenth five-year plan.

He summed up the manifold work of the Party and its Central Committee in the principal areas of bringing about the new society and indicated the indivisible link between all the stages of the road travelled thus far, between all the Soviet *pyatiletki,* each of which was a milestone in the history of the USSR. In their main tasks and targets, the ninth and tenth five-year plans can be viewed as a whole. The 25th Congress specified and enlarged upon the guidelines of the preceding congress on fundamental questions of Party economic policy in the mature socialist society with reference to the latter half of the 1970s and even beyond.

'Just as any other strategy,' Brezhnev observed, 'the Party's economic strategy begins with the formulation of tasks and identification of fundamental long-term aims. The most important of these has been and remains a steady improvement of the national standard of living and culture. Economic strategy also covers a precise determination of the ways and means of attaining the set aims.'

The chief target of the tenth five-year plan, as defined by the 25th Congress, was the consistent implementation of this Party policy of raising the national standard of living and culture through the dynamic and proportionate development of social production and the enhancement of its efficiency, the acceleration of scientific and technological progress, the rise in labour productivity, and the greatest possible improvement in the quality of work in all areas of the national economy.

The drive for efficiency and high quality is the key component of the CPSU's economic strategy. During the tenth five-year plan, higher labour productivity must ensure approximately 90 per cent of the increment in industrial output and the entire increment in agricultural output and construction.

Another essential feature of the Party's economic policy is its call for the further build-up of the USSR's economic might, for the extension and fundamental renewal of production assets, and the maintenance of a stable, balanced growth of heavy industry, which is fundamental to the socialist economy. This is due above all to the gigantic increases in the scale and potentialities of that economy.

In 1976-90 the USSR will have approximately double the material and financial resources compared with the preceding fifteen-year period. 'New possibilities,' Brezhnev told the 25th Congress, 'are thereby being created for the solution of the basic socio-economic problems set by the Party programme and by the last few congresses. This concerns, notably, a further rise of the Soviet people's well-being, an improvement of the conditions of their work and everyday life, and considerable progress in public health, education and culture—in fact everything that helps to mould the new man, the harmoniously developed individual, and to improve the socialist way of life.'

In order to carry out the diverse social and economic tasks, a rapid growth of labour productivity and a drastic increase of efficiency in the whole of social production are the only options. Profound qualitative changes must be effected in the structure and technical level of the national economy, and its very image must be substantially altered. The key problems of the Party's economic policy during the tenth five-year plan are to speed up scientific and technological progress, achieve a further growth of agriculture, increase the output of consumer goods, improve economic planning and management, and promote economic relations with foreign countries.

The basic principles of the Party's economic strategy are aimed at improving production efficiency and performance. They proceed from the realization that the supreme goal of social production under socialism is the maximum satisfaction of the people's growing material and cultural requirements.

The Soviet economy as a single integrated national economic complex embraces all the constituents of social production, distribution and exchange throughout the Soviet Union.

Economic management is based on state plans of social and economic development with due account being taken of varying circumstances within individual industries and areas, alongside centralized management on the one hand and economic autonomy and initiative of individual enterprises, production associations and similar economic units on the other. In this process extensive use is made of such economic levers and incentives as 'cost accounting', profit, prime cost, etc.

Relying on the creative activity of the working people, socialist emulation, the advances of scientific and technical progress, by improving the existing forms and methods of economic management, the state ensures the continuing growth of labour productivity, boosting production efficiency and performance, all of which contributes to a dynamic, planned and balanced development of the country's national economy.

Brezhnev's propositions on the content of the Party's economic strategy are of fundamental significance for theory and policy. He defined the chief factors of economic growth, the main trends in restructuring agriculture, and the ways of bringing the life styles in town and village closer together. He stressed the necessity for improving the economic mechanism to suit the needs of developed socialism, the necessity for orienting economic management and the planning system towards end-results, and for perfecting the methods of comprehensively resolving the country's major problems.

In agriculture, practice has conclusively shown that inter-farm co-operation and agro-industrial integration offer tremendous possibilities for raising the efficiency of farming and putting crop and animal farming on an up-to-date industrial basis. And at the 25th Party Congress Brezhnev urged more vigorous promotion of this policy.

In June 1976 the Party's Central Committee discussed their General Secretary's proposals and adopted a decision on the 'Further development of specialization and concentration in agriculture through inter-farm co-operation and agro-industrial integration'. The decision noted that the sweeping agricultural measures approved by the 25th Congress are a pressing necessity and an undertaking of great political, economic, and social significance—not a short-term campaign but a far-reaching process for the future, a new stage in realizing Lenin's co-operative plan under conditions of developed socialism.

The country has tackled a historic task—blending the achievements of the scientific and technological revolution with the advantages of the socialist economic system, which ensures success in building the material and technical basis of communism. Speaking at the 25th Congress, Brezhnev drew the important conclusion that this process was tied up with changes in social relationships. 'We Communists,' he said, 'are acting on the belief that only under socialism can the scientific and technological revolution find a course consistent with the interests of man and society. Conversely, the final objective of the social revolution, the building of a communist society, is attainable only on the basis of accelerated scientific and technical progress.'

The idea that working people play the decisive part in carrying out the plans of building communism and that there is a continuity of revolutionary traditions runs through the Central Committee report to Congress. With more than four-fifths of the country's population born after the October Revolution, this continuity is seen first of all in the close ideological bonds between the older and younger generations, in their deep-rooted community of outlook and their common beliefs. In the final analysis this continuity of traditions is attested by the continuity of deeds, by each new generation's ability to project and develop the achievements of earlier ones in line with the new tasks of building communism.

An important item for Congress was communist education—the education of working people in a spirit opposed to any manifestation of bourgeois ideology. Congress stressed that positive changes in world affairs, and *détente*, are creating favourable opportunities for a massive spreading of socialist ideas. On the other hand, the ideological contention of the two systems is becoming more intensive and imperialist propaganda more subtle.

'There is no room for neutralism or compromise in the struggle between the two ideologies,' says the Central Committee report. 'There must be a high degree of political vigilance, active, efficient, and convincing propaganda, and quick reaction to hostile ideological subversion.'

The increasingly close social, political, and ideological unity of Soviet society is a reliable basis for the further development of socialist democracy and the political system of mature socialism. Socialist democracy implies unity of rights and duties, genuine freedom and civil responsibility, a harmonious balanced blend of the interest of society, the collective and the individuals. 'In our concern for the full development of the individual and of his rights,' said Brezhnev, 'we also give due attention to strengthening social discipline and the fulfilment by all citizens of their duties to society.' Conscious and free socialist discipline is no more conceivable without democracy than is socialist democracy without good organization and discipline.

It is precisely the organic interaction in the relationship of rights and duty, the responsible attitude of each citizen to his duties and the interests of his people that furnish the only secure durable basis for the fullest expression of the principles of socialist democracy, the genuine freedom of the individual. The socialist system ensures the extension of rights and freedoms and the steady improvement in living standards and quality of life as programmes of social economic and cultural development are implemented. As our society advances along the road of building communism, the creative energies of the people are coming out more and more fully and vividly.

It was true praise for the Soviet people, the people that entrusted the country's guidance to the Communists, that Brezhnev, speaking at the Congress, should have called them 'a people of extraordinary industry, courage and stamina; a people of generous spirit, talent, and intellect; a people that does not flinch in times of hardship; a people that is concerned over the smallest slip in its gigantic undertaking. It is not given to boasting, but neither does it play down its achievements. It is responsive to the joys and sorrows of other peoples, and is always ready to help them in their struggle for justice, freedom, and social progress. The Soviet people is a truly great and heroic people.'

The Soviet people has been building a new life under the guidance of Lenin's Party for a full sixty years. The Great October Socialist Revolution ushered in a new era in the history of mankind—that of the transition from capitalism to socialism on a world scale. It marked the beginning of the collectivist system, of a new mode of life for hundreds of millions of people. 'Six decades is less than man's average lifespan,' observed Brezhnev, 'but in that time our country has travelled a road equalling centuries.'

The General Secretary defined the three decisive results achieved by Party and people. In the USSR a new society has been created the like of which mankind has never known—a society with a crisis-free and continuously growing economy, mature socialist relations, and genuine freedom. It is a society with a scientific materialist world outlook, with infinite confidence in the future, with radiant communist expectations. Boundless horizons of further general progress lie before it. That is the first result of the country's development in six decades.

The second result is the Soviet way of life, meaning true collectivism and comradeship, growing unity and friendship among all the country's nations and nationalities, and the moral health that makes the Soviet people strong and persevering whether labouring or fighting.

The third result of the past sixty years is Soviet man himself. His freedom won, he has been able to safeguard it even in the bitterest battles. He has given all his strength and spared no sacrifice to build the future. Withstanding all trials, he has changed beyond recognition, and now combines ideological convictions, tremendous vital energy, culture, and knowledge with the ability to use them. An ardent patriot, he has been and always will be a consistent internationalist.

Mature socialism, established on one-sixth of the world's surface, is, for all the world to see, the most dynamic social system. It embodies freedom from exploitation and oppression, the sovereignty of the working people, the all-round development of democracy, a flourishing culture, steadily rising living standards, and equality and unity among all the country's nations and peoples.

The achievements of the homeland of the October Revolution are conclusive evidence to the effect that socialism has made possible rates of progress in all fields of social life without precedent in history.

The national income in 1976 was 65 times that of before the revolution, although some two decades in the history of the Soviet state were periods of war imposed on our people and of economic rehabilitation. Taking the fiftieth anniversary of Soviet government, 1967, as a point of reference, the country's economic potential has practically doubled. Today industry produces in two and a half days as much as during the whole of 1913.

Between 1965 and 1975 industrial production grew 120 per cent—a seventeen-fold increase since 1940. We are now producing more than the whole world was producing a quarter-century ago. The Soviet Union has outstripped the United States and ranks first in the world in output of oil, coal, manganese, chrome and iron ore, pig-iron, steel, coke, mineral fertilizers, diesel and electric-powered locomotives, tractors, prefabricated reinforced concrete sections and parts, cement, sawn timber, woollen cloth, leather shoes, sugar, and butter. In 1975 the country produced 141 million tons of steel (against 18.3 million tons in 1940) as compared with the USA's 110 million tons.

Agricultural development, the extension and improvement of the material and technical side of farming, is being conducted on an unparalleled scale. Under the seventh five-year plan, for example, investments in agriculture totalled 48,600 million roubles, under the eighth 82,200 million, and under the ninth (1971-5) as much as 131,500 million, or more than in the preceding two five-year periods combined.

Under the tenth plan, more than 170,000 million roubles have been earmarked for investment in agriculture, with land improvement claiming more than 40,000 million of this sum, or as much as was spent in the preceding two five-year periods combined. This scale of investment is unparalleled anywhere.

The Party is taking steps to achieve a radical solution to the food problem and meet the country's growing demand in a situation where population and demand are steadily growing while cropland acreage remains the same. This is why, Brezhnev points out, it is planned to accelerate the intensive development of all branches of agriculture in future. Great investments are being made in agriculture, and the industries catering to it are being built up.

Successful economic development and rising labour productivity have steadily pushed up the living standard and cultural level of the people. For instance, the average monthly earnings of factory and office workers during the ninth five-year plan increased from 122 roubles to 146. Their real incomes have grown 50 per cent over the last decade. The social consumption funds have more than doubled over the period. Housing construction is being carried out on an immense scale. On average more than 6000 flats become ready for occupation per day, that is, more than 100 million square metres of floor space every year. Over 110 million people have moved into new homes in the past decade.

Educational standards are rising rapidly. In 1975 the number of qualified engineers employed in the national economy was 230 per cent more in the Soviet Union than in the United States. The educational standards of the country's social groups are gradually converging.

In handling the key problems of the country's economic and social development, the Party, its Central Committee and the Politburo led by Brezhnev display constant concern for strengthening national defence and enhancing the combat-preparedness of the Soviet armed forces. Speaking at the 25th Party Congress, Brezhnev stated that the Soviet people may rest assured that the fruits of their constructive work are reliably protected. He went on to say that nobody should have any doubt that the Soviet Communist Party would do everything in its power to provide the Soviet armed forces with everything they need to perform their noble mission of safeguarding the constructive work of the Soviet people and world peace.

The problems involved in supplying the Soviet army, navy and air force with up-to-date weapons and equipment, training and educating members of the armed forces and officer cadres, developing Soviet military science and the art of warfare are being tackled under Brezhnev's personal direction as Chairman of the Defence Council.

Loyal to their patriotic and internationalist duty, the Soviet armed forces along with the armies of the other Warsaw Treaty member states are contributing effectively to the defence of socialism and peace. Strengthening the defence capability of the USSR and other nations of the socialist community is the key factor in averting war and promoting international security.

The 25th Party Congress has outlined new objectives which will add still more to the country's might. This Congress has been a major event in the life of Party and country, and also in the history of world communist, working-class, and national liberation movements. No fewer than 103 delegations from 96 countries attended, representing communist and workers', national democratic, and socialist parties. There have never been so many friendly delegations at any previous congress. This testifies to the enduring vigour of the life-giving internationalist bonds that securely link the Soviet Communist Party with all the other participants on the worldwide battle-front for peace, the freedom of nations, and social progress.

The Congress made a signal contribution to the theory of scientific communism. Its results, and the speeches made by representatives of the fraternal parties, struck a devastating blow at hostile propaganda myths of a 'crisis' in the world communist movement. It was also a demonstration of the movement's closer unity and solidarity with other progressive forces all over the world.

The 25th Congress unanimously elected Leonid Brezhnev to the Party's Central Committee, and a Central Committee plenum elected him its General Secretary. This was more than a mere acknowledgement of his outstanding personal qualities: it was also an expression of approval and support of the Leninist policy followed with scrupulous consistency, energy, and perseverance by the Party's operational headquarters—the Central Committee—under his leadership.

Congress gave a powerful impetus to the political activity and work motivation of Soviet people, who welcomed its decisions as their own programme of action and rallied still closer behind the Party and its Central Committee.

The revolutionary spirit of innovation, the ideas of the 25th Congress are alive in the day-to-day activities of the Communist Party and the Soviet people. Once the mass of the people has realized and accepted them, they are turning increasingly into a material force and a powerful factor of social development.

Inspired by the decision of the 25th Congress, the Soviet people have already made great efforts to accelerate economic, scientific and cultural progress, modernize industry and agriculture on the basis of advanced science and technology, enhance its efficiency and perfect economic management and planning.

7

Mature Socialism

In his speech at the October 1976 Central Committee plenum, the General Secretary summed up the results of the work done by Party and people since the 25th Congress. The plenum detailed the ways of implementing the Congress decisions, and produced an in-depth study and political evaluation of the tenth five-year plan and the next economic year. It singled out and summarized the decisive sectors requiring special attention and the greatest concentration of energy by Party, government, trade union, and economic bodies. In his speech Brezhnev gave a comprehensive review of present-day international relations, and thoroughly examined the current tasks of Party and government in foreign policy and the further struggle for peace, the national independence of peoples, and social progress.

Never before has the Soviet Union enjoyed such objectively favourable opportunities for rapid advance. It has a powerful economic potential, a high level of culture, advanced science and technology, and fully educated, skilled cadres devoted to the great ideals of communism.

The spectacular achievements of socialism in being, the central immediate and long-range tasks of further construction were reflected in the historic decisions of the May 1977 Central Committee plenum, which approved the new draft Constitution of the USSR.

The Constitution was drafted on the basis of extensive theoretical research carried out by the Party in analysing the historical laws governing the development of Soviet society, the specific features of its current stage, the international position of the Soviet Union and world socialism. The Constitution rests on a solid theoretical foundation provided by the concept of developed socialist society, evolved jointly by the Soviet Communist Party and the fraternal communist and workers' parties. The new Constitution was drafted under the immediate direction and with the active participation of the Party Central Committee, its Politburo, and General Secretary Brezhnev as Chairman of the Constitutional Commission.

At the plenum Brezhnev made a report on the draft new Constitution. He substantiated by scientific arguments the need for a new constitution, and described in detail its main features expressing the Soviet people's epoch-making achievements under the leadership of the Communist Party, and the immense importance of the new Constitution both for the country's domestic life and for consolidating the positions of socialism, peace and progress on the international scene.

In his report Brezhnev reviewed and summed up the far-reaching changes that had been taking place in the Soviet Union, in the whole of Soviet society, since the adoption of the Constitution of 1936. At that time merely the foundations of socialism had been laid. The collective farm system was still young and immature. Technologically the Soviet economy still lagged behind that of the leading industrial powers. The leftovers from the pre-revolutionary period were still in evidence in various fields. Today a mature socialist society has been built in the Soviet Union. Brezhnev emphasized that fundamental changes on a large scale have affected all aspects of social life.

The economy of the country, where socialist property has unchallenged domination, has changed beyond recognition. A powerful integrated economic organism has formed, which is operating and developing effectively on the basis of a combination of the scientific and technological revolution with the advantages of the socialist system.

The social image of society has also changed. The working class today consists of scores of millions of educated, technically competent, and politically mature members. Their social activity has grown considerably as has their participation in the administration of the state. The peasantry has also changed, and its psychology has formed on the basis of socialist social relations. The collective farmers use up-to-date machinery, and their educational standards and way of life differ but little from those of urban residents. The intelligentsia has truly become flesh and bone of the people, and its proportion in society is growing. The social uniformity of Soviet society continues to increase steadily.

Not only has the equality of nations been proclaimed constitutionally but it has become a reality. All Soviet Republics have now attained a high level of development. The essential distinctions between the basic social groups are being gradually erased, and all of the country's nations and peoples are drawing closer together. A new historical community—the Soviet people—has come into being.

Brezhnev pointed out in the report that, as was laid down in the draft, just as in the Constitution of 1936, the sovereign rights of the Union Republics were to be under the protection of the Union state. The guarantees of these rights were to be continued. What is more, they were to be widened, for instance by authorizing the Republics to have a vote in matters within the jurisdiction of the Union state. The Union Republics as represented by their supreme bodies of government were to be guaranteed the right of legislative initiative in the Supreme Soviet of the USSR.

Now that developed socialism has been built and all the sections of the population have adopted the ideological and political platform of the working class, the Soviet state, born as it was as a state of the dictatorship of the proletariat, has developed into a state of the whole people.

Brezhnev also analysed the fundamental changes that had taken place in the international positions of the Soviet Union and in the socio-political image of the world as a whole. The capitalist encirclement of the Soviet Union has long become a thing of the past. Socialism has grown into a world system. The positions of capitalism have deteriorated considerably. Dozens of young sovereign states have sprung up in what were formerly colonial possessions. The Soviet Union's international prestige and influence have increased immeasurably. As a result a new alignment of forces has taken shape in the world arena. It has become feasible to avert another world war. Brezhnev stressed, however, that although the menace of such a war had been greatly lessened, much work and a stubborn struggle lay ahead.

The draft was prepared in full conformity with the directives of the 25th Congress, which pointed out the need for the new Constitution to reflect the great achievements of socialism, to formalize not only the general principles of the socialist system expressing the class essence of the Soviet state but also the basic features of developed socialist society, its political organization, the principles of management of the national economy, the role of the state in the spiritual life of society, and the continued development of socialist democracy.

'In our work on the draft', Brezhnev emphasized, 'we firmly abided by the principle of continuity. In it the characteristic features of the Constitution of a socialist type outlined by Lenin in his time have been preserved and developed.' The Constitution rests on Soviet legislation renewed and perfected during the last few years and consummates what has been done in this field. Brezhnev pointed out another essential element in the new Constitution: its draft drew widely on the experience in constitutional law gained by other nations of the socialist community.

The USSR Constitution opens with a preamble to the effect that the Great October Socialist Revolution carried out by the workers and peasants of Russia under the leadership of the Communist Party headed by Lenin overthrew the power of the capitalists and landlords, shattered the bonds of oppression, established the dictatorship of the proletariat in the form of the Soviet state—a state of a new type, which is the main instrument for defence of the revolutionary gains and for building socialism and communism. Mankind began its historic transition from capitalism to socialism.

In the process of its heroic revolutionary struggle and work of construction, the Soviet people led by the Communist Party has built a developed socialist society. This society is a historically legitimate stage on the path towards communism.

The ultimate goal of the Soviet state is the construction of a classless communist society based on public communist self-government. The central tasks facing the socialist state of the whole people are as follows: building up the material and technological basis for communism, perfecting socialist social relations to the level of communist relations, moulding the new man of communist society, advancing the material and cultural standards of life of the working people, safeguarding national security, promoting peace and international co-operation.

The USSR is a socialist state of the whole people expressing the will and the interests of workers, peasants, and the intelligentsia, the working people of all Soviet nations, large and small. This is the most complete and consistent democracy in the world today. All power in the USSR is vested in the people, which exercises its sovereignty through the Soviets of People's Deputies making up the political foundation of the USSR.

The General Secretary of the Soviet Communist Party described the main features of the new Constitution, which formalizes the construction of a developed socialist society in the USSR. He pointed out that the main innovative element contained in the draft was the widening and advancement of socialist democracy.

Government by the Soviets is truly government of the people. All Soviet citizens who have attained the age of 18 are eligible to vote and to be elected to the Soviets. The age qualification for election to the USSR Supreme Soviet is 21. Elections are carried out on the basis of universal, equal and direct suffrage by secret ballot. Citizens of the USSR are equal before the law regardless of their origin, social and property status, race or nationality, sex, education, language, religious beliefs, occupation, residence, and other circumstances.

The equality of Soviet citizens is guaranteed in all political, economic, social, and cultural fields.

Brezhnev indicated in his report that the new Constitution defined a much wider spectrum of the political rights and freedoms of Soviet citizens.

Under the new Constitution citizens of the USSR enjoy unabridged social, economic, political and individual rights and freedoms proclaimed and guaranteed by the USSR Constitution and Soviet laws.

Soviet citizens are fully fledged members of society, enjoying the right to employment, holidays, medical care, material security in old age and in the event of disability, and the right to housing. They have the right to education, access to cultural achievements, freedom of scientific, technical and artistic creation. They have the right to take part in the management of the affairs of state and society, to submit suggestions to government bodies and public organizations for improving their work performance, to criticize flaws in their activities, and to associate in public organizations. In accordance with the interests of the people and with a view to consolidating and developing the socialist system Soviet citizens are guaranteed freedom of speech, the press, assembly, public processions and demonstrations, freedom of conscience, personal immunity, inviolability of the home, privacy of correspondence and telephone conversations.

Respect for the individual, protection of the rights and freedoms of citizens is the duty of all Soviet government bodies, public organizations and officials. In addition to this important provision it is stipulated that the rights and freedoms of citizens shall not be misused so as to prejudice the socialist social system and the interests of the Soviet people. It is necessary, Brezhnev emphasized, that every Soviet citizen should be clearly aware of the fact that the most effective guarantee of his rights is, in the final analysis, the power and prosperity of the homeland. Therefore, Soviet citizens should realize their responsibility to society and conscientiously fulfil their duty to the state and the people.

The General Secretary said further: 'Against the interpretation of concepts of democracy and human rights, distorted and profaned by bourgeois and revisionist propaganda, we set the fullest and most real spectrum of the rights and duties of a member of socialist society. We submit to the judgment of history the truly historic achievements of the working people made possible by government of the working class led by the Communist Party.'

At the end of his report, General Secretary Brezhnev expressed his firm assurance that the adoption of the new Constitution, a veritable manifesto of developed socialist society, would be another historic contribution of the Leninist party and the entire Soviet people to the building of communism, to the internationalist cause of the struggle waged by the working people of the world for freedom, mankind's progress, and lasting peace on earth.

The May plenum of the Central Committee approved in general the draft Constitution of the USSR submitted by the Constitutional Commission, forwarded it to the Presidium of the USSR Supreme Soviet and recommended that the draft should be published for nationwide discussion.

The plenum unanimously agreed to nominate General Secretary Brezhnev to the post of President of the Presidium of the USSR Supreme Soviet, this to be held simultaneously with his Party office. Speakers at the plenum presented exhaustive arguments in favour of this decision, referring to Brezhnev's outstanding role in the activities of the Communist Party and the Soviet state, in the international communist and working-class movement—his selfless service of the people and the great cause of communist construction. By his indefatigable struggle for *détente*, for lasting peace and social progress, he has won great prestige and respect among all honest people on earth. Brezhnev is a worthy representative of the Soviet Communist Party, the Soviet people as a whole, the great socialist state in the international arena.

The growth of the Party's leading and organizing role in Soviet life, in all activities of the Soviet state on the home and international scene, as well as Brezhnev's outstanding personal qualities and selfless work for the benefit of his homeland have had the result that for many years now he has truly been the most prestigious representative of the Communist Party and the Soviet state in the eyes of the Soviet people and indeed of the whole world.

The election of Brezhnev as President of the Presidium of the USSR Supreme Soviet meets the supreme interests of Soviet society and the state, and will contribute to the fulfilment of the decisions of the 25th Congress, to new achievements in building communism.

The Central Committee of the Party, the Presidium of the USSR Supreme Soviet, and the Councils of Elders of the Soviet of the Union and the Soviet of Nationalities of the USSR Supreme Soviet submitted in June 1977 to the sixth session of the ninth USSR Supreme Soviet a proposal nominating Brezhnev to the Presidency. Unanimously and with enthusiasm the deputies elected Brezhnev President of the Presidium of the USSR Supreme Soviet.

The President-elect acknowledged his gratitude to the Supreme Soviet for its high appreciation of his merits and said in part: 'It is certainly not easy to combine these lofty and responsible duties of a statesman with my duties as General Secretary of our Party. However, the will of the Party and the Soviet people, the interests of our socialist homeland have always been to me the supreme law I have honoured all my life.'

Brezhnev assured the audience of his willingness to devote all his energies to the achievement of the great goals pursued by the Party and people on the path towards communism. 'I will do everything in my power', he said, 'to help make our beloved homeland stronger and more prosperous, improve the life of the Soviet people, strengthen the peace of the world and develop friendly co-operation among nations.'

The Soviet people enthusiastically and unanimously approved Brezhnev's election to the Presidency. Cordial messages of congratulation poured in from all over the Soviet Union. In their congratulatory telegrams world statesmen and public leaders expressed their recog-

Wartime memories: visiti

nition of the high international prestige of the tireless fighter for peace and social progress.

The decisions of the May plenum evoked a powerful upsurge of the working people's activity in all spheres of social life throughout the

ctory in Novorossiisk 1974.

country. It was with a feeling of patriotic pride that the Soviet people welcomed the new draft Constitution. Its discussion took on enormous scope and was conducted in an atmosphere of vigorous political activity and enthusiastic work. It was a milestone in the country's political life, a nationwide forum at which millions of working people learned how to decide the cardinal problems involved in the development of society and the state.

The nationwide discussion of the draft Constitution, which lasted for almost four months, demonstrated the acute political awareness of the Soviet people, their profound interest in the affairs of the Soviet state. Over 140 million people, that is, more than four-fifths of the country's adult population, took part in the discussion.

People from all walks of life, of different ages, nationalities and ethnic groups, Communists and persons without party affiliation, as true masters of the country analysed the draft and suggested changes. They proposed some 400,000 amendments to individual articles aimed at clarifying and extending the formulations in the draft Constitution. At the same time, Soviet citizens expressed their views on various aspects of the development of Soviet society and the state, made critical remarks on the different aspects of the activities of government bodies and public organizations and suggested measures to be taken to improve their functioning and eliminate shortcomings. This was a frank and truly nationwide discussion of the most crucial problems of Soviet life, another triumph of socialist democracy. As Brezhnev put it: 'We can say confidently and proudly that the Soviet people as a whole is the true author of the new Constitution.'

The discussion of the draft Constitution demonstrated again the strength and vitality of the unity of all classes and social groups; all nations and peoples of Soviet society rallied behind the Communist Party. It awakened new creative powers in the Soviet people and gave a new dimension to their drive to implement the decisions of the 25th Congress.

The draft Constitution held the attention of all mankind. It was enthusiastically supported in the other socialist countries. The new Constitution is an inspiring example to the young socialist-oriented states. It excited keen interest among the working people in the capitalist world, primarily within their vanguard—the communist and workers' parties.

The plenum of the Central Committee held early in October 1977 heard a report 'On the Draft Constitution of the USSR and the Results of its Nationwide Discussion' delivered by Brezhnev in his capacity as General Secretary of the Party, President of the Presidium of the USSR Supreme Soviet, and Chairman of the Constitutional Commission. The plenum approved in the main the draft Constitution submitted by the Constitutional Commission with additions, clarifications and amendments suggested during its nationwide discussion, and ruled to submit the draft to the extraordinary seventh session of the USSR Supreme Soviet. Brezhnev was asked to report at the session on the draft Constitution and the results of its nationwide discussion.

The ninth Supreme Soviet of the USSR went into session on 4 October 1977. This was an event of truly historic importance. The attention of the Party and people and indeed of the world public as a whole was focused on Brezhnev's report. It was a central document of creative Marxism-Leninism, a statement of policy principles, which gave a profound scientific insight into the laws governing the development of Soviet society at the present stage and the prospects for further communist construction.

Brezhnev dwelt in the first place on the historic significance of the new USSR Constitution. He said in particular: 'We are adopting the new Constitution on the eve of the 60th anniversary of the Great October Socialist Revolution. This is not just a coincidence of two crucial events in the life of the country. The link between them is much more deep-rooted. The new Constitution may be described as the epitome of the development of the Soviet state over six decades. It strikingly demonstrates that the ideas proclaimed by the October Revolution and Lenin's behests are being successfully translated into life.'

The report showed conclusively that the drafting and nationwide discussion of the new Constitution had been a splendid example of consistent application of the principles of genuine, that is socialist, democracy. The main political outcome of the nationwide discussion may be illustrated by this comment of Soviet people: this is the Constitution we were waiting for. It accurately reflects our achievements, aspirations and hopes and accurately defines our rights and duties.

Brezhnev presented a thorough, comprehensive analysis of the most important additions, clarifications and amendments to the draft submitted during its nationwide discussion, which made it possible to improve the wording of a number of provisions with a view to the continued development of socialist democracy. Brezhnev oriented Party and government bodies and public organizations on specific practical conclusions to be drawn from this nationwide discussion and on measures to be taken to improve work performance in all spheres of life throughout the country.

He brought up and analysed in a creative spirit the vital theoretical problems involved in the continued steady advance of Soviet society towards communism. The report comprehensively substantiated the new Soviet Constitution as a law of life in developed socialist society. By summing up theoretically the experience in building developed socialist society in the Soviet Union and the progress made in this direction by the other socialist countries, Brezhnev developed and specified along scientific lines the essence and distinctive features of mature socialism, the laws and trends of its development, and showed its place in the process of the emergence of communist society.

Brezhnev pointed out that developed socialism is the stage of maturity of the new society completing the restructuring of the whole pattern of social relations on collectivist principles intrinsic to socialism. This brings into full play the laws of socialism, and its advantages are realized in all spheres of social life. Hence the organic integrity and dynamism of the social system, its political stability, its indestructible unity. Hence the growing consolidation of all classes and social groups, all large and small nations into a new social and international community—the Soviet people. Hence also the emergence of new, socialist culture, the advent of the new, socialist way of life.

Brezhnev underscored that the definition 'developed socialism' applies only to a socialist society based on powerful, advanced industry and on large-scale, highly-mechanized agriculture, which makes it possible in practical terms to set as the main immediate goal of social development the increasingly complete satisfaction of the varied requirements of citizens.

Having discussed the specific historical conditions and ways of building developed socialism in the Soviet Union and other nations of the socialist community, Brezhnev drew an important general theoretical conclusion of immense practical political significance for all countries taking the socialist path in the future. He stated in this context: 'Whatever specific conditions may prevail in the countries building socialism, the stage of its advancement on its own basis, that of mature, developed socialist society, forms an indispensable stage in social transformation, a relatively long stretch of the road from capitalism to communism. The future does not lie beyond the limits of the present. The future has its roots in the present, and so while solving the tasks of today's socialism we are gradually entering the communist morrow.'

In his report Brezhnev further developed the important theoretical propositions he had made earlier at congresses of the Communist Party and at plenary meetings of its Central Committee on the leading and organizing role of the Party in the struggle for the triumph of communism, on its place in the political system of Soviet society, on the transformation of the state of the dictatorship of the proletariat into a socialist state of the whole people and on the prospects of its further development into communist social self-government, and on the objective process of the growing unity and all-round development, the mutual spiritual enrichment, of the different nations and peoples of the USSR.

Brezhnev described in detail the leading and organizing role of the Soviet Communist Party in the struggle for the victory of communism and gave the lie by well-grounded arguments to the fabrications of imperialist propaganda about the 'proclamation of the dictatorship of the Communist Party' and other fables of this kind. He stated in this context that the Communist Party is the vanguard of the Soviet people and their most class-conscious contingent inseparably linked with theory. The Party has no other interests but the interests of the people. To seek to oppose Party and people to one another is tantamount to trying to separate, say, the heart from the rest of the body.

Brezhnev stated that the Soviet Union today is a legitimate stage in the development of the state created by the October Revolution, the stage characteristic of mature socialism. Therefore, the tasks of the government bodies, their structure and functions, and the procedure of their activities should conform to the stage achieved in the development of society. Such conformity is definitely ensured by the new Soviet Constitution. Once we have adopted it we are fully entitled to say that another important step has been taken, bringing our country nearer to the great goals of our Party and our people.

Exposing the distortions by bourgeois ideologists of the Marxist-Leninist doctrine on the withering away of the state in the conditions of building socialism and communism, Brezhnev proved conclusively that the ideological adversaries of socialism are unwilling to see the main thing—the dialectics of the development of the Soviet state and society. As he put it: 'With the development and advancement of the socialist state millions of citizens are increasingly involved in the activities of government and people's control bodies, in the management of production and distribution, in social and cultural policies and in the administration of justice. In short, along with the development of socialist democracy our statehood is gradually being transformed into communist social self-government. This is, of course, a long process, but it is proceeding along a steady course. We are convinced that the new Soviet Constitution will contribute effectively to the attainment of this important goal of communist construction.

Brezhnev paid great attention to the international significance of the formulation, discussion and acceptance of the new Soviet Constitution. He stressed that its discussion was not merely national but international. And this was further clear proof of the enormous part that socialism had to play in today's world. 'The lively comments, the great and sincere interest and warm approval of the draft Constitution by the working masses of the world fill our hearts with pride in the Soviet people's achievements and illustrate even more strikingly their great international significance.'

The report brought devastating criticism to bear on the attempts by imperialist propaganda to distort the new Constitution's content, to play down and where possible ignore it, concealing from their own working masses its major provisions. Noting that specially hostile attacks were reserved for provisions of the Constitution on the rights, freedoms and duties of Soviet citizens, Brezhnev said: 'The critics of the Soviet Constitution have found themselves here in an unenviable situation. They cannot escape the fact that the draft Constitution defines the social, economic and political rights and freedoms of citizens and the specific guarantees of these rights more widely, clearly and fully than ever before and anywhere else.'

The extraordinary session of the Supreme Soviet's work was carried out amid general enthusiasm. In the deputies' speeches resounded pride for the historic achievements of the Soviet nation given concrete expression in the draft Constitution, and approval for the domestic and foreign policy of Party and government. Discussion of Brezhnev's report demonstrated the unity of the thoughts and aims of Soviet people, whose collective intelligence and will, whose solidarity around Lenin's party, was embodied in the draft of the new Constitution of the USSR.

The deputies greatly valued Brezhnev's report, filled as it was with concern for the welfare of the Soviet people and for the widening and deepening of socialist democracy. They also emphasized the great personal contribution he had made to the formulation of the new Soviet Constitution. The determination of the working class, collective farmers and intelligentsia to strengthen by confident work the power of their socialist homeland, to bring about the decisions of the 25th Congress, was also voiced by the deputies.

The highest organ of government, the USSR Supreme Soviet, unanimously approved the new Constitution of the Soviet Union on 7 October 1977. The unanimous Declaration read: 'The Supreme Soviet of the Union of Soviet Socialist Republics, acting in the name of the Soviet people and expressing its sovereign will, accepts the Constitution (Fundamental Law) of the Union of Soviet Socialist Republics and declares it put into effect from 7 October 1977.'

Summarizing the Supreme Soviet session, Brezhnev said in conclusion: 'Expressing the will of the Soviet people and carrying out its commission, the USSR Supreme Soviet has accepted the new Constitution of the USSR. The Fundamental Law of the first all-people's socialist state is confirmed. A new and historic landmark in our move towards communism has been constitutionally strengthened—the building of developed socialist society.

'Years and decades will pass, but this October day will live forever in the national memory as shining evidence of the triumph of Leninist principles of people's power.'

The 7th of October was declared a national holiday—the Day of the Soviet Constitution. The new Constitution began to take effect, to live, to work.

The Soviet Constitution makes an enormous contribution to Marxist-Leninist theory and to the growth of doctrine on the state. It not only marks a new historic stage in the life of the country but also reveals bright future developments in communism.

The new Constitution met with total and unanimous approval from the Soviet people, as was shown by widely attended meetings and assemblies confirming the historic document of the USSR Supreme Soviet. Reports of new labour victories by work forces at factories, on building

At a Yaroslavl factory, 5 October 1977: 'Together wi

'Deputies, we vote for the new Soviet Constitution!'

projects, in collective and state farms and in educational institutions added weight to support for the Constitution.

The Soviet people note the outstanding role of the Party, its Leninist Central Committee, and the personal efforts of Leonid Brezhnev in preparing the Fundamental Law of the Land of the Soviets. This nationwide approval of the USSR Constitution strengthened yet further the indestructible unity of Party and people.

World society as a whole has judged the new Soviet Constitution to be a highly important contemporary political document. In telegrams of congratulation sent to the CPSU Central Committee, to Brezhnev himself as its General Secretary and as President of the USSR Supreme Soviet, the leaders of fraternal socialist countries termed the new Constitution an expression of the richness of the universally valid experience of Great October's homeland. The people of the socialist countries link their morrow with the Soviet Constitution that incorporates their experience too.

In those countries which have recently freed themselves from the yoke of colonialism and are now shaping their own future, the Constitution of developed socialism was received with particular interest. The progressive press in the capitalist world, especially of the communist and workers' parties, noted the Constitution of the world's first all-people's socialist state as an exceptional contribution to the international cause of the struggle of the peoples of the whole world for freedom, true democracy and social progress, for a lasting peace on earth and the happy future of mankind.

The place of the Party in Soviet society and the state is defined by the new Soviet Constitution in these words: 'The leading and guiding force of Soviet society and the nucleus of its political system, of all state organizations and public organizations, is the Communist Party of the Soviet Union. The CPSU exists for the people and serves the people.

'The Communist Party, armed with Marxism-Leninism, determines the general perspectives of the development of society and the course of the home and foreign policy of the USSR, directs the great constructive work of the Soviet people, and imparts a planned, systematic and theoretically substantiated character to their struggle for the victory of communism.

'All party organizations shall function within the framework of the Constitution of the USSR.'

In an interview for French television on 5 October 1976 Leonid Brezhnev said: 'The nature of my work, and indeed that of the entire Politburo, is primarily determined by the role in our country of the Communist Party. In our country the Party comprises the most advanced, politically conscious, and active sections of the working class, peasantry, and intelligentsia. Its policy stems from a scientific approach and deep study of the actual needs and wishes of the people. It welds all strata of our society, all nationalities, and gives the people the will, motivation, and ability to fight for the ideals of the most progressive and most just society — the communist society.'

In the conditions of developed socialism the Party faces new tasks. The content of its work is growing deeper and its forms and methods are becoming more varied. It is shouldering a greater responsibility to the people of its country, to the international working class, and to the other revolutionary forces of the day. Setting a consistently scientific political course in line with the objective laws of social development in our time, which abounds in revolutionary opportunities and events, the Soviet Party is doing its utmost to embody in its policy and activity the thought and will of all Communists and to align the Party's internal life and the forms and methods of its work with the now much greater challenges of building communism.

The Communist Party, its Central Committee, and Politburo constantly concern themselves with questions of internal Party development, which are regularly discussed at congresses and Central Committee plenums. Of bearing on questions of principle were the decisions of the 20th Party Congress, the October 1964 plenum, and the 23rd, 24th and 25th Party Congresses.

The Central Committee plenum of November 1964 decided to revert to the principle of structuring Party branches and their leading organs on the territorial/production model, restoring the unified regional and territorial Party organizations and thus bringing all Communists together in those regions and territories where formerly they had been separated into industrial and rural branches. The plenum reactivated district committees in rural districts, took steps to extend the role of the primary Party branches, and helped to improve the forms and methods of Party work.

The March and September 1965 Central Committee plenums called the attention of Party branches to the key economic problems and to furthering the Leninist principles of leadership. The 23rd, 24th and 25th Congresses worked out the Party's economic and social strategy, reaffirming and furthering the scientific approach to economic, political, and ideological matters and to organizing and educating the masses. They raised the responsibility of Party cadres for their work and extended the role of the Party committees as organs of political leadership.

All these years were highlighted by a further growth of the Party's leading and directing role in building communism, primarily in such areas as the following:

- Economic development, higher efficiency of social production and labour, and scientific and technical progress aimed at substantially raising the living standard and cultural level of the peoples of the USSR.
- Improving of socialist social relations, consolidation of the leading role of the working class, of its alliance with the kolkhoz farmers and the people's intelligentsia, of the social, political, and ideological unity of the Soviet people.
- Furtherance of closer relations among the Soviet nations and nationalities, ensuring their progress and gradual convergence in the context of the new historical community of people—the single multi-national Soviet people.
- Extension and deepening of socialist democracy and further consolidation of the socialist state of the whole people, of the political system of a developed socialist society; efficient interaction under the Party's guidance of all state and public organizations, all-out development of their initiative, and of the social activity of the masses in administering production and state and public affairs.
- Development of the socialist way of life, moulding the new man, raising the role of labour collectives in effecting the economic and social policies of the CPSU, and enriching the forms of the socialist emulation movement.

The striking Soviet successes under the Party's leadership show that its policy line is correct. The standards of the Party's guidance in all sectors of building communism have risen considerably. This has fostered the unbreakable unity of the Party and people, the high level of the Soviet people's socialist consciousness, their dedication to work, their political involvement and boundless loyalty to the communist cause; their high degree of organization and sense of responsibility to society; the successful fulfilment of the communist construction plans; and the constantly growing socialist patriotism and internationalism.

The measures relating to the Party's internal development have been of a comprehensive nature, suiting the conditions and needs of developed socialism. The thrust in Party work is always towards greater scientific grounding and efficiency. As a result the Party is functioning more effectively and purposefully, this being in many ways furthered by the re-registration of Party cards on Brezhnev's initiative between the 24th and 25th Congresses.

Party organizations benefit continuously from new experience in organizational and political work among the masses. Strict observance of Lenin's standards of Party life and principles of Party leadership, notably democratic centralism, have lent new vigour to the ideological and organizational unity of the CPSU.

The Communist Party is a mighty force. At present its ranks number over 16 million members. Its composition is kept strictly to Leninist principles of Party membership. Guided by these principles, the CPSU regulates the growth of its ranks and the Party's composition so as to ensure the best possible performance of current tasks.

Although in the conditions of developed socialism it has become a party of the whole people, the CPSU retains its class character and by nature continues to be the party of the working class. It expresses the aims of the working class and follows a working-class policy, extending these to encompass all classes and strata of the people that took part in building socialism.

In the Central Committee report to the 25th Congress, Brezhnev noted that the recommendation of the 23rd and 24th Congresses to ensure industrial workers the leading place in the Party's social composition is being consistently carried out. This is consistent with the class character of the Party and with the leading role of the working class in Soviet society.

Party ranks are being continuously augmented through admission of the foremost kolkhoz farmers; this is adding strength to the alliance of the working class and the peasants. The Party also absorbs the finest elements from among the intelligentsia. This reflects its growing part in the scientific and technical revolution, in the country's economic growth, in raising the people's cultural level, and in the performance of the tasks of building communism.

The Party's membership will continue to grow. This is an objective tendency resulting from society's course of development under socialism and the enlargement of the Party's leading role and prestige. But the CPSU does not artificially stimulate numerical growth. It admits by individual selection only those whose conduct has shown that, to use Lenin's phrase, they are joining the Party not for any self-serving reasons but for dedicated work in the name of communism. Concern for the integrity of the Party's ranks and for every Communist's justifying his or her membership in Lenin's Party is an inflexible rule.

An important feature of the present phase in the Party's development is the streamlining of its structure, which reflects the further growth of its role in building communism. Acting on Lenin's unshakable principles, the Central Committee is taking steps to strengthen the ranks of the CPSU organizationally and to heighten the operational efficiency of all Party branches.

The continuous development and consistent instilling of democratic principles in the life of the Party is especially important when socialist democracy is expanding and millions of people are becoming involved in the administration of production and of state and public affairs. The Party's political decisions express the vital interests of all classes and social groups, all nations and peoples, all generations of Soviet society. Developing as a profoundly democratic body of Leninists, the Party stimulates the exercise of democratic principles in all state and public organizations.

The Central Committee and Brezhnev personally show constant concern for the further development of internal Party democracy and for the observance of Lenin's principles of Party life. Consistent extension of internal Party democracy and a more exigent attitude to every Party member—these Leninist principles, as the Central Committee report to the 25th Congress stressed, are highly relevant as the basis for the Party's development today.

The great work done by the Party and the Politburo of the Central Committee headed by Brezhnev has helped eliminate the consequences of the personality cult and manifestations of subjectivism and voluntarism, thus ensuring observance of Lenin's standards of Party life.

All this has furthered within the Party a comradely, creative, and at the same time exigent atmosphere, fidelity to principle, and the steady growth in activity and initiative of Party members in elaborating and implementing the policy of the CPSU. The Party's ideological and organizational unity and the operational efficiency of all its branches enable it to tackle and accomplish the increasingly complex tasks of building communism.

All Party matters are settled democratically on a strictly collective basis. The work of Party branch committees is regularly reviewed by the branch members, and elections held when due. The composition of all elective Party organs from top to bottom is systematically renewed, with proper consideration for the continuity of leadership which safeguards and extends Lenin's Party traditions.

The dynamic social development, the depth and scale of the economic and social changes, and the more complex administrative functions in the mature socialist society all oblige the Party to improve its guidance in every area and also its style and methods of work. Concern for this marks the entire activity of the Party, its Central Committee, the Politburo, and General Secretary Brezhnev.

At the 25th Congress Brezhnev stressed that universal establishment of the Leninist style of work is an important condition for successful Party leadership. It is a creative style imbued with a scientific approach to all social processes, a style that rules out subjectivism and requires people to be strict with themselves and others—a style incompatible with smug complacency and intolerant of bureaucratism and red tape.

The manifold activity of the Central Committee and Politburo headed by Brezhnev, the way in which they promote the country's home and foreign policy, is a model of the Leninist style of work. It is marked by profound realism and a scientific approach to current economic, political, organizational, and ideological matters; by collectivism, sense of purpose and efficiency, close bonds with local organizations, and a readiness to help them effectively at all times; by the continuous promotion of everything new that is collectively created by the masses; and by wise boldness, resolve, and breadth of vision.

The Central Committee plenums and Politburo and Secretariat sessions work on vital matters of state, economic and cultural development, the improvement of economic management, the raising of living standards, and the basic tasks of stepping up the Party's organizational and ideological work, invigorating its foreign policy activities, and ensuring the country's defence capability. The Central Committee examines and sums up the experience of local Party organizations. It studies the reports of central committees of communist parties in the constituent republics and those of territorial, regional, city, and district Party committees on matters of economic and cultural guidance, and also on Party organizational and ideological-educational work. The experience of the primary Party branches and labour collectives is thoroughly analysed. Many useful initiatives by Party branches, collectives, and individuals in Moscow and Leningrad, the Ukraine and Kazakhstan, the Urals and Byelorussia, Central Asia, the Baltic republics, the Transcaucasus, and Moldavia have been commended by the Central Committee and widely introduced throughout the country, thanks to the Party's intensive political and organizational work.

The Central Committee affords to Party organizations and cadres an instructive example of Leninist consistency and sense of purpose in work generally and in carrying out adopted decisions. The Central Committee, its Politburo and Secretariat work intensively and unremittingly as a harmonious, smooth-running collective. Credit for this belongs to the Central Committee's General Secretary—to his skill in organizing efficient and creative activity by the most competent and authoritative leaders of Party and State. Many questions are entered for discussion at Central Committee meetings on Brezhnev's own initiative.

The Central Committee Politburo, its Secretariat, and Brezhnev personally devote unfailing attention to ensure the efficient functioning of the Central Committee apparatus and local Party organs, which play a prominent part in implementing the policy and decisions of the CPSU. The General Secretary makes it his daily concern to ensure that the Party machinery copes with its tasks and that Party workers tackle each problem creatively and with initiative, showing concern not merely for their own sector but also for the common cause. Of fundamental importance in this respect are Brezhnev's speeches at conferences called by the Central Committee in 1974 and 1976 of the personnel of regional and territorial committees and the central committees of the communist parties of the constituent republics.

Following the example of the Central Committee, local Party organizations are also constantly improving their style and methods of work.

They are increasingly efficient. Their approach to complicated social and political matters is increasingly creative. They show perseverance and sense of purpose, and are more exacting towards their cadres and all Communists. They have stepped up their organizational, educational, and ideological work and are showing a deeper involvement in economic and cultural matters. They devote close attention to the key economic and political problems and are furthering the growth and effectiveness of social production. Their great merit, as bodies of political leadership, is that in recent years they have made many more proposals of nation-wide importance than previously.

The primary Party branches, which constitute the foundation of the CPSU, are an object of special concern to the Party and its Central Committee. And this is natural because, as Brezhnev has put it, the standard of Party leadership depends directly on the initiative and dedication of the primary Party branches. They are in the front line of economic and cultural development and operate right among the people. Their activity helps to combine Party policy with the creative energies of the masses and ensures success in the economic, political, and ideological - educational fields.

The Party and its Central Committee teach people to see the flaws as well as the achievements, and to rectify them as soon as possible. As the size and complexity of the tasks increase, a self-critical approach to all things becomes especially important. The CPSU always encourages criticism and self-criticism—the proven way to eliminate shortcomings and train cadres correctly.

A creative approach and the ability to spot faults and correct them without delay are all characteristic of the Central Committee, the Politburo, and Brezhnev himself. This entirely matches the nature of the Soviet Communist Party, which displays an inherent fidelity to principle and a sense of responsibility to the people.

The Communist Party never hesitates openly to criticize mistakes and shortcomings or to tackle subjectivism and dogmatism in theory and practice. Thorough and self-critical analysis of achievements and faults, it holds, is essential to the progress of society. It attaches supreme importance to sound criticism of bureaucracy, red tape, parochialism, outdated work methods, and everything else that impedes progress.

The 25th Congress, while discussing the impressive successes achieved in building communism's material and technical basis, developing social relations, moulding the new man, and in the field of foreign policy, also heard delegates speak honestly and frankly of the snags, as true Bolsheviks should. They raised unsolved problems, and in a principled and direct fashion were critical of shortcomings noted in work.

'He who has lost the ability to critically assess his own acts, who has lost touch with the masses, who spawns toadies and bootlickers and has lost the trust of the Communists cannot be a Party leader,' Brezhnev said at the Congress. These words show how exacting the Party is to its cadres. Returning to the subject in his summing up and noting the delegates' self-critical and demanding approach to their own jobs, Brezhnev said: 'We shall do right and act as befits Leninists if, with due credit to what has been achieved, we concentrate our attention on the shortcomings still there and the tasks still to be carried out.'

Every speech by Brezhnev, especially his reports and speeches at Party congresses and Central Committee plenums, all his many diverse activities, are instructive examples of the skilled use of criticism and self-criticism, of intolerance towards shortcomings and self-complacency, and of matching words with deeds.

The Communist Party, keeping always to Lenin's principles of Party leadership, attaches prime importance to scientific grounding in its work with cadres. It considers cadre policy a powerful means of influencing society's course of development. Through their consistent cadre policy, the Party and its Central Committee are being successful in raising the standard of leadership in all areas of society and mass organizational and political work, and heightening the Party's leading role in all spheres.

The main feature of Party cadre policy today is the more demanding selection, appointment, and training of leading cadres. The present-day leader, Brezhnev holds, must blend together a commitment to the Party with a high degree of proficiency, and discipline with initiative and a creative approach to his work. He must never fail to bear in mind all the social, political, and educational aspects; he must be considerate to people, to their needs and wishes; and must always set an example at work and in everyday life. These are the Leninist principles which the Central Committee, its Politburo, and the General Secretary apply to cadres, requiring all Party organizations to exercise the utmost care in selecting, appointing, and training personnel.

An atmosphere of trust and respect for cadres prevails in the Party and country, and an inestimable part in creating it belongs to Brezhnev. He is considerate and understanding, shows constant concern for people's development, has the knack of fostering valuable and useful initiatives, and is at the same time—as befits a Communist—highly demanding.

The facts show that a cadre policy based on trust and respect, on considerate treatment of cadres plus rigorously high standards and a sense of responsibility on the part of each person for the assigned job, is best suited to meet the needs of developed socialist society.

The Communist Party devotes a prominent place to questions of ideological and ethical training, to the moulding of the new man. 'It is the Party's constant concern,' said Brezhnev at the 25th Congress, 'to promote communist consciousness and the readiness, will and ability to build communism.' An extensive programme of communist education, of raising the people's cultural level, is contained in the Party's decisions and the speeches of the General Secretary. Its keystone is cultivation of the communist world outlook, lofty ideological and moral qualities, patriotism and socialist internationalism, a high sense of responsibility, a creative attitude to work, and intolerance of all elements of bourgeois ideology.

The main purpose and function of ideological work, Brezhnev stresses, is to make Marxist - Leninist ideas the deep-rooted conviction of every citizen, inspiring active involvement in the great common cause. The Communist Party can legitimately be proud of the success of its ideological work, moulding the new man and shaping communist relations between people, and in educating the mass of the people in the spirit of Marxist - Leninist ideals.

The whole world can now see that in the years of Soviet power a new society has been built and a new man formed in the Soviet Union in accordance with Lenin's precepts. The millions of Soviet citizens feel personally responsible for the destiny of their country and the world. This growing communist consciousness and selfless devotion to Marxist - Leninist ideas finds vivid expression in the labour achievements of the Soviet people, the immense scale of the socialist emulation movement, and the promotion of a communist attitude to labour. Socialist emulation is not only vast in scale, encompassing large masses of the people, but has also developed a new dimension, serving as an increasingly effective means of stimulating economic practice and the country's social-political life, making a tremendous moral impact, helping to advance social relations, and drawing greater numbers of people into administering production. All this is the fruit of the Party's titanic organizational, ideological, and educational activity under the day-to-day direction of its Central Committee and the Politburo headed by Brezhnev.

The Soviet people, brought up by the Party, are proud of their identification with the destiny of their socialist homeland. And to cultivate in people—notably in the rising generation—ideas of Soviet patriotism and socialist internationalism, pride in the Soviet Union, and readiness to defend the gains of socialism has been and remains one of the Party's most important tasks.

A number of Central Committee decisions taken in recent years have summed up the Party's accumulated experience of ideological work and defined main lines of further improvement. As a result, the Party organizations have become much more active. They are paying more attention to ideological and educational work, are looking deeper into its content and tying it up more closely with economic and cultural development.

On the whole we have advanced and we have made good progress in the field of ideological and educational work. But this is not to say that there is reason for us to be complacent. The continuing growth in the political awareness of the people and greater access to information, plus the need to form a timely rebuff to the ideological subversion of imperialist propagandists, combine to make more exacting demands on all ideological activity, and the task of improving its quality and effectiveness is more relevant than ever.

The General Secretary has laid particular stress on a comprehensive approach to the communist education of the masses and on securing the close fit of ideological, political, labour, and ethical training. This is exactly what is required by the present level of Soviet society's social and economic development and by its objective of moulding harmoniously developed individuals.

The new Soviet constitution emphasizes that the State shows concern to safeguard, add to the cultural heritage and ensure free access to this heritage for purposes of the moral and aesthetic education of the Soviet people with a view to raising their cultural standard. Every encouragement is given in the USSR to the promotion of art and amateur artistic activities by the people.

Deeds are the only measure of ideological work, of the effectiveness of such training. Communist ideological equipment is a blend of knowledge, conviction, and practical action. The higher the people's ideological, ethical, and cultural level, the more substantial is their contribution to the Party's plans and the building of communism. 'Nothing adds so much to the stature of the individual,' Brezhnev has said, 'as a constructive attitude to life and a sense of one's duty to society, so that matching words with deeds becomes a general rule of behaviour.'

It is man and his work, life, and cultural world that stand at the centre of the Party's organizational and ideological task. The Party is seeing to it that the propaganda of communist ideas should reach the heart and mind of every Soviet citizen.

Brezhnev's correspondence with the foremost production groups and innovators elicits a lively response all over the country. His letters are warm-hearted messages of Party concern for the development of the urban and rural workers' creative initiative and the widest possible spread of advanced production techniques. 'Words fail me when I try to describe how I felt when I received Leonid Ilyich Brezhnev's congratulations on being decorated with the Order of Lenin and my second Golden Hammer and Sickle Medal,' so the twice-times Hero of Socialist Labour A.V. Chuyev, turner at the Ordzhonikidze Shipbuilding Yards in Leningrad, informed the 25th Congress. 'It was a big event for all my comrades too . . . a tremendous incentive for us to work still better and devote all our strength to the homeland we love so much.'

The steady development of Lenin's standards of Party life and principles of Party guidance, the further extension of socialist democracy and rule of law, the broadening of the rights of the constituent republics in economic and cultural development, and the heightening of the role of public organizations—these and many other measures by the Party and its Central Committee in recent years have helped enormously to extend the Party's ties with the masses and to stimulate them politically and in production activity.

Thanks to the unflagging efforts of the Party, its Central Committee, the Politburo and those of Leonid Brezhnev personally, an atmosphere of genuine collective leadership, comradely confidence, respect for and at the same time an exacting attitude to one's colleagues has been produced, such as helps every man and woman to display full creativity in contributing to the building of communism.

Of all the factors determining the vitality and strength of the CPSU and the success of its revolutionary activity, the Party's close ties with the masses, its boundless trust in the working class and in all working people, are the most important and decisive. In all its undertakings, current and long-term, the Party draws on the inexhaustible initiative and support of the broad mass of the people. Soviet citizens were stirred by Brezhnev's inspired words at the 25th Congress: 'Every morning tens of millions of people begin another ordinary working day. . . . They probably don't spare a thought for the grandeur of what they are doing. But in carrying out the Party's plans it is they and they alone who are raising the Soviet Union to new and ever higher summits of progress.'

The Soviet people know that where difficulties arise the Communists are sure to be in the forefront. Whatever happens, the Communists never falter. Where the Party is, there also are success and victory. The people trust the Party and support its home and foreign policy. And this adds to the Party's strength and is the source of its inexhaustible energy.

Leaning on, generalizing, and popularizing the collective experience of the masses, the CPSU, its Central Committee, and the General Secretary hold that no plans or decisions will have the desired effect unless the people take them to their heart and the effort to implement them is adopted as their own cause by workers, kolkhoz farmers, and the intelligentsia.

The Communists and the entire Soviet people take an active part in working out the home and foreign policy of the CPSU. Nationwide discussion of the most important Party and government documents has become general practice. As noted at the 25th Congress, this is a striking indication of the effectiveness of socialist democracy. The Party always consults the people on vital questions of building communism. This enables it to sum up, reflect on and use the people's vast stock of experience, and to find optimum solutions matching the situation and the needs of society's development.

For the same purpose, the Party and its Central Committee hold meetings, consultations, and conferences. As in Lenin's day, the CPSU turns to the people—especially at times of great moment—explaining the current tasks and looking with them for potential reserves, making these reserves operational, and thus achieving success.

Extensive press, television, and radio coverage of the work of Party congresses, conferences, and election meetings helps strengthen and extend the Party's ties with the masses. The accounts rendered by Party organs to the Party rank and file, Brezhnev notes, are in fact accounts to the people. This makes good sense. The Party has no secrets from the people. It is vitally concerned that the Soviet people should be familiar with its work and plans, should have its own opinion of them, so that the masses should know about everything and (in Lenin's phrase) go into everything with their eyes open.

Working people's letters are an indication that the Party, its Central Committee, and the local Party organs have close ties with the masses. For example, the 25th Congress received more than 600,000 letters and telegrams in which Soviet people, moved by civic concern for the affairs and further progress of their country, expressed their thoughts, feelings, and explicit support of the Party's Leninist policy. Behind this epistolary chronicle, as Brezhnev described it to Congress, is the tremendous enthusiasm of millions of working people, the pulse-beat of a great and mighty power building communism.

The Central Committee is systematically informed about everything of substance contained in letters received from working people. The more important suggestions are examined by its Politburo and Secretariat and taken into account in the elaboration of decisions and the activity of leading Party and government organs.

On Brezhnev's initiative the Central Committee adopted a decision on 'Further improvements in dealing with working people's letters in the light of the 25th Party Congress decisions'. The General Secretary urges Party workers to treat working people's letters with true Leninist consideration. He himself always shows a deep interest in such letters and the action taken on them. He often issues specific orders to the appropriate departments or officials concerning working people's suggestions sent in to the Central Committee.

'I am in the habit of acquainting myself not only with the official business papers coming to the Party's Central Committee,' he says, 'but also with letters arriving at the Central Committee in vast numbers from Party members and working people not in the Party. When reading these letters, I am thrilled as a human being and as a Communist that, whether coming from Party members or not, they tell us of public matters as well as personal. They show involvement in everything concerning our country. I often ask my comrades: let me see the negative as well as the positive letters. This helps me and all of us. It is like drawing new ideas for our practical work from the prime source. . . . The letters that come to us, to the Party's Central Committee and to local Party organizations, are clear evidence that our Party and the Soviet people are united. This we must cherish.'

True to the tradition started by Lenin, Party and government leaders appear regularly before the working people at meetings, conferences, and congresses. Brezhnev's own steady contact with the people is exemplary. His speeches are always considerate of the working man, and show deep knowledge of the needs, wishes, and sentiments of the Soviet people. They are an ardent and vigorous call to new achievements in building communism.

The General Secretary has visited most of the republics of the Soviet Union and many of the country's territories and regions. His meetings with Party activists, with rank-and-file Communists, with workers, kolkhoz farmers, and intellectuals make a tremendous impact and give the masses a better understanding of current questions of building communism. His direct contacts with working people in turn enable Brezhnev to raise and solve new questions of social and political life. As an example, consider his visit to Kazakhstan in September 1976 at the height of harvesting, when the country was rallying to fulfil the decisions of the 25th Congress.

The Kazakh Republic is one of the country's biggest grain-producing areas. In many ways the entire harvest campaign in the first year of the tenth five-year plan depended on Kazakhstan's keeping its socialist pledges on how much grain it delivered to the state granaries. The General Secretary's speech to Kazakh Party activists and economic executives was filled with optimism and firm confidence that the country would achieve its tasks. It was received with great enthusiasm by millions of urban and rural workers, inspiring them in their work.

Speaking in Alma-Ata, the capital of Kazakhstan, Brezhnev stressed that, with all due credit to considerable successes thus far, it was important to concentrate on shortcomings, on the unsolved problems, and to do so in a principled and truly Leninist fashion. The meeting of Kazakhstan's activists provided a splendid example of this. Kazakh farmers bound themselves to deliver at least 1100 million poods of grain, and kept their promise to the letter. During his stay in Alma-Ata,

Brezhnev inspected the city's recently completed building projects and spoke to workers and experts and to Party and government workers.

At the 25th Congress Brezhnev said that the greater leading role of the Party is no abstract concept but is reflected in everyday practice. The Party's role as organizer and leader of the masses is especially evident at difficult times. The General Secretary cited the example of the drive to overcome setbacks in agriculture caused by unfavourable weather in 1972 and 1975.

In those inclement days, the energy, organization, and will of millions of people was ranged against the elements. The Central Committee and the local Party organizations rallied, inspired, and led the working people in a Herculean effort to save the harvest.

Brezhnev visited the decisive areas—among them the Ukraine, Uzbekistan and Kazakhstan, the Omsk and Novosibirsk regions, and the Altai and Krasnoyarsk territories. His appearances at meetings of Party activists and economic executives, his friendly talks with kolkhoz and state-farm workers, and his competent advice and instructions were an invaluable contribution to the successful outcome of the harvesting. 'The people had a hard time,' Brezhnev recalled at the 25th Congress, 'but they worked with extraordinary enthusiasm and energy. They accomplished everything that could possibly be accomplished. I'll even say they did more than many had thought possible. Looking at it one was filled with legitimate pride for our Party and our remarkable people.'

Speaking at the October 1976 plenum of the Central Committee, Brezhnev thanked the leading kolkhoz and state-farm workers, operators of farming machinery, and Party, Komsomol, and Soviet workers—all of them staunch organizers of the campaign to save the harvest, to secure bread for their homeland. He outlined ways and means of implementing the 25th Congress decisions in the period to come.

In many of his speeches Brezhnev exposes the utter falsity of the charges of bourgeois ideologists and right and 'left' revisionists that the Marxist - Leninist proposition on the growth of the Party's leading role is anti-democratic and encroaches on the competence and functions of other public organizations and the interests of the people. In reality the ruling Marxist - Leninist Party draws all citizens into administering the affairs of the socialist state. Far from interfering in the work of government and public organizations, the Party encourages and supports this by directing their efforts to building the new society. It is the

Party's main task, in fact, to stimulate the activity of all the links in the socialist political system, to improve their work, and to heighten their responsibility for matters within their competence.

The new Soviet Constitution states: 'The principal direction in the development of the political system of Soviet society is the extension of socialist democracy, namely ever broader participation of citizens in managing the affairs of society and the state, continuous improvement of the machinery of state, heightening of the activity of public organizations, strengthening of the system of people's control, consolidation of the legal foundations of the functioning of the state and of public life, greater openness and publicity, and constant responsiveness to public opinion.'

Growth of the Party's leading role and of the influence of the Soviets of People's Deputies, of the trade unions, the Young Communists, and all other mass organizations is an interconnected and mutually determined process reflecting the profoundly democratic nature of the socialist system. As the role of the Party increases under mature socialism, so do the rights of government bodies and public organizations. That is the dialectic of the socialist political system's development.

The activity of the Central Committee and its Politburo under Brezhnev is for all Party organs a model of the truly Leninist guidance of mass organizations. While encouraging their initiative, the Central Committee sets them the specific objectives they must accomplish, supplies them with cadres, and exercises systematic control over their fulfilment of the Party's policy and decisions.

The Central Committee pays special attention to bettering the work of the Soviets as organs of state power and as the largest of public organizations. Some fundamental aspects of their work, their guidance by the Party, were recently examined on Brezhnev's personal initiative. Laws have been enacted on the rights and duties of rural, town, city, and district Soviets. In the Central Committee report to the 25th Congress, the General Secretary proposed that laws should also be adopted to define the competence of territorial, regional, and area Soviets. And earlier, also at his suggestion, the Supreme Soviet of the USSR passed a law on the status of Soviet deputies at all levels, defining the powers and rights of these people's representatives and detailing the obligations of state organs and public organizations towards them.

In his report to the plenum held in May 1977, Leonid Brezhnev pointed out that the new Soviet Constitution further strengthened the role of Soviets in tackling the major tasks of running public affairs. In the words of the report: 'The tremendous potential of the two million strong army of Soviet Deputies representing every section of the population, every trade and profession and every nationality should be used to the full. This mighty collective brain of Soviet power has decided and will go on deciding ever more complex and varied tasks. It can and must exercise effective supervision over the operation of executive bodies at every level'.

Speaking at the meeting of the Presidium of the USSR Supreme Soviet on 17 June 1977 Leonid Brezhnev defined the priority tasks facing every body of state power and administration in the country, ranging from local Soviets to the Presidium of the Supreme Soviet, the country's supreme body of people's power made up of elected representatives from over fifty thousand local Soviets. Emphasizing the need for continuing efforts to improve the performance of Soviets, Brezhnev said: 'Lenin repeatedly stressed that nothing can be more stupid than converting the Soviets into a rigid, fossilized and self-perpetuating entity. Indeed, comrades, the Soviets are the living, dynamic organization of the people that is constantly rejuvenating itself.'

The democratic principles and standards of work within the Soviets are being increasingly established. The prestige and activity of deputies are growing as is their responsibility to the electorate. At the initiative of deputies far more questions of all-state significance are being tackled by the Soviets than ever before.

As President of the Presidium of USSR Supreme Soviet, Brezhnev emphasized the importance of developing further the law-making activity, improving supervision over the enforcement of law, over the implementation of the national economic development plan and the way the state budget is fulfilled. In fully developed socialism the performance of Soviets should be even more effective. In the words of the new Constitution: 'Soviets of people's deputies shall function publicly on the basis of collective, free, constructive discussion and decision-making, of systematic reporting back to them and the people by their executive-administrative and other bodies, and of involving citizens on a broad scale in their work.

'Soviets of People's Deputies and the bodies set up by them shall systematically inform the public about their work and the decisions taken by them.'

The influence of the trade unions, that crucial link in the system of socialist democracy, is substantially greater in the conditions of developed socialism. They have become a still more active and action-worthy force in the tasks of building communism. Their work directly helps extend democracy in production. They participate actively in running the economy.

Guidance by the Communist Party was, is, and ever will be the source of success in all trade union work. Union activity, as Brezhnev stressed at the 25th Congress, must be organized in full accord with the rights of and the degree of responsibility borne by the trade unions.

The 16th Congress of Soviet Trade Unions was held in March 1977. Leonid Brezhnev made an important speech at the congress in which he defined the tasks facing the country's trade unions at the present stage. Once again he emphasized that the Soviet Trade Unions which from their inception have been guided by the Communist Party remain the school of economic management, the school of communism. Brezhnev spoke of their important role as a force accelerating the country's development: 'The trade unions represent a deep source of creative activity, initiative and the labour enthusiasm of millions. This, in turn, represents a major advantage offered by socialism, one of the main secrets of success which throughout Soviet history have enabled the USSR to achieve the seemingly impossible, to surprise the rest of the world by unprecedentedly rapid growth of a new society, with its vitality and dynamism'.

At this congress Brezhnev presented the Soviet Trade Unions with the order of the October Revolution in recognition of their considerable services in advancing the revolutionary movement and carrying out the Great October Socialist Revolution, of their contribution to the resolution of major tasks of economic and cultural development, and in recognition of their active participation in educating the working people in the spirit of communist ideals.

The CPSU, its Central Committee, and Brezhnev himself devote much attention to the Lenin Young Communist League, or Komsomol, the Party's battle aide and standby. The General Secretary shows truly paternal concern for the rising generation. His speeches at the Central Committee of the YCL plenum on the League's fiftieth anniversary, at the 15th, 16th, and 17th Congresses of the YCL, and at the Union-wide Students' rally in 1971 made a great impression on Soviet youth. 'The young,' Brezhnev said, 'are our future. We want them always to feel their link with our revolutions, to be aware of the depth and complexity of life, to be conscious of their own role and of their responsibility for building communism.'

Speaking at a meeting with leaders of the Youth Leagues of socialist countries on 5 November 1976, Brezhnev again referred to the immense responsibility they bear in forming the new man. The Party and its Central Committee are helping the Komsomol organization and Soviet youth as a whole to match up creditably to the great things expected of them. The Party's message inspires the young and calls on them to scale new summits.

Principles governing the Party's guidance of the Komsomol have been further elaborated in Party documents and in Brezhnev's speeches defining its action programme and clarifying, in the light of the present conditions, Lenin's call to young people 'to learn communism'. The Central Committee and its General Secretary help the Komsomol daily in various ways, provide it with experience in political and organizational work, and give every support to the many valuable undertakings and initiatives of the young. Komsomol building projects, student construction teams, the Komsomol's help in building the Baikal - Amur railway, a young people's emulation drive marking the 30th anniversary of the Soviet people's victory in the War, and other patriotic initiatives met with their wholehearted approval and support.

In the Central Committee report to the 25th Congress, Brezhnev noted that the Komsomols had launched many splendid undertakings and accomplished many glorious deeds. But our times make increasingly exacting demands on the content, forms, and methods of Komsomol work. Listed as the Komsomol's tasks of the day are education of youth in a communist spirit, more active enlistment of young people in the affairs of society, their closer involvement in the economic and political tasks, and further enhancement of the Komsomol's role in organizing for youth its work, education, leisure, and everyday life.

The staunchness, creativity and ideological toughening of Soviet youth have emerged particularly strikingly at the great development projects of recent years. Carrying on the fine traditions begun by their fathers and grandfathers, the Komsomols of today are in the front ranks of the builders of communism as they mature in day-to-day work, learn the art of economic management and of running the affairs of state.

By its devoted service to the communist cause, the CPSU, led by its Leninist Central Committee, is winning new prestige as the universally recognized and tested collective leader of the Soviet people. It treasures this prestige as its most valuable attribute. For us, Brezhnev said, it is not only a well-deserved tribute to the Party's past and present services to the people; it is also a mighty, all-conquering weapon helping us to unite the broad masses and rally them for the tasks facing the country.

The celebrations marking the 60th anniversary of the Great October Socialist Revolution developed into an impressive review of the record of achievement scored by the Soviet people under the leadership of the Communist Party, tangible proof of the unconquerable strength and vitality of the ideas of Marxism - Leninism, proletarian internationalism and the might of the socialist system. The Soviet people, Communists of all countries and progressives everywhere celebrated with enthusiasm this landmark event of contemporary history. The celebrations took on a truly international character. A total of 123 delegates from 104 different countries arrived in the Soviet Union to take part. They represented Party and government delegations from fraternal socialist countries, delegates from communist, workers', national democratic, socialist and social democratic parties the world over, as well as Party and government delegations from the newly independent countries and many different international democratic and national public associations and organizations of the progressive type.

The joint anniversary session of the CPSU Central Committee, the USSR Supreme Soviet and the Supreme Soviet of the Russian Federation was addressed by Leonid Brezhnev as Party General Secretary and President of the Presidium of the USSR Supreme Soviet. The session adopted 'An Appeal to the Soviet people' and 'An Appeal to the peoples, parliaments and governments of the world'.

In his report entitled 'The Great October Socialist Revolution and the progress of mankind' Brezhnev developed in a creative spirit some of the basic problems of Marxism - Leninism in today's world. The report contained a thorough scientific analysis of the results of the Soviet Union's record of achievement since 1917 and outlined the tasks to be tackled in further efforts to enhance the economic and cultural potential of the Soviet Union's fully developed socialism.

The report gave an in-depth and all-round assessment of the permanent significance of the first victorious Socialist Revolution in human history which ushered in a new era: that of the revolutionary rejuvenation of the world, an era of transition from socialism to communism. The road which hundreds of millions of people are following today, and which all mankind will eventually take, began with the October Socialist Revolution of 1917.

Brezhnev emphasized: 'The October Revolution naturally tackled above all problems facing Russia, problems arising from her own history and circumstances. For all that, these problems transcended purely local bounds and assumed characteristics that made them common to all mankind, being essentially the result of the entire course of social development. The significance of the October Socialist Revolution in the context of world history lay precisely in the fact that it opened the way to the resolution of these problems, thereby setting the stage for a new type of civilization on earth.'

The meaning of the October Revolution in the context of world history and the significance of subsequent victories of socialism for all peoples, for the international workers' movement and the entire world development was emphasized by the leaders of socialist countries, communist parties, newly independent countries and representatives of the national liberation movements in their contributions to the anniversary session. Their speeches testified to the fact that the ideas of the Great October Socialist Revolution are as valid today as they ever were, and are a source of inspiration for today's fighters for freedom and the happiness of working people throughout the world.

In his report to the anniversary session Brezhnev described in vivid detail the proud record of achievements scored by the Soviet people under the leadership of the communist party founded by Lenin. Contemporary social development is posing ever-more challenging tasks in different areas of the life of society. The increasing complexity of these tasks calls for correspondingly greater co-ordination, discipline, and everything which may be termed well-organizedness. Brezhnev went on to stress that a high sense of organization displayed by people at all levels, at every work place, at every link in the chain of Party, state and economic management, was an absolutely essential precondition if the tasks set by the 25th Party Congress were to be fulfilled successfully. To use the potential of developed socialism to the full—this was the task of our day, this determined the measure of responsibility placed on us by history.

Brezhnev spoke of the need to foster public-spiritedness and educate the new man as an all-important task in building communism. In his own words: 'The level of consciousness, of cultural standards, and of the sense of responsibility shown by Soviet people as citizens will be playing an increasing role in every area of the life and progress of the Soviet Union's socialist society. To foster in Soviet people a desire to aspire to lofty ideals of contributing to the common good, to foster idealistic commitment and a genuinely creative attitude to work is a task of the first importance. This work is a vital battle-area in the struggle for communism, and the success we score there will largely determine the course of economic construction and the country's social and political progress.'

Speaking of the Soviet Union's consistent and unchanged peace-oriented foreign policy, of its course aimed at peaceful coexistence of countries with different social systems, Brezhnev outlined a series of important new proposals aimed at averting the threat of nuclear war, the greatest menace hanging over mankind today.

He issued an appeal to the Soviet people's brothers in class throughout the world: 'As we mark the 60th anniversary of our revolution, we Soviet Communists declare once again that we will always be faithful to the concept of the great brotherhood of the world's Communists. We wish the communist and workers' parties, and the allies in the struggle against the dictatorship of capital and for freedom, peace and social progress, every success. You may rest assured that in this struggle you can always count on our friendship, solidarity and help.'

Brezhnev's report at the anniversary session was imbued with the spirit of revolutionary, class-motivated optimism. It described the prospects and current trends in the world revolutionary process which originated with the October Socialist Revolution in Russia, and sketched the bright contours of the communist society of the future and the historic role played by the world's first country of developed socialism.

Brezhnev went on to say: 'The victory of the Great October Socialist Revolution made our country and people the vanguard of social progress. Today, sixty years later, we still are in an honoured place in its front ranks. We were the first to build a fully developed socialist society, and we are the first to build a communist society.'

Finally Brezhnev concluded: 'The achievements of the Great October

Red Square, Moscow: at the anniversary celebrations, 7 November 1977.

Revolution and the potential of socialism are today the best guarantee of mankind's further progress. The October Socialist Revolution is the banner of great change held aloft over the 20th century by the will and hands of the working masses.

'We are approaching an era when socialism in one or another historically determined form will be the dominant social system in the world, bringing peace, freedom, equality and prosperity to mankind's working masses.

'This is no utopia, no pipe-dream, but rather it is a realistic prospect. And by our daily work and struggle, by our common efforts, comrades, we are bringing that day nearer, as is the work and struggle of millions upon millions of men and women throughout the world. This is the continuation of the great project launched by the October Socialist Revolution.'

In the appeal 'To the Soviet people', the Party Central Committee, the USSR Supreme Soviet and the Council of Ministers of the USSR called upon the people to spare no efforts in building up the power of their great homeland and to devote their energy and strength to the struggle for the triumph of peace and communism in the world.

The celebrations marking the 60th anniversary of the Great October Revolution proved that the Soviet people associate all their achievements and victories with the Communist Party. They fully endorse the Party's domestic and foreign policy, the untiring activities of its Central Committee and Politburo led by Leonid Brezhnev, Party General Secretary and President of the Presidium of the USSR Supreme Soviet.

The CPSU is the party of scientific communism. All its work for revolutionary change rests on the dependable foundation of Marxist - Leninist theory. This enables it not only to restore current problems but also to anticipate the future correctly. 'Marxism - Leninism derives its power from constant and creative development,' Brezhnev stresses. 'That is what Marx taught us. That is what Lenin taught us. Our Party will always be faithful to their precepts.'

The main results of the Party's tremendous ideological and theoretical work are seen in its documents and in the works of Brezhnev and its other leaders. They contain in-depth studies of the broad range of topical questions concerning social development and creative generalizations from practice. They are imbued with the Leninist spirit and Lenin's methods and have enriched Marxist - Leninist teaching with important new propositions.

In recognition of his outstanding contribution to the development of Marxist - Leninist theory, the scientific elaboration of current problems of developed socialism and to the historic struggle for the realization of communist ideals, for a durable peace throughout the world, by decision of the Presidium of the USSR Academy of Sciences, Leonid Brezhnev was awarded the Karl Marx gold medal, the Academy's highest award for outstanding achievements in the field of social sciences.

The Party and its Central Committee under General Secretary Brezhnev elaborate on the strategy and tactics of the country's economic and political development and look deeply into factors within domestic and international life when working for new achievements in building communism. This contributes creatively to the theory of scientific communism. Successes of the Party's domestic measures, the continuously growing Soviet economic, scientific, and technical potential, the moral and political unity of socialist society, the people's dedicated labour, and the Party's clear-sighted foreign policy—all these go to consolidate yet further the international positions of the USSR and the world socialist community, the successes of the movement for peace and mankind's social progress.

The Great October Socialist Revolution began far-reaching changes throughout the world. The lightning-flashes of the tempest of that revolution illuminated the path into the future of the peoples of many different countries. Mankind has now entered upon the era marked by transition from socialism to communism.

8

Towards Detente

The historic victory of the Soviet people in the war paved the way for the further development of the world revolutionary process, and generated a mighty new upsurge. There were radical changes in world affairs. The Soviet Union's prestige abroad rose immeasurably. Its position in foreign affairs became much stronger. Socialism transcended the limits of one country and became a world system. This was the biggest event in history since the October Revolution. The precipitous rise of the national liberation movement brought about the collapse of the imperialist colonial system. The working class in capitalist countries stepped up its struggle against monopolies and for profound democratic change.

A new stage began in humanity's transition from capitalism to socialism, marked by a steady growth of socialist power and influence on world events and by an ever-visible change in the world balance of forces in socialism's favour.

Thus placed, the Communist Party and the Soviet state applied themselves to strengthening and consolidating the world socialist system, increasing aid to national liberation movements, and still more vigorously promoting the struggle for peace through steady observance of Lenin's principles.

Combating the danger of a new world war and neutralizing imperialism's aggressive designs was the key foreign policy aim of the Soviet Union and the People's Democracies in the early post-war years. By building up their economic and defence potential and promoting a policy of peace and international co-operation consistent with the interests of all nations, the socialist countries countered the adventurist designs of the cold war and 'policy from strength' advocates.

It was in these difficult years that Brezhnev's natural endowments as Party leader and statesman showed themselves more and more strikingly. He devoted all his knowledge and energy to restoring and building up the economy. A consistent and staunch internationalist, he also regarded the work of the Party organizations in his charge as the fulfilment of their internationalist duty. When speaking to working people he never failed to stress the deep-seated connection between Party domestic and foreign policy.

Questions of foreign policy and international relations took a specially prominent place in Brezhnev's activity when he was elected a member of the Presidium of the Party Central Committee, its Secretary, and later (in 1960) President of the Presidium of the USSR Supreme Soviet. In his capacity as head of the country's supreme organ of state power, Leonid Ilyich Brezhnev contributed substantially to the fraternal co-operation of the socialist countries, to friendly ties with countries that had flung off their colonial yoke, and to establishing good-neighbour relations based on principles of peaceful coexistence with capitalist countries.

Important events in 1960-4 were the visits of Party and government delegations headed by Brezhnev to Bulgaria, the German Democratic Republic, Czechoslovakia, and Yugoslavia. Brezhnev took part in the 12th Congress of the Communist Party of Czechoslovakia, in the celebrations of the 20th anniversary of Bulgaria's liberation, and the 15th anniversary of the GDR. He was also directly involved in working out the co-ordinated policy of socialist states touching important international issues.

At the head of such Party and government delegations, Brezhnev visited many Asian and African developing countries. His visits to Guinea, Ghana, Morocco, Sudan, India, Afghanistan, and Iran furthered the Soviet Union's relations with these countries.

In his capacity as Presidium President of the USSR Supreme Soviet,

Brezhnev also negotiated with many foreign statesmen in Moscow, making a constructive contribution to international co-operation.

Acclaimed by progressive forces, the peace policy of the CPSU and the Soviet Union and the good results of friendly visits paid by Brezhnev and other leading Soviet statesmen to the developing countries infuriated the colonialists. There were even provocations. Once, the plane flying the President of the USSR Supreme Soviet to the Moroccan capital Rabat was fired on while over neutral waters.

In his meetings with leaders of Asian and African states, Brezhnev discussed topical problems of the struggle against imperialism, colonialism, and neo-colonialism, and also questions related to the development of the national liberation movement. The meetings promoted close mutual understanding between the Soviet Union and the states that had risen on the ruins of colonies and semi-colonies. Also dealt with were certain practical questions such as Soviet aid to developing states in building their national economy and Soviet support of their independent policy aimed at safeguarding peace and promoting social progress.

Friendship with the Soviet Union ever more effectively united the newly free countries in the fight against imperialism and colonialism. Unstinting Soviet aid helped many an Asian and African state build up its economic potential, protect and extend its progressive gains, and consolidate its sovereignty. In a number of these countries the ruling revolutionary democratic parties opted for the socialist orientation and established ties with the CPSU and other communist and workers' parties. Brezhnev's activity as Central Committee Secretary and President of the Supreme Soviet was always directed to furthering inter-Party co-operation, that vital component in world socialism's alliance with the movement for national liberation.

The President of the Supreme Soviet gave much of his attention to Soviet relations with capitalist countries. He headed many Soviet delegations in talks with statesmen of capitalist countries. His meeting with President Urho Kekkonen had a beneficial effect on good-neighbour Soviet-Finnish relations, which went far towards consolidating peace and security in the north of Europe.

In those years Brezhnev participated in preparing many important foreign policy documents, including the Soviet draft of the declaration on the granting of independence to colonial countries and peoples which the UN General Assembly adopted in December 1960; the treaty banning nuclear weapons tests in the atmosphere, outer space, and under water; the treaties of friendship, mutual aid, and co-operation between the Soviet Union and the Democratic People's Republic of Korea and between the Soviet Union and the German Democratic Republic; and the protocol renewing for another twenty years the Soviet-Czechoslovak treaty of friendship, mutual aid, and post-war co-operation.

By the time the Party put Brezhnev at the head of the Central Committee, the sphere of its foreign policy activity had expanded considerably. As the Central Committee's General Secretary, Brezhnev is making an outstanding personal contribution to formulating and implementing the foreign policy of Party and country.

The growth of the role and scale of the Party's work in foreign policy was influenced by a number of factors, such as the establishment of a developed socialist society in the Soviet Union and of socialism in a number of other countries, and the vital need for a still higher level of co-operation between the USSR and these countries. The collapse of imperialism's colonial system and the growing influence of the newly free states in world affairs, plus the radical changes in the world balance of forces in favour of peace, democracy, and socialism—this, too, enlarged the scope of the Soviet Communist Party's activity on the world scene. Imperialism was impatient to take revenge for its setbacks, creating a dangerous situation in a number of world regions and accentuating the need to combat imperialist reaction, bourgeois ideology, and opportunism of both the right and 'left' varieties. This doubled the progressive forces' burden of historical responsibility for maintaining world peace and for frustrating the designs of reactionary forces.

Questions of foreign policy, its elaboration and implementation, always hold an important place in the activities of the CPSU. In present conditions this has taken on extra significance for the success of socialist and communist construction in the Soviet Union and the other countries of the socialist community, and for peace and social progress throughout the world.

Now that the Soviet Union's foreign policy activity has expanded in volume and scale and become more intensive, now that Soviet prestige and influence have soared, no international problem of any weight can be solved without Soviet participation. In specific terms this means that almost every day there arise foreign policy questions requiring the immediate attention of the Central Committee, its Politburo, and

General Secretary.

The success of the Party's foreign policy reflects its wealth of experience and collective wisdom. The Party works diligently to ensure the practical implementation of its chosen course. 'The international activity of the CPSU,' Brezhnev said at the 25th Congress, 'involves the whole people. . . Behind its successes are the experience and knowledge, the spiritual energy and strenuous work of many representatives of Party and state: members and alternate members of the Politburo; Central Committee secretaries; members of the Central Committee; a large number of staff workers of the Central Committee apparatus, of the Foreign Ministry, the Ministry of Foreign Trade, the State Committee for Foreign Economic Relations, of other ministries and departments; leaders and workers of republican Party central committees and of territorial and regional committees; comrades from city and district committees; and primary Party organizations in towns and villages. I think I shall not be wrong in saying that most of the delegates to our Congress have in one way or another worked in the international sphere. Our parliamentarians and the local and central government bodies, the trade unions, public organizations, workers in science and culture and, of course, the press, radio, and television are doing important work in this area. Thousands of Soviet people work abroad—as staff members of embassies and other missions, as geologists and builders, doctors and teachers, metallurgists and chemists, transport workers, and other specialists.'

The principles, the strategy, and the most important positive measures in the field of foreign policy are elaborated by the Party and its Central Committee under Brezhnev on the basis of a profound Marxist-Leninist analysis of world trends and a thorough consideration of the balance of world forces.

The new Soviet Constitution for the first time in world legislative history elevates the aims and tasks of the Soviet Union's Leninist foreign policy to the level of basic constitutional principles.

Article 28 states: 'The USSR steadfastly pursues a Leninist policy of peace and stands for strengthening of the security of nations and broad international co-operation.

'The foreign policy of the USSR is aimed at ensuring international conditions favourable for building communism in the USSR, safeguarding the state interests of the Soviet Union, consolidating the positions of world socialism, supporting the struggle of peoples for national liberation and social progress, preventing wars of aggression, achieving universal and complete disarmament, and consistently implementing the principle of the peaceful coexistence of states with different social systems.

'In the USSR war propaganda is banned.'

Lenin's ideas on the class nature and peace-loving character of Soviet foreign policy, whose principles embody the essence of the socialist system, have been taken further in the speeches and statements of General Secretary Brezhnev. They show how the constructive activity of the Soviet people led by the CPSU blends organically with the world revolutionary process, and stress that the interests of Soviet people building the communist society are inseparable from the cause of world peace and social progress. 'The foreign policy of the CPSU, of our Central Committee,' Brezhnev points out, 'is imbued with deep concern for the welfare of the Soviet people. At the same time, it fully corresponds to the interests of all revolutionary forces and the cherished aspirations of all peoples. It is a class-oriented, socialist, truly internationalist policy.'

Directed to furthering socialism, to strengthening international peace and security, and powered by a spirit of solidarity with the revolutionary progressive forces of the world, the foreign policy of the CPSU is now an important factor of social development. This policy, with its socialist content—truly internationalist, democratic, and peaceful—is an important source of strength and international prestige for the USSR and world socialism. 'It is a mighty weapon,' Brezhnev has said, 'and we shall use it to the full in our struggle for peace and communism.'

The distinguishing mark of Soviet foreign policy is its active recognition of the equality of all races, nations, and peoples. Following Lenin's precepts, it addresses itself not only to governments but also and directly to peoples. The general line of the Party's foreign policy and that of other fraternal parties is ensuring favourable international conditions for building socialism and communism. It is therefore essential to reinforce the unity, cohesion, friendship, and fraternity of the socialist countries. Soviet foreign policy is also aimed at bringing about cooperation in every sphere with the liberated countries and at supporting the national liberation movement. The CPSU and the Soviet state are consistently asserting the principles of the peaceful coexistence of states with different social systems, decisively throwing back aggressive imperialist forces and championing world peace and security.

Brought up by Lenin's Party in the spirit of proletarian internationalism and a staunch advocate of fraternity and friendship with all peoples of other countries, the Soviet people actively participates in the battle for lasting peace—the greatest battle of our time. Addressing his constituency on 14 June 1974, Brezhnev said: 'War is hateful for every Soviet person. All our plans and intentions tie up with the maintenance of peace. The first generation of Soviet people not to have fought in the last war or gone through the hardships and adversities of war-time is now at its bloom and maturity. To put it in the simplest terms, comrades, we dearly wish that our children and grandchildren should never experience what war is like.'

These stirring words could only come from someone who had given a good account of himself in war, who had endured all its hardships, whose eyes had seen the pain and suffering war brought to the Soviet people and other peoples.

Jointly with the communist and workers' parties of the other socialist countries, the CPSU is working on the central theoretical problems of international relations, of strengthening the socialist community, of the growth of its might, political influence, and internationalist unity. The Central Committee, its Politburo, and the General Secretary are engaged in work of wide scope and significance in this area.

Speaking at the 24th Congress of the CPSU, Brezhnev enthusiastically stated the aims of the Central Committee and the many millions of Soviet Communists. He said: 'We want the world socialist system to be a close-knit family of nations building and defending the new society hand in hand and enriching each other's experience and knowledge—a united and strong family in which people everywhere will see the prototype of the future world community of free peoples.'

Analysis of the present-day world role of the socialist states occupies an important place in the General Secretary's reports and speeches. These demonstrate that the birth and growth of the socialist community is a qualitatively new, truly revolutionary development. The socialist community is the very greatest gain for the international working class, for all revolutionary forces. It is the decisive factor in the anti-imperialist struggle and in efforts to prevent a new world war, the bulwark of today's liberation movements, and a power to accelerate historical progress.

Brezhnev emphasizes: 'We can say with a clear conscience that our alliance, our friendship and our co-operation are those of sovereign and equal states, united by common goals and interests, by bonds of comradely solidarity and mutual assistance. We are marching forward together helping one another, pooling our efforts, knowledge and resources for a more rapid advance.'

The practice of world socialism has been enriched by new experience. Each of the countries following the socialist path tackles to some extent in its own way the problems of building a new society. The transition to socialism by peoples and countries with different levels of development and their own national traditions will doubtless generate a rich variety of concrete forms of socialist construction. However, the record to date indicates that common essential and unmistakable features of socialist revolution and socialist and communist construction retain their validity.

Brezhnev provided a brief and generalized definition of these features in his report 'The Great October Socialist Revolution and Progress of Mankind':

'The combined experience of the development of world socialism persuades us of the following conclusion:

—The question of power is, as always, the crucial question of revolution. Either the working class in alliance with the rest of the working people takes power, or the bourgeoisie does. There is no third way.

—The transition to socialism is only possible when the working class and its allies, after gaining real political power, use it to eliminate the social and economic domination of capitalists and other exploiters.

—Socialism can conquer when the working class with the Communists as its vanguard succeed in inspiring and uniting the working masses in the struggle to build a new society, to remodel the economy and the entire fabric of social relations on socialist lines.

—Socialism can only become established when working people's power is capable of defending the revolution against all attacks of the class enemy (such attacks being inevitable both from within and, which is more likely, from outside).'

These are but a few of the lessons taught by the contemporary development of socialism. They are added proof of the enormous international significance of the experience of the October Revolution, irrespective of all its specific circumstances. They once again bear out Lenin's conclusion when he wrote, 'The Russian example shows to *all* countries something, an essential something, from their inevitable and not too distant future'.

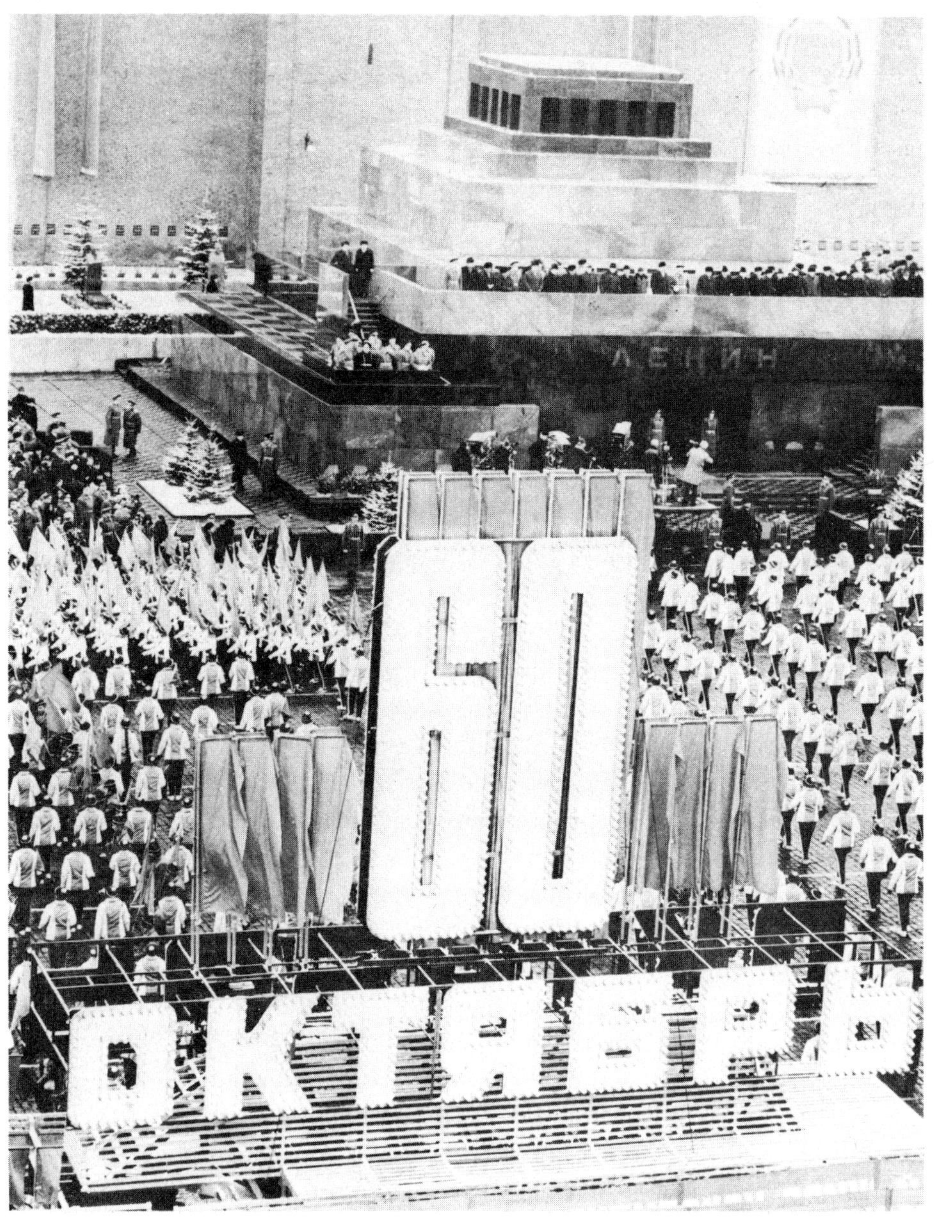

The 60th anniversary of the October Revolution, Moscow, 1977.

The unity and fraternal co-operation of the socialist countries are an inspiring example for the working people of the entire world. The successes of the socialist community conclusively prove socialism's advantages over capitalism. They are decisive in the competition of the two opposed social systems and make for a reduction of imperialist influence. They are crucial for preventing a world nuclear holocaust and for curbing aggressors. The socialist countries have restricted imperialism's ability to pursue an aggressive foreign policy, to export counterrevolutions, and to exploit nations.

The socialist countries' achievements and their influence on world affairs require unity and co-ordination. 'We need unity, co-operation, and joint action now in order, first of all, to ensure the swifter and more effective development of socialist society and the building of communism,' Brezhnev has observed. 'They are also needed in order the more successfully to safeguard and consolidate the peace so necessary for all nations, to reinforce international *détente*, and repulse effectively all aggressive imperialist designs and all attempts to encroach on the interests of socialism.'

Brezhnev's writings identify the objective factors behind the unity of the socialist countries. The socialist nations, he points out, are brought together by common vital interests. They have the same type of economic basis—public ownership of the means of production; the same type of political system—power of the people headed by the working class; the same ideology—Marxism - Leninism; a common interest in safeguarding world peace and security and in defending their revolutionary gains against imperialist encroachments; and the same great goal—communism.

The fundamental principles underlying the Soviet Union's relations with fraternal countries of the socialist community have for the first time found legal enactment in the new Soviet Constitution. 'The USSR, as part of the world system of socialism and of the socialist community, promotes and strengthens friendship, co-operation, and comradely mutual assistance with other socialist countries on the basis of the principle of socialist internationalism, and takes an active part in socialist economic integration and the socialist international division of labour.'

The community of socialist countries is founded upon the ideological and political unity of their Marxist - Leninist parties, on their dependable alliance. The principles governing relations between fraternal parties are also applied to relations between fraternal governments and peoples. 'The main basis of our close co-operation, its soul, the guiding, organizing force, is the indissoluble militant alliance of the communist parties of socialist countries, the identity of their world outlook, their aims and their will,' said Brezhnev at the 25th Congress.

The unity of the Marxist - Leninist parties of the socialist states is a guarantee of the further success of peace and socialism. Brezhnev has stressed repeatedly that converting the potential of the socialist system into reality depends first of all on the ruling Marxist - Leninist parties and on their ability to solve in Lenin's style all vital problems.

The inception and development of fraternal relations between socialist countries is a complex and many-sided process. Today's socialist world is a young and growing organism. Not everything in it has ripened as yet, and many things still bear the imprint of past eras. The development of the socialist community as a whole and of each separate country is taking place in a struggle between the new and the old, through the overcoming of contradictions as they arise.

Analysing the development of the socialist community, Brezhnev has said: 'The emergence and development of this alliance has needed time and considerable collective effort. Answers had to be found to many fundamentally new questions of theory and practice, and reactions, well considered and timed, had to be ready against the shifting course of events. The facts have shown beyond doubt that with the correct Marxist - Leninist approach we have solved and can solve even the most difficult problems, helping to strengthen every socialist country and the socialist community as a whole.'

Socialist internationalism implies a deep sense of responsibility for socialism's future all over the world, not only in one's own country. It implies deep respect for the national and historical peculiarities of every country and readiness to give one another the broadest possible support. It implies a deep understanding of the historical role played by socialist countries in the world revolutionary process and in supporting the people's anti-imperialist struggle of liberation.

Brezhnev's speeches stress that the countries of the socialist community are now entering a qualitatively new stage of co-operation in economy, science, technology, ideology, and culture, and in political relations and international affairs.

The Central Committee report to the 25th Congress carries an important theoretical conclusion based on deep analysis of the development of the socialist community. 'The ties between the socialist countries,' it says, 'are becoming ever closer with the flowering of each socialist nation and the strengthening of the sovereignty of them all. In policy, economy, and society they have more and more common interests. In development they grow steadily more level. This gradual drawing-together of socialist countries is now operating quite definitely as an objective law.'

In each separate country, building socialism and communism requires stronger forms of co-operation and mutual assistance including intensive exchange of advanced experience in social reconstruction. This all-round and equal interchange of experience is in the vital interests of the individual country and also helps strengthen the world socialist system as a whole. It furthers the advance of peace and socialism, allows each side to know of the other's achievements in various aspects of building the new life, and helps bring about the drawing-together of peoples of the socialist countries. A most important area of relations between socialist states from the very outset, exchange of experience is an objective factor in their ideological and political unity. It serves the common cause of building communism and the further development of Marxist - Leninist theory.

The historical experience of world socialism has added to the treasure chest of Marxism - Leninism new conclusions stemming from revolutionary theory and practice. It has once again indicated the need to apply basic laws governing socialist revolution and the building of a new society in a creative way with due account of the concrete circumstances and special features of individual countries.

In pursuance of the Party's political line, Brezhnev and the other members of the Politburo and the Central Committee devote constant attention to strengthening the socialist community and increasing its influence on world events.

Brezhnev took an active part in preparing and concluding new bilateral treaties of friendship, mutual aid, and co-operation—as the terms of the previous ones expired—between the Soviet Union and the GDR (June 1964), Poland (April 1965), Mongolia (January 1966), Bulgaria (May 1967), Hungary (September 1967), Czechoslovakia (May 1970) and Romania (July 1970).

A Soviet - Cuban declaration was signed during the General Secretary's official visit to Cuba in January - February 1974, summing up the experience of the past fifteen years of internationalist co-operation between the two countries and outlining a programme of further bilateral ties.

All these treaties are charters of friendship, embodying the long experience and the maturity, warmth, and lofty internationalist spirit of the relations prevailing between allied fraternal peoples. They represent an extensive system of mutual commitments. The relations formalized in them exercise a beneficial effect on the course of socialist reconstruction in fraternal countries and the building of communism in the Soviet Union.

The unity, solidarity, and mutual support of the socialist countries is helping them resolve the most difficult problems and put into effect what they have long been working for.

The heroic people of Vietnam have scored a glorious victory. The biggest post-war imperialist attempt to destroy by force of arms a socialist state and the national liberation movement in South-East Asia has collapsed. The unremitting struggle and complete victory of the Vietnamese was greatly helped by the international solidarity and fraternal aid of the Soviet Union and other socialist countries.

As the result of the Vietnamese people's historic victory and the completion of the reunification of the country, the Socialist Republic of Vietnam has become a major factor for peace and progress in Asia. With the victory of the patriotic forces of Laos and the coming to power of the Marxist - Leninist People's Revolutionary Party in that country, the socialist community of nations has acquired a new member.

Imperialist designs to isolate the German Democratic Republic on the world scene have fallen through. The joint efforts of the socialist states have helped that country win universal recognition of its sovereignty, admission to the United Nations, and international confirmation of its western frontiers along with those of Poland and Czechoslovakia. The most important results of the liberation struggle of the European peoples in the Second World War have thus been consolidated and formalized; the way has been paved for stable peace and good-neighbour co-operation in Europe and the rest of the world, and for a healthier international climate.

During the situation that endangered Czechoslovakia's socialist gains in 1968, the Soviet Union, Bulgaria, Hungary, the GDR, and Poland acted on principles of socialist solidarity. Performing their internationalist duty, they came to the aid of a fraternal nation. 'This internationalist act,' states a 1970 document of the Czechoslovak Party's Central Committee, 'saved the lives of thousands of people, ensured conditions internally and externally for peaceful and untroubled labour, strengthened the western frontiers of the socialist camp, and put an end to imperialist hopes of altering the results of the Second World War.' The 15th Congress of the Czechoslovak Communist Party in April 1976 again expressed profound gratitude to the fraternal parties for their aid and support in that hour of crisis.

The international position of Cuba, the first socialist country in the western hemisphere, has grown stronger. The internationalist solidarity of the Soviet Union and the other socialist countries has helped the Cuban people to withstand the incursion of the imperialists, break their economic blockade, safeguard Cuban freedom and independence, and successfully build the new society.

In his report to the 1st Congress of the Communist Party of Cuba, Fidel Castro, its First Secretary and Prime Minister of the Cuban Republic's Revolutionary Government, said: 'We shall always preserve in our hearts a sense of gratitude to the glorious Communist Party of the Soviet Union and its heroic people. Its solidarity with Cuba—a country thousands of miles distant from the USSR—embodies the internationalist visions of Marx, Engels, and Lenin. . . . In future there will be many changes . . . but our feelings of friendship with the nation that assisted us in those decisive and critical years when we faced hunger and annihilation will live forever.'

Brezhnev has visited all the countries of the socialist community, many of them several times. Every meeting with representatives of the people of the fraternal countries and his friendly and heartfelt discussions on a wide range of subjects have always culminated in joint decisions of great political significance.

At the 25th Congress Brezhnev said: 'I am happy to report to Congress that the leaders of the communist parties of the socialist community keep up close contacts. . . . Regular multilateral and bilateral meetings enable us to consult on all major problems and, as they say, share in each other's joys and sorrows and jointly map out the course of our future progress.'

On three occasions since the 25th CPSU Congress the leaders of fraternal parties have met—in Berlin, Bucharest, and Moscow. In recent years Brezhnev has several times conferred in the Crimea with leaders of the communist and workers' parties of fraternal socialist countries. These meetings have helped develop and deepen co-operation between the governing parties of the socialist countries concerned, and have enabled common positions to be worked out.

Thus, the CPSU Politburo examined the results of the friendly meetings in the Crimea in July - August 1977 between General Secretary of the CPSU and President of the USSR Supreme Soviet Leonid Brezhnev and Erich Honecker, General Secretary of the Socialist Unity Party of Germany; Gustav Husak, General Secretary of the Communist Party of Czechoslovakia and President of the Czechoslovak Socialist Republic; Janos Kadar, First Secretary of the Hungarian Socialist Workers' Party; Edward Gierek, First Secretary of the Polish United Workers' Party; Nicolae Ceausescu, General Secretary of the Romanian Communist Party and President of the Socialist Republic of Romania; Todor Zhivkov, First Secretary of the Bulgarian Communist Party and Chairman of the State Council of the People's Republic of Bulgaria; Yumzhagiin Tsedenbal, First Secretary of the Mongolian People's Revolutionary Party and Presidium Chairman of the Great People's Khural. The Soviet Politburo fully approved the outcome of these meetings and judged them to be useful for further developing all-round co-operation between the CPSU and the Soviet state and the fraternal parties and countries, and for co-ordinating their actions on the world scene.

In November 1976 Leonid Brezhnev made a friendly visit to Yugoslavia where he conferred with Josip Tito, President of the Socialist Federal Republic of Yugoslavia and Chairman of the League of Communists of Yugoslavia, and other leaders. In the same month Brezhnev paid a friendly visit to Romania, where he held talks with Nicolae Ceausescu.

In October 1976 a Party and government delegation of the Mongolian People's Republic led by Yumzhagiin Tsedenbal paid a friendly visit to the USSR. A month later a Party and government delegation of the Polish People's Republic led by Edward Gierek likewise came to the USSR on a friendly visit.

Fidel Castro, First Secretary of the Cuban Communist Party and Chairman of the State Council and Council of Ministers of the Republic of Cuba, paid an unofficial friendly visit to the USSR at the invitation of the Central Committee, the Presidium of the USSR Supreme Soviet and the Soviet government.

In late May and early June 1977, a Bulgarian Party and government delegation led by Todor Zhivkov, First Secretary of the Bulgarian Communist Party and Chairman of the Republic's State Council, paid an official friendly visit to the USSR.

In August 1977 Tito paid an official friendly visit to the USSR. In November 1977 there was a friendly meeting between Leonid Brezhnev and Le Duan, First Secretary of the Workers' Party of Vietnam, who led the Party and government delegation of the Socialist Republic of Vietnam attending the celebrations for the 60th anniversary of the October Revolution.

1977 saw similar friendly meetings between Leonid Brezhnev and Pak Sung Chul, Member of the Political Committee of the Korean Workers' Party and Premier of the Administrative Council of the Korean Democratic People's Republic; Phomvihane, Prime Minister of the Laotian Democratic People's Republic and General Secretary of the People's Revolutionary Party of Laos; Pham Van Dong, Prime Minister of the Socialist Republic of Vietnam; and leaders of other fraternal socialist countries.

All these meetings and visits, whose participants examined matters relating to the further progress of co-operation between the USSR and other socialist countries, have significantly strengthened friendship, unity and cohesion between the fraternal parties and peoples of the countries concerned.

The countries of the socialist community follow co-ordinated policy on all central international issues. The Warsaw Treaty's political consultative committee is the chief medium of co-operation between their Party and government leaders. Brezhnev heads the Soviet delegation at committee sessions, which draw up this policy of the fraternal countries and prepare their joint international measures.

The CPSU and its General Secretary contribute constructively to the work of the political consultative committee which, in Brezhnev's words, 'dependably serves the interests of peace and socialism'. As long as the NATO bloc lasts, as long as militarist circles in the capitalist world continue the arms race, the Soviet Party and the communist and workers' parties of the other socialist countries will continue to devote due attention to strengthening yet more the Warsaw Treaty Organization.

In the meantime, the Warsaw Treaty countries have come forward with a variety of proposals aimed at furthering *détente,* consolidating security, and promoting international co-operation.

The declaration of the Warsaw Treaty countries of 26 November 1976 states: 'Wishing to make a new, active step towards eliminating the danger of a nuclear war, we offer to conclude with all states that have signed the Final Act [of the Conference on Security and Co-operation in Europe—*Ed.*] a treaty directed to this aim, pledging not to be the first to use nuclear weapons against one another; we hope that this proposal will elicit a favourable response.'

The Warsaw Treaty members also said in the Declaration: 'Every kind of effort must be built up to increase *détente,* to eliminate all remnants of the "cold war", to consolidate peace and promote international co-operation. Active involvement of all states and all political and public forces conscious of their responsibility to present and future generations is required to ensure further progress in resolving these historic problems. All those who really wish to participate in the shaping and carrying out of such actions will find dependable and faithful allies in the socialist countries and their peoples.'

The socialist solidarity of the Warsaw Treaty countries in the Council for Mutual Economic Assistance (COMECON) is invincible. Their common policy has become decisive for peace and the independence of nations.

The CPSU Central Committee, its Politburo, and Brezhnev personally give constant attention to questions of economic co-operation among the socialist countries. Internationalization of the economy is objectively necessary; under socialism it occurs not spontaneously but through the conscious activity of the masses led by Marxist - Leninist parties.

The peoples of the socialist community of nations exemplify an effective solution of problems facing the whole of mankind. As Brezhnev emphasized in his message of greetings on the occasion of the 25th anniversary of COMECON, 'The Council for Mutual Economic Assistance has given the world a unique example of co-operation within a large group of countries based on full equality, a balanced blend of national and international interests, and co-operation resting on a practical implementation of the principles of socialist internationalism.'

The fraternal parties of the socialist countries are continuously improving the content and forms of those of their relations that directly

Brezhnev on a visit to Poland, with Edward Gierek and Silesian coal-miners, 1974.

concern material production and scientific research, and that are aimed at the long-term and comprehensive solution of major economic development problems. In July 1971, acting on the decisions of the leading Party organs of the socialist states, the 25th session of COMECON adopted the comprehensive programme for the further extension and improvement of co-operation and the development of socialist economic integration of COMECON member countries. This programme is the socialist community's strategic plan of economic co-operation, a graphic example to working people in all countries of socialism's tremendous advantages over capitalism and of the great benefits of co-operation based on friendship, mutual aid, and socialist internationalism.

The Politburo of the CPSU Central Committee and the USSR Council of Ministers have acclaimed the comprehensive programme as an important step in developing internationalist co-operation between the sovereign economies of the fraternal countries. 'Fulfilment of the measures contained in the programme,' runs their decision, 'enables COMECON member countries to make fuller use of the advantages of the socialist economic system and the socialist international division of labour, in the interests of strengthening the economic and defensive might of COMECON member countries and raising the living standard of their peoples. This will give added strength to the unity and cohesion of the socialist community and reinforce socialism's positions in the struggle for social progress, peace, and international co-operation.'

The very first results achieved under the comprehensive programme in fulfilment of the national economic plans for 1971 - 5 show that the socialist countries have indeed found an effective means of ensuring joint economic, scientific, and technical progress. Productive forces are expanding rapidly, efficiency of social production is rising, and the people's wellbeing is steadily improving.

Socialist economic integration plays an ever-increasing part in the execution of the national economic plans of the fraternal countries and in augmenting the might of the socialist community as a whole. Seen against a backdrop of the worst crisis of the capitalist economy for forty years, it is obvious that COMECON countries have become the world's most dynamic economic force. Their present share in world industrial output is about one-third.

The 31st Session of COMECON was held in June 1977. The joint communique issued at the end of the Session emphasized that the comprehensive programme to deepen and improve co-operation and develop the socialist economic integration of COMECON members was being successfully implemented. As this programme was fulfilled and each socialist country was speeding up its economic progress, the interaction between the national economy of the fraternal countries was acquiring greater depth and the gap between levels of their economic development was being gradually narrowed.

After approving the work of the Soviet delegation to the 31st Session of COMECON, the Politburo and the USSR Council of Ministers stressed the importance of working out and carrying into effect long-term co-operation programmes. These would be geared to the achievement of greater depth in economic co-operation between COMECON members, and of successful solution of social and economic tasks set by congresses of their Communist and workers' parties as part of efforts to enhance the essential material foundation of the socialist community of nations. It was noted that to solve by joint efforts key economic problems identified during work on co-operation programmes would expand the basis for working out and co-ordinating the national economic development plans of the countries concerned for the next and subsequent five-year periods.

The ties between the fraternal peoples of the socialist countries, and their co-operation in science and culture, are becoming closer and more diverse. 'The life of our splendid community of socialist states,' said Brezhnev at the October 1976 plenum of the CPSU Central Committee, 'is rich and full-blooded. This is of tremendous significance, and our Leninist Party will spare no effort to ensure it should also hold true in the future.'

Close co-operation and mutual assistance have become a standard feature of relations of friendship existing within the family of equal fraternal socialist countries; they have become part of the consciousness of the fraternal peoples who see them as a living embodiment of the principles of international socialism. Initiative such as that taken by the Cepel Iron and Steel Works and engineering complex in Hungary, or by the work force of an engineering firm in the town of Policka in Czechoslovakia, well illustrates the strengthened vitality of these fraternal relations. These workers started a socialist emulation drive to mark the 60th anniversary of the October Revolution and undertook to meet delivery deadlines for export shipments to the USSR.

Speaking at the 16th Congress of Soviet Trade Unions, Leonid Brezhnev said: 'Allow me from the rostrum of this Congress to thank from the bottom of my heart the workers in fraternal socialist countries for this effective and touching demonstration of their solidarity with the cause of the October Socialist Revolution, with our country and Party, and our great project of building communism. I think I'll be speaking for all of us if I say that the Soviet working class, the entire Soviet people will meet the high-minded initiatives of their comrades in other socialist countries in suitable fashion, and will respond with new successes in the building of communism and the development of close co-operation between our countries.'

The rapid economic and social progress of the USSR and other socialist countries, the successes scored by socialism in the peaceful competition between the two world systems are playing an increasing role in the social life of today's world. The moral and political prestige enjoyed by socialism has never been greater, and socialism is having an ever-increasing impact on broad sections of working people in every country of the non-socialist world. The proud record of achievements by the socialist countries is convincing proof that the future belongs to socialism.

Soviet foreign policy is actively contributing to the elimination of colonialism and its aftermath. Following the adoption on Soviet initiative of the 1960 United Nations' Declaration on the prompt granting of independence to colonial countries and peoples, the Soviet Union has repeatedly pressed for its fulfilment. The principled policy of the USSR and, alongside other socialist countries and the newly independent states, its steady efforts have substantially helped the rapidly growing movement for national liberation.

By and large the colonial system of imperialism in its classic forms can be regarded as finished. This is a phenomenon of significance for world history. Dozens of new independent states have come into being, whose role in world development is steadily growing. As Brezhnev has put it: 'Today we can safely declare that no force in the world can destroy the results of the heroic national liberation struggle waged by teeming millions in the former colonies and semi-colonies of imperialism. The tide of national liberation is irresistible; the future belongs to it. The torch lit by October will never be extinguished on this front of world history.'

Recent years have seen the liberation of the peoples of Mozambique and of other Portuguese colonies. The victory of the patriotic forces of Angola who relied on the solidarity and fraternal assistance of the USSR and Cuba, of all countries in the socialist community of nations, of progressive forces on the African continent and throughout the world, has come as a major success for the revolutionary movement. This victory has provided fresh impetus to the struggle of African peoples against the racialist regimes of South Africa and Rhodesia.

The Soviet Union is giving and will continue to give selfless fraternal support to the liberation struggle of the nations. It seeks no political domination and wants no concessions or military bases. Soviet Communists, Brezhnev notes, act as they are bidden by conviction and revolutionary conscience.

However, after gaining national independence the liberated countries have still to fend off neo-colonialist encroachments and imperialist attempts to exploit their economic backwardness. In these conditions, co-operation with the socialist world is important for the fledgling national states in achieving genuine sovereignty. Brezhnev has repeatedly stressed Soviet readiness and resolve to make their task easier. The Central Committee report to the 25th Congress stated: 'The Soviet Union fully supports the legitimate aspirations of the young states, their determination to put an end to all imperialist exploitation, and to take full charge of their own national wealth.'

Supporting young states and aiding their economic and social development is implicit in the very nature of the Soviet social and political system and in the principles of proletarian internationalism underlying the foreign policy of the CPSU. This policy rests on the identity of the basic longterm interests and aims of the socialist world and the movement for national liberation, on the need to unite all forces in the struggle for peace and social progress.

Soviet relations with the developing countries follow the principles of equality, mutual benefit, and consideration for each other's interests. The USSR regards economic ties with the Asian, African, and Latin American countries as a form of world socialism's alliance with the national liberation movement. Soviet economic and technical assistance to countries that have freed themselves from colonial slavery helps strengthen their national independence and overcome the one-sidedness of their economy; it also facilitates the establishment and consolidation of a state sector. The Soviet Union actively supports the industrialization of the liberated countries and helps train their scientific and technical personnel.

Elaborating on Lenin's ideas about the alliance of socialist forces with peoples fighting for independence, the CPSU Central Committee and Brezhnev personally are doing their utmost to further the Soviet Union's friendship and co-operation with countries that have taken the non-capitalist road and are the foremost units of the present-day movement for national liberation. Alongside inter-state contacts, ties are proliferating between the ruling communist and revolutionary democratic parties.

Brezhnev is active in negotiations with the leaders of Asian and African governments and ruling parties. His visit to India in 1973 opened a new chapter in friendly Soviet-Indian relations, which are of tremendous international importance. A Soviet-Indian treaty of peace, friendship, and co-operation was signed, the provisions of which are being success-

With Dr. Agostinho Neto, Moscow, 1976.

fully implemented. Similar treaties have been concluded with a number of other Asian and African countries. In October 1976, following on the negotiations between Brezhnev and Agostinho Neto, Chairman of the MPLA and President of the People's Republic of Angola, important Soviet-Angolan documents were signed at summit level—a Treaty of

Friendship and Co-operation and an agreement of co-operation between the CPSU and the MPLA. During the talks between Soviet and Angolan leaders held in Moscow in September 1977 the progress of friendly Soviet-Angolan relations was given a high appraisal and the determination of both sides to strengthen them in every way was reiterated.

In 1977 Brezhnev took a personal part in talks with President Mohammed Daud of Afghanistan; Hafez al-Assad, president of the Syrian Arab Republic and General Secretary of the Party of Arab Socialist Renaissance; Lieutenant-Colonel Mengistu Haile Mariam, Chairman of the Council of Ministers of Socialist Ethiopia and Chairman of the Provisional Military Administrative Council; and leaders of other newly independent countries.

In October 1977 Prime Minister Morarji Desai of the Republic of India paid an official friendly visit to the USSR. The joint Soviet-Indian declaration issued at the end of the talks expressed the determination of both sides to go on strengthening friendship and co-operation, which match the interests of the peoples of India and the USSR and which serve the cause of international mutual understanding and agreement.

Friendly relations between the Soviet Union and the newly free states exert a positive influence on world affairs and help consolidate the positions of the forces of peace, democracy, and socialism.

The important changes witnessed on the international scene in the late sixties and early seventies are in very large measure attributable to the tireless activity of the CPSU, the Soviet Government, and the Central Committee's Politburo headed by Brezhnev. The CPSU performed a historic service to world socialism, to the communist, working-class, and national liberation movements, by proving—in a thorough analysis of present-day social development and on the basis of a precise study of the relation of class forces in the world arena—that a relaxation of international tension is possible, and by specifying the practical moves that would consolidate international security. This led the way towards a radical improvement of the international climate.

At that time the world situation was still very tense. America's war in Vietnam was escalating. In 1967 Israel perfidiously attacked Egypt, Syria, and Jordan, and occupied large sections of their territory. On the European continent, too, an explosive situation persisted due to reactionary intrigues.

The Soviet Union frustrated the aggressive imperialist designs and supported the just struggle of the peoples for freedom and independence. It was becoming increasingly apparent that imperialist 'from a position of strength' policy was in deep crisis. It began to dawn on the ruling circles of the capitalist world that the socialist countries could not be destroyed by force and that the politics of cold war were utterly bankrupt. All the same, to exploit the opportunities that arose on the world scene for lessening the danger of war and buttressing peace was no simple matter. It required a flexible yet principled approach and a creative search for mutually acceptable solutions.

The Soviet Union came forward with initiatives that could improve and fundamentally restructure the entire system of international relations. And it is also in the broad context of the international political scene of the sixties and seventies that we should view the efforts of the Soviet Union and the other socialist countries to win recognition of the territorial and political realities resulting from the Second World War, and thus reinforce European security.

Co-operation between the Soviet Union and France has made good headway in the past decade. A new chapter in Soviet-French relations was opened by the negotiations between L. I. Brezhnev, along with other Soviet leaders, and President de Gaulle in Moscow in 1966. From that time on, the two countries began to work together in the most varied fields. The General Secretary's visits to France and his meetings with Presidents Georges Pompidou and Valéry Giscard d'Estaing were seminal in the growth of co-operation between the two countries. Much of what was conceived in the process of Soviet-French co-operation passed subsequently into more general international practice.

Of fundamental importance was the fact that the co-operation between France and the Soviet Union, based as it is on mutual benefit, has developed into a stable and useful element of international affairs, a factor for securing a durable peace and advancing *détente*. Each new successive Soviet-French summit contributes to the climate of mutual trust prevailing in relations between France and the USSR and brings the two positions of the two countries closer together. Added proof of this was provided by the official visit to France paid by Leonid Brezhnev at the invitation of President Giscard d'Estaing in June 1977. On that occasion Brezhnev and Giscard d'Estaing stated that friendship and co-operation between the USSR and France would remain an essential and permanent component of the foreign policies of their two countries.

Important political documents were signed at the end of the visit, along with a series of agreements furthering co-operation between the USSR and France in the political, commercial, and industrial fields as well as in science and engineering.

As the decision of the Soviet Politburo, the Presidium of the USSR Supreme Soviet, and the Council of Ministers of the USSR subsequently emphasized, Leonid Brezhnev's visit to France was a major contribution to the realization of the programme of further efforts for peace and international co-operation, for freedom and independence of nations mapped out by the 25th Congress. Its importance went far beyond Soviet-French relations. In the course of talks held as part of the visit, a wide range of key issues of present-day international affairs was discussed: how to strengthen world peace and advance *détente*, to eliminate hotbeds of war danger, to end the arms race and avert the menace of nuclear war. The outcome of these Soviet-French talks confirmed once again the fruitful and effective nature of the foreign policy formulated by the 24th and 25th CPSU Congresses.

In 1970 a treaty was concluded between the Soviet Union and the Federal Republic of Germany, and this resulted in a noticeable shift towards the normalization of Soviet-West German relations. Bonn recognized the inviolability of Europe's borders. Brezhnev's negotiations with Chancellor Willy Brandt, later with Helmut Schmidt, were important milestones in the subsequent fruitful development of Soviet-West German relations. They helped to consolidate peace and mutually beneficial co-operation on the European continent.

Brezhnev's talks with the American President in May 1972 were a turning point in Soviet-American relations, so significant as these are for world peace. The documents signed as a result of the negotiations spelled out the peaceful coexistence principles governing Soviet-American relations and the basis of bilateral co-operation in different fields. They contain a commitment by both countries to 'do their utmost to avoid military confrontations and to prevent the outbreak of nuclear war'.

The agreement on preventing nuclear war, signed in Washington in 1973 during General Secretary Brezhnev's official visit to the USA, responds to the aspirations of all mankind. And the understanding reached during his 1974 meeting with President Ford in Vladivostok was a new step forward in efforts to curb the arms race.

As subsequent developments in international affairs showed, the Peace

Programme, annunciated in 1971 by Leonid Brezhnev at the time of the 24th Party Congress, was of truly historic importance for the cause of freedom, security and progress of the nations of the world. It became a potent factor in ameliorating international relations, in turning towards *détente* and establishing ever more firmly the principles formulated by Lenin of peaceful coexistence between countries with different social systems. This highly realistic programme was a creative application, developed for modern conditions, of Lenin's ideas on peace and friendship between peoples. It embodied the consistently peace-loving policy of the Soviet Union promulgated by the Decree on Peace after the October Revolution. The Peace Programme—the battle-standard in the fight against the danger of a new, thermonuclear war—was justly viewed throughout the world as an outstanding document of our time. The battle for its implementation became known as 'the Soviet peace offensive'.

The Peace Programme outlined a detailed series of measures. In particular, it set the following objectives:

- Elimination of military flashpoints in South-East Asia and the Middle East; furthering political settlements there on the basis of respect for the legitimate rights of the states and peoples subjected to aggression.
- Final recognition of the territorial changes that resulted in Europe from the Second World War; furthering a radical change of course towards *détente* and peace on the European continent; summoning and successfully holding a European conference on security and co-operation.
- Conclusion of treaties outlawing nuclear, chemical, and bacteriological weapons.
- Greater efforts in the struggle to end the arms race of all types of weapons.
- Full implementation of United Nations' resolutions on the abolition of colonial regimes.
- Promotion of mutually beneficial co-operation between the Soviet Union and all interested states.

The peace-loving initiatives of the Soviet Union received and still receive support from the peoples of all countries, since they mirror their basic interests and desires.

The CPSU and the Soviet Government were eminently successful in implementing the Peace Programme in the period between the 24th and 25th Party Congresses. Realization of the Programme brought about substantial changes in international relations in favour of peace and social progress.

As the Peace Programme proceeded to take effect, more and more capitalist governments acknowledged the principles of peaceful coexistence as the norm for relations between states with different social systems. Economic, scientific, technical, and cultural co-operation among peoples made good headway. International tensions relaxed considerably. Objective conditions appeared for a European security system.

In recent years the changes in world affairs have been truly impressive. The seat of war in South-East Asia has been stamped out. The treaties signed by the Soviet Union, Poland, and Czechoslovakia with West Germany have ratified in terms of international law the inviolability of the frontiers in Europe. A four-power agreement on West Berlin has been signed by the USSR, USA, Britain, and France, alleviating the main tensions and creating conditions under which West Berlin could change from a source of dispute into a constructive element of peace and *détente*.

A positive change has occurred in Soviet-American relations. This took the form of a whole package of Soviet-American treaties, agreements, and other documents, including the extremely important 'Basic principles of relations between the Union of Soviet Socialist Republics and the United States of America'. These cover a wide range of topics, from the prevention of nuclear war and the limitation of strategic offensive arms and anti-ballistic missile systems to co-operation in the fields of health and environmental protection. The normalization of relations between the USSR and the USA—two countries of opposite social systems, each with tremendous economic, scientific, technical, and military potential—has had a highly positive influence on the course of world events.

There was a further expansion of bilateral Soviet ties with France, West Germany, Italy, Britain, Japan, Canada, Finland, and other capitalist countries. A number of important measures were put into effect to curb the arms race, including the signing of treaties on banning and destroying bacteriological weapons, and banning the siting of nuclear arms in outer space and on sea and ocean beds. Negotiations are at present under way in Vienna on the mutual reduction of armed forces in

Central Europe.

In May 1977 representatives of thirty-three UN member countries meeting in Geneva signed the convention banning environmental modification for military or potentially hostile purposes.

All these developments are inseparably linked with the peace policy of the Soviet Union, the fraternal socialist countries, and of other progressive forces. Brezhnev's tireless efforts to strengthen international security and assert the principles of peaceful coexistence have been hailed by wide sections of the world public. They have been highly important in rallying the mass of the people to fight for peace. Brezhnev's speech 'For a just, democratic peace, for the security of the peoples and international co-operation' at the World Congress of Peace Forces in Moscow on 26 October 1973 won a lively response in all countries.

The Conference on Security and Co-operation in Europe was an event of outstanding historic importance. It was convened at Helsinki in July 1975 on the initiative of the socialist countries, and became the biggest political and diplomatic forum of representatives of countries with different social systems ever held in Europe.

The Soviet delegation to the European Conference was headed by Brezhnev in person. His speech in Helsinki made a galvanizing impact on the struggle for international peace and security. The whole world responded to his call for the further materialization of *détente,* for making it irreversible, and for matching political with military *détente.* He put his signature to the Final Act of the Conference on behalf of the Soviet Union.

This Act, signed by thirty-three European countries and by the United States and Canada, embodies and details the principles of peaceful coexistence and mutually beneficial co-operation. Its ten agreed principles are a virtual code of international conduct to ensure peace and security for all the European nations. The Conference outlined an extensive programme of co-operation in commerce, economy, science, and culture.

Interviewed by a *Pravda* correspondent a year after the Helsinki Conference, Brezhnev said of the Final Act: 'By formalizing what has been achieved in improving the European political climate, this collectively worked-out document has given a long-term perspective for realistic and responsible conduct of inter-state affairs, first of all with regard to Europe and also in large measure from the standpoint of the likely opportunities for settling problems of a worldwide character. It is aligned on international *détente*, on terminating armed conflicts wherever these still exist, and on peaceful co-operation between states without interference in their internal affairs.'

The success of the Conference created fresh opportunities for resolving the main problem of the times—to strengthen world peace and international security.

On examining the results of the Helsinki Conference, the Politburo, the Supreme Soviet Presidium, and the USSR Council of Ministers adopted a resolution noting Brezhnev's outstanding contribution to the foreign policy of the Communist Party and Soviet Government and to the implementation of the Peace Programme. 'His single-minded activity, motivated by deep concern for world peace,' the resolution stated, 'was of great significance for the convocation and success of the European Conference. Our Party and the Soviet people set a high value on this selfless activity and express total approval of L. I. Brezhnev's speech at the Helsinki Conference.'

Delegates and foreign guests at the 25th Congress stressed the outstanding part played by the Peace Programme in the radical restructuring of international relations in favour of peace and social progress. 'Like many other participants in the Congress,' said A. V. Gitalov, a prominent Ukrainian farmer, 'I have been a soldier and fought in the war; I have seen blood and tears, and lost relatives and close friends. So I know the high price paid for peace. I also know how difficult it is to safeguard and make firm a lasting peace in our troubled times. We Congress delegates can say with every right that our Leninist Party and its Central Committee are doing their utmost and showing tremendous perseverance, firmness, and patience to achieve this historic goal. 'And it is small wonder that our Peace Programme, the greatest achievement in the struggle for peace, is associated by all honest people on earth first of all with your name, Leonid Ilyich. I am pleased to convey to you the deepest respect of the war veterans and their gratitude for your fine work.'

Brezhnev's observation that the march of events had completely confirmed the timeliness and realism of the Peace Programme was received by Congress with pride and satisfaction. Thanks to the co-ordinated moves of the socialist countries, the fraternal communist and workers' parties and progressives all over the world, mankind is now struggling

Signing the Final Act at Helsinki, 1975.

out of the mire of the Cold War onto the firm soil of *détente*. Though there is as yet no guarantee of world peace, one can safely say, in Brezhnev's words, that 'the healthier international climate is convincing evidence that lasting peace is no hollow wish but an entirely realistic goal. One can and must continue working for it energetically.'

After analysing the conditions for international progress, Brezhnev put forward at the 25th Congress a programme of future struggle for peace and international co-operation, for the freedom and independence of peoples. This programme came as an embodiment of the combined will of the CPSU and the Soviet people to maintain and strengthen the cause of peace and mankind's progress, to avert the menace of a nuclear world war. The new proposals represent the direct extension and further elaboration of the Peace Programme. They were enthusiastically endorsed by the Soviet Communist Party, the entire Soviet people, and by the world communist, workers', and national-liberation movements, by peace-loving peoples throughout the world. The proposals may be summarized as follows:

- To invigorate the unity of the fraternal socialist states; to further their all-round co-operation in building the new society, and by so doing to increase their joint contribution to the consolidation of peace.
- To work for an end to the expanding and dangerous arms race and for the reduction of arms stockpiles; to work for disarmament.
- To concentrate the efforts of the peace-loving states towards eliminating the remaining seats of war and, first of all, towards securing a just and lasting settlement in the Middle East.
- To actively promote the full implementation of the Final Act of the European Conference and greater peaceful co-operation in Europe; to step up the efforts increasing *détente* and to give it concrete shape in mutually beneficial co-operation between states.
- To work for Asian security through the joint efforts of the Asian states.
- To work for a world treaty on non-use of force in international relations.
- To seek the elimination of all remnants of the system of colonial oppression, all seats of colonialism and racialism, and to further the equality and independence of the peoples.

—To work against discrimination and all other artificial obstacles to international commerce and seek abolition of all inequality in international economic relations, the dictation of terms and exploitation.

This programme of further struggle for peace, international co-operation, and the freedom and independence of nations advanced by the 25th Congress is inspiring and rallying millions of people to work for a lasting and dependable peace.

All people of good will have acclaimed such Soviet peace initiatives as the draft of a world treaty on the non-use of force in international relations and the memorandum on ending the arms race and promoting disarmament which were submitted by the Soviet Government to the 31st UN General Assembly, and the Soviet statement on restructuring international economic relations made at that session.

In 1977 the Soviet Government proposed to place on the agenda of the 32nd UN General Assembly as a matter of great urgency the topic 'On deepening and consolidating international *détente* and averting the menace of nuclear war'.

In his report 'The Great October Revolution and the progress of mankind' Brezhnev advanced fresh important peace initiatives aimed at averting the menace of nuclear war. He proposed a plan to agree on the simultaneous cessation by all nuclear powers of the manufacture of any kind of nuclear weapons, and simultaneously to undertake a progressive reduction in the available stock-piles of nuclear weapons, moving on to complete '100 per cent' destruction of these weapons; and also to agree that, alongside a ban on all nuclear arms tests for a specified period, there should be a moratorium on nuclear explosions for peaceful purposes.

Faithful to its revolutionary duty, the Soviet Communist Party persists in its efforts for peace—the greatest boon for all peoples and an important condition for human progress. It holds, however, that *détente,* strict observance of the principle of non-interference in the affairs of other states and respect for their independence and sovereignty concern interstate relations only; they do not and cannot repeal or change the laws of the class struggle.

The outlook for mankind has never been more favourable, since the revolutionary potential of the international working class and the anti-imperialist forces has grown considerably. However, the world revolutionary process is complex and full of dialectical contradictions.

The Soviet Communist Party is fully aware that today's stage in world development is characterized by an intensification of class struggle on the world scene. Aggressive imperialist forces are whipping up the arms race which poses serious danger to the peace and security of nations, and are doing their best to sabotage *détente*. Reactionary circles are busy organizing ideological subversion against the Soviet Union and other socialist countries, are engineering all manner of slanderous anti-Soviet and anti-communist campaigns, and are even attempting to meddle in the internal affairs of socialist and other countries. Whipping up anti-communist hysteria, the reactionaries in imperialist countries are strengthening the campaign of terror and persecution against democratic and progressive movements.

Interviewed by the French newspaper *Le Monde* in June 1977, Leonid Brezhnev said: 'The latest recommendations emanating from NATO headquarters are designed to get the member countries of this alliance to increase their military expenditure, to keep the American military budget ever growing and encourage the USA to continue developing new weapons of war. All this is evidence that the ground is being prepared for a new phase of the arms race. We are convinced that curbing the arms race is crucial to maintaining world peace and developing *détente*. If we should fail to check this devilish race, we will again find ourselves on the brink of the unpredictable, as in the years of the Cold War.'

As the Soviet Union and other fraternal socialist countries resolutely rebuff the intrigues and designs of the enemies of peace and socialism, they help bring about further progress in creating in international affairs an atmosphere favourable for the cause of peace and social progress, for turning *détente* into a stable, increasingly viable, general and irreversible process affecting all continents, a process of transition to a stable pattern of fruitful, peaceful co-operation between states and of practical steps forward in disarmament—above all, in nuclear disarmament.

In the complex conditions of world social development, it is important that one should find the determinant trend. Brezhnev identified it as the growth of world socialism,of forces fighting against imperialism and for the socialist transformation of society. From this flows the historical optimism of the Marxists - Leninists and their unshakable confidence in the ultimate victory of the new system. Of tremendous importance today is the ability of the working-class parties to call upon the revolutionary energy of the masses and direct it against imperialism and in favour of peace and social progress.

The Communist Party of the Soviet Union, its Central Committee and General Secretary follow very closely the development of the world communist movement, the most progressive and influential political force today. They base their relations with fraternal parties upon Marxist - Leninist principles and proletarian internationalism. Participation in each other's Party congresses is highly effective, as are the friendly meetings of the CPSU Central Committee and Brezhnev personally with representatives of communist, workers, and national democratic parties. Those who have been present on such occasions invariably respond warmly to his sincerity, comradeship, and cordiality, and his deep understanding of problems of the revolutionary movement and of trends in social development.

Problems of the international communist movement were thoroughly examined by Brezhnev in the Central Committee's reports to the 23rd, 24th, and 25th Congresses, and also in his reports to many Central Committee plenums.

The conference of communist and workers' parties in Moscow in June 1969 was an important landmark in the development of the present-day world communist movement. It was the third such communist forum since the war and was attended by representatives of seventy-five fraternal parties.

At this meeting, Brezhnev presented a searching analysis of the world's economic and political situation and criticized in convincing fashion the policy and ideology of imperialism. The general crisis of capitalism, he showed, was becoming increasingly acute, and the system of private enterprise was to an ever-increasing extent inhibiting and retarding the progressive development of mankind. In contrast to this, said Brezhnev, socialism as it matures is giving ever greater scope to the advantages of its economic, social, and political system, and is setting an example of genuine democracy.

The question of united anti-imperialist action by communist and workers' parties figured prominently in Brezhnev's address as leader of the CPSU delegation. 'Joint action by communist and workers' parties,' Brezhnev said, 'is a pressing need of the times which bears on vital interests of the entire revolutionary movement. The strength of every communist party and the effective functioning of every national contingent of Communists come not only from their influence within the home country but also from their ability to act jointly with other contingents of the communist movement.'

In a world where Communists bear direct responsibility for their own peoples' future and for that of mankind, differences of opinion on particular questions should not prevent joint action against imperialism. 'The important thing in our practical activity is to put first that which unites the Communists of all countries,' emphasized Brezhnev.

Today, special importance has become attached to bilateral and multilateral meetings of representatives of communist and workers' parties. Regional conferences, too, have become a form of collective work in the new conditions. Always a defender of the communist movement's political and ideological unity as based on Marxist - Leninist principles, the Soviet Communist Party is ready at all times to join with other fraternal parties in specific moves to cement this unity. It holds that theoretical work—the creative development of revolutionary teaching and protection of it against distortions—is among the most important tasks of Communists in all countries.

General Secretary Brezhnev refers, with deep and outspoken fidelity to principle, to the danger of right and 'left' opportunism, stressing the need for combating it. Whether right or 'left', opportunism tends to lessen the communist parties' capability and to undermine the revolutionary positions of the working class and the unity of anti-imperialist forces. At present, concessions to nationalism, and occasionally downright nationalist postures, are as a rule the common symptom of 'left' and right revisionism.

The CPSU is combating all types of bourgeois ideology, opportunism, and nationalism, and is working for the further extension of the communist movement's role in the development of society and for its closer political and ideological unity.

In his analysis of the motive forces of the modern world revolutionary process, Brezhnev presents incontrovertible proof of the increasing role of the working class as the leading force in the struggle for the people's interests and for democracy and socialism.

Important ideas on the development of revolution under present conditions were advanced by the General Secretary in the Central Committee's report to the 25th Congress. He tied in the key problems of international relations and the consolidation of world peace with the growth of the world revolutionary process. The report exhaustively analyses the peculiarities of the current phase of capitalism's general crisis, and how the struggle for democracy relates to the struggle for socialism. It examines peaceful and non-peaceful forms of revolution, and demonstrates the need for protecting and consolidating revolutionary gains and for international *détente.* It makes clear that *détente* does not and cannot repeal or alter laws of the class struggle. All these points contribute greatly to solving the central problems of the present world revolutionary process and world communist movement, and provide a scientific ground for its strategy and tactics.

The expansion of the communist movement's social basis in the capitalist world, the greater role played by Communists in social development, and their wider influence among the mass of the people have been among the most remarkable developments of our time. The international unity of Communists is especially important in today's conditions when the world revolutionary process has grown to unparalleled dimensions and when the forces of reaction and counter-revolution, dreading its successes, are co-ordinating their anti-communist activities on an international scale.

Proletarian internationalism is a crucial tried and tested principle in the activity of Communists. The Central Committee's report to the 25th Congress describes it as one of the main principles of Marxism - Leninism. All the gains of the communist movement are associated with proletarian internationalism. To defend it with all available resources is to work for the closer unity of the working class and all communist parties under the Marxist - Leninist banner and to give added power to their joint struggle for peace and social progress.

The entire course of world revolutionary movements confirms that the observance of common principles of Marxism - Leninism and proletarian internationalism is an essential precondition for strengthening the positions, authority and influence of each and every communist party, and alone can enable it to perform its duty before the working class of its own country and the people of the world.

In 1976 Brezhnev took part in the Berlin Conference of European communist and workers' parties. In his speech he stressed that proletarian internationalism, solidarity of the working class and Communists of all countries in the struggle for common aims and their solidarity with the peoples fighting for national liberation and social progress, and free co-operation of the fraternal parties on the basis of strict equality and independence are and always have been a mighty and reliable weapon of the communist parties and the working-class movement. Examining the important aspects of the situation in present-day Europe and elsewhere, and the greater role played by the world socialist system, he showed why co-operation by Communists of socialist and capitalist countries is needed.

The Berlin Conference found a wide resonance all over the world. Brezhnev's speech in Berlin is regarded by the communist and workers' parties of Europe and other continents as a document of profound theoretical and political significance. The forum showed that the movement for peace, security, national independence and democracy is inseparably linked with fundamental tasks in the struggle for social progress and socialism.

In its resolution on the results of the Berlin Conference, the Politburo commended the activity of the CPSU delegation headed by Brezhnev and noted that the conference had contributed significantly to the struggle for a Europe of peace, security, co-operation, and social progress. The unanimously adopted conference document, the resolution said, rests on Marxist - Leninist principles and contains the joint assessments and conclusions of the communist and workers' parties on a number of topical and vital problems. The Politburo expressed its conviction that the Soviet people with its constructive work will continue to contribute honourably to the common internationalist cause of the communist movement and of anti-imperialist and peace forces, to the struggle for peace, security, democracy, and socialism.

The October 1976 plenum of the CPSU Central Committee took note of the fact that in recent years substantial results have been achieved, through the joint efforts of the peace forces with active participation by the Soviet Union, in reducing the danger of nuclear war. These results must be consolidated and developed in order to end the new arms race instigated by the imperialist powers and to secure progress towards disarmament.

In a restatement of the Soviet Union's unwavering determination to maintain world peace, develop international co-operation and strengthen the security of nations, Leonid Brezhnev at a reception given in July 1977 for the diplomatic corps in Moscow asked the foreign ambassadors to pass on to the leaders of their respective countries the following message: 'There is in today's world no country and no people with which the Soviet Union is reluctant to have good relations. There is no international problem to the solution of which the Soviet Union is reluctant to contribute. There is no hotbed of war danger the elimination of which by peaceful means does not interest the Soviet Union. There is no type of weapon, and more especially no weapon of mass destruction, which the Soviet Union is reluctant to limit or ban on a reciprocal basis in agreement with other countries and eventually remove from the stockpiles.'

The Soviet Union has always been and will continue to be an active participant in any negotiations, any international action aimed at fostering peaceful co-operation and strengthening the security of nations, or creating favourable conditions for a durable world peace.

Speaking at the anniversary meeting in Moscow to mark 60 years of Soviet power, Leonid Brezhnev pointed out: 'Today the principles of peaceful coexistence have become fairly well established in international affairs as the only realistic and sensible ones.' Brezhnev emphasized that in following a policy of peace aimed at strengthening the security of nations, in developing relations based on mutual understanding and good-neighbourliness, 'the Soviet Union is attaching great importance to its co-operation with the USA, France, West Germany, Britain, Italy, and with all countries big and small. If the major problems facing mankind today are to be successfully resolved, well-designed and purposeful efforts are required of the people of every country. This demands wide-based and constructive co-operation between all countries and peoples. The Soviet Union, for its part, is all for such co-operation.'

Our position in this matter wins the hearts and minds of working people everywhere. Which is why progressives throughout the world speak so highly of the foreign policy activities of the Central Committee of the CPSU, the Politburo, and the untiring personal efforts of Leonid Brezhnev aimed at strengthening the peace and security of nations.

The activity of the Communist Party, its Central Committee, Politburo, and General Secretary Brezhnev is marked in foreign relations by a truly scientific and creative approach and by deep insight into the substance of vital aspects of world affairs. This activity stands out in its fidelity to principle, its profound commitment to the class interests of the working people, and its skill in picking out the really decisive points from amid a mass of intricate and contradictory developments, in holding course through the most complex and confusing situations, and in choosing the most effective methods of promoting a peaceful course in foreign affairs.

As a leader of the Leninist type, Brezhnev is true to the spirit of democracy and revolution and to class principles in evaluating the crucial issues of world policy. He is sincerely fond of the working people, with whom he has close ties. He has an objectively correct understanding of the new developments in world relations and of the perspectives of social progress, and he is unfailingly realistic in the way he handles foreign policy. His tireless efforts to strengthen world peace and security and to promote the principles of peaceful coexistence have won high praise and universal recognition. In 1973 Leonid Brezhnev was awarded the international Lenin Peace Prize.

This met with wholehearted approval both at home and abroad. Democratic spokesmen are unanimous that in world affairs Brezhnev speaks not only for his own country and people, but for millions of peace-loving men and women all over the world. People of different nationalities and political beliefs refer with deep appreciation to the constructive, far-sighted, and consistent policy of the CPSU and its Central Committee under Brezhnev.

Le Duan, First Secretary of the Workers' Party of Vietnam, who attended the Lenin Peace Prize ceremony, said: 'This high award is a profoundly meaningful event. It is an appreciation of the tireless efforts of Comrade Brezhnev, the Communist Party of the Soviet Union, and the Soviet Government in the struggle for world peace against the warlike imperialist policy and on the side of the lofty revolutionary aims of all peoples, for peace, national independence, democracy, and socialism.'

Addressing representatives of Moscow's public organizations, factory and building workers, farmers from rural areas near the capital, and prominent scientists and cultural workers, Renato Guttuzo, Central Committee member of the Italian Communist Party, himself a laureate of the Lenin Peace Prize, and also a member of its international committee, declared: 'There is tremendous significance in the activity of a person who is shouldering responsibilities of global dimensions and working energetically, consciously, and bravely for peace and international understanding. He embodies the ideals of human brotherhood and peace which are the main content of Leninist policy, of the aims that faced the October Revolution, and the determining factor in Soviet man's actions and moral stance.'

In his reply to the many messages of congratulation, Brezhnev said: 'For me, as a Communist, there can be no reward more precious than one bearing the name of the great Lenin—our teacher, our theorist of genius, and a brilliant and far-sighted statesman. . . . The foreign policy of the Soviet Union is the fruit of the collective reason and activity of our Communist Party. In this award to me of the Lenin Prize, I therefore see acknowledgement of the whole Party's merits and international recognition of the rightness of its Central Committee's policy. And I am happy that, in the ranks of the Party that has shaped and strengthened me, I can take part in the struggle for the great aims of a lasting peace and international security—aims aspired to by working people in the entire world.'

The Soviet people and the peace-loving citizens of all countries were deeply gratified that the Presidium of the World Peace Council conferred on Brezhnev the highest award of the peace movement, the F. Joliot-Curie Gold Medal of Peace. The award was acclaimed by many statesmen, leaders of political and public organizations, and people of different views and convictions.

Congratulating Brezhnev on behalf of the national organizations of 125 countries from all continents serving on the World Peace Council, its General Secretary, Romesh Chandra, said: 'In recent years no single individual has done so much in so many countries for peace, independence, justice, and social progress as Comrade Brezhnev.' The respect that Brezhnev had always shown for the opinion of the peoples, for the peace movement, Romesh Chandra went on to say, had gone a long way in helping the World Peace Council to its present prestige and influence. Brezhnev's participation in the Peace Movement had found its most vivid expression in his speech to the World Congress of Peace Forces in October 1973, which Romesh Chandra described as 'a guide to action for peace fighters to which they can turn again and again in order to make their struggle for peace more effective.'

Thanking the Presidium of the World Peace Council for the high award, Brezhnev said: 'The conviction that peace is the greatest boon to working people and to all nations, the resolve to fight against its enemies and to promote its consolidation to the best of my ability have,

I can say, been part of me all my life. Today, as I receive this high international award, I wish to reassure you, dear friends, that I shall always be true to this conviction.'

Leonid Brezhnev's consistent and fruitful activity in this matter has been recognized by the United Nations. UN Secretary-General Kurt Waldheim during his official visit to the Soviet Union in September 1977 awarded Brezhnev the gold medal of peace of the United Nations Organization.

In a message of greeting to the participants in the World Forum of Peace Forces held in Moscow in 1977, Brezhnev emphasized that the main task today is to act, to look for sensible solutions that facilitate rapid progress towards real disarmament, towards real *détente,* with the aim of converting it into a truly universal and irreversible process. Political parties, trade unions, women's and youth's organizations, parliamentarians, scientists and art workers, all peace supporters, active participants in the struggle to avert a new world conflict—all builders of durable peace and the security of nations have an important contribution to make to this effort. Today, new and better opportunities are opening for their work.

Brezhnev has won the respect of millions of people of good will in all corners of the world. When handing him a second Gold Star of Hero of the Czechoslovak Socialist Republic and the Order of Klement Gottwald on 2 November 1976 for outstanding services in the liberation of Czechoslovakia from the Nazis, in promoting Soviet - Czechoslovak friendship and the fight for peace and social progress, Gustav Husak, General Secretary of the Czechoslovak Communist Party and President of Czechoslovakia, said: 'Our people see you as their true and sincere friend, a loyal and devoted patriot and internationalist, a party leader and statesman who rightly enjoys exceptionally high prestige throughout the world. We set a high value on your unsparing efforts to strengthen the great community of socialist states. . . . Your work as General Secretary of the Central Committee of a Party that has accumulated such a wealth of experience in building socialism and communism and fighting for world peace and social progress is an outstanding contribution to the successful development of the world communist and working-class movement and the action solidarity of all progressive, democratic, and anti-imperialist forces.'

Brezhnev's visits to the socialist countries never fail to become vivid

At a Cuban-Soviet Friendship meeting, Havana, 1974.

demonstrations of the unbreakable friendship of the fraternal peoples and parties, and of the deep and sincere respect enjoyed by the leader of the CPSU and the Soviet people. Those who witnessed his visit to Cuba in January - February 1974, for example, felt at once the rapport that established itself between Brezhnev and Cuba's working people the moment he stepped on Cuban soil. The people of Cuba had, of course, known of Brezhnev before his visit; they had always respected him and appreciated his work for peace and socialism. But this was the first time the Cubans had seen him at close hand and they took him to their hearts for his charm, friendliness, sincerity, modesty, and personal warmth.

Even during Brezhnev's visits to capitalist states, friendly feelings for the Soviet Union and its leader are to be seen in various forms every-

With Giscard d'Estaing.

where, despite the rigid framework of diplomatic protocol.

During his stay in France in October 1971, Brezhnev visited the Lenin Museum in the house on the rue Marie-Rose where Lenin once lived. Thousands of people gathered in the street, carrying red flags and streamers in honour of Brezhnev, and there were posters inscribed in Russian 'Greetings to Comrade Brezhnev'. Hundreds of voices shouted 'Long live the Soviet Union' and 'Druzhba' ('Friendship'), and the *Internationale* was sung. Warm greetings were showered on the CPSU's

General Secretary. An elderly man held up a home-made placard pasted with war-time newspaper photographs of Brezhnev in military uniform. 'Welcome,' the man shouted, 'welcome to our comrade-in-arms.'

Americans responded warmly to Brezhnev's visit to the USA (June 1973). On hearing Brezhnev on television, a Chicago building worker said to reporters: 'I don't usually waste my time watching television. But on 24 June, when Leonid Brezhnev addressed the American nation, which also means me, John Pershing, I had my Zenith on and followed every word. I have a bullet scar on my left arm. I got it in the Ardennes in 1945, and I have a worker's rough hands. He spoke from the heart. I'll never forget what he said about the cold war—that it's a wretched substitute for real peace, and that the world has outgrown the cold war straitjacket.'

These are just a sample of the millions of tokens of respect and gratitude offered to Brezhnev for his tireless efforts to strengthen the might and influence of the world socialist system, tighten the unity of the communist and workers' movement, and consolidate world peace. The Leninist foreign policy of the CPSU and Soviet Government conducted under his leadership accords with the vital interests of the working class, all working people, and the nations of the whole world.

9

The Leninist Leader

ALL his life, LEONID ILYICH BREZHNEV has been associated with the Communist Party, which its founder and leader, the great Lenin, described as the mind, honour, and conscience of the era. He was elected head of the Central Committee at the time when the Party faced the task of working out a political line consistent with the present stage of Soviet society — the stage of mature socialism.

On the basis of Marxist - Leninist teaching, taking into account the trends of social development and drawing on the practice of socialist and communist construction, the Party, its Central Committee, and the Politburo headed by Brezhnev have worked out and unswervingly followed a course that receives the full support of the Soviet people. It is designed further to increase the country's economic, social, and cultural potential; to ensure the intensification of industry and agriculture; and to put to full use the potentialities of developed socialism to the ends of a steady rise in the standard of living, a stimulus to social activity and initiative among the people, and a yet firmer consolidation of the positions of world socialism and the friendship and co-operation of nations.

Today, with the Soviet Union entered upon a new stage in its development when it is tackling ever more ambitious and challenging tasks of building communism and the all-important task of securing durable world peace, the Soviet Communist Party's consistent and undeviating Leninist policy emerges with new strength. In a new historical situation the Party, relying on unprecedentedly great opportunities, is taking the heritage of the October Revolution a stage further. The cause of October, in whose name Russia's workers and peasants had fought under Lenin and the Bolshevik party that was the glory and pride of Russia's proletariat, lives on.

Fidelity to Leninism is an immutable law for the Communist Party of the Soviet Union. The Party is constantly engaged in improving the scientific principles of leadership and enriching Marxist - Leninist theory through revolutionary practice. Dedicated to the interests of the people, it meshes creative development of theory with the current tasks of building communism in the USSR and with the progress of world socialism and the entire international communist and workers' movement. In Lenin's name, under the leadership of the Party, the people of the Soviet Union are going from success to success, scaling new summits and putting Lenin's immortal teaching into practice.

'All of Lenin's life,' Brezhnev stresses, 'was ceaseless creation—creation in theory, in politics, in organizing the class struggle, and in Party and state construction. He also cultivated the quality of creator and builder in the great Party that holds aloft the banner of Leninism, the banner of communism.'

The policy and actions of the CPSU and its Central Committee are strictly scientific. Their approach to new developments in a rapidly changing situation is unfailingly concrete and historical, yet marked by a bold Leninist vision of the future. They are clear and precise in formulating practical tasks in keeping with the objective laws and with socialist humanism. The unity of these closely interconnected elements is guarantee of and decisive factor in the success of the revolutionary transformations undertaken by Party and people.

The multi-volume collection of Brezhnev's speeches and articles, *Following Lenin's Course*—a title that faithfully expresses its central idea—is a concentrated expression of the Party's collective theoretical work and its main lines of practical activity. Summing up the vast experience of the CPSU, the collection bears the clear stamp of the General Secretary's endowments as leader of the Party and the Soviet people, an outstanding figure of the world communist movement, and a dedicated

A tribute to Brezhnev — part of the commemoration of Great October, Moscow, 1977.

fighter for communism. These qualities include revolutionary optimism and realism, humanity, a high sense of Party principledness. Brezhnev's speeches and articles contain penetrating thoughts on topical issues of the day and warm words of greeting and support to workers, scientists, farm workers, and cosmonauts—to all people of action and creative thought, to all actively building the new life.

The history of the Soviet Union, the other socialist states, and the world communist movement demonstrates that the wider the scope of the people's historical creativity and the more complex the tasks of revolutionary construction, the greater is the role of leaders in the mass movement.

Particularly important for society's successful advance are experienced leaders of the masses promoted by the Party and people in the struggle for the revolutionary reconstruction of society and for communism—leaders capable of determining the vital needs of social development in line with Marxist - Leninist science and finding ways of meeting these needs, organizing the masses, and leading them boldly forward to new objectives. And these requirements are amply met by Brezhnev's personal qualities and versatile activities, which are based on exhaustive scientific analysis of current developments and main trends and on consistent observance of the principles of collective Party leadership.

Brezhnev has travelled a long way from rank-and-file Communist to General Secretary of the CPSU Central Committee, from steelworker to Soviet Head of State. Wherever he has worked he has lived up honourably to the title of Party member and to the Party's trust in him, never faltering in his self-sacrificing struggle for its noble cause and for the triumph of communist ideals. In the strenuous days and nights of the early five-year plans when the foundations were being laid for the might of the Soviet Union; in the battlelines during the war when the country's future hung in the balance; amidst all the heroic labour effort of the post-war period when a war-ravaged economy was being rapidly raised from the ruins, and, later, during the glorious virginland development; and in the highest Party and government offices— everywhere, at all times, Brezhnev has been at the centre of things, sharing the people's joys and sorrows.

He devotes all his vast experience, knowledge, and ability to the people, to the building of communism and the cause of world peace and social progress. The activity of the CPSU, its Leninist Central Committee, the Politburo, and the General Secretary is imbued with concern for man's good and the well-being of the people. Addressing a workers' meeting at the Likhachev car factory in Moscow on 30 April 1976, Brezhnev said: 'Whatever the Party deals with, whether in foreign policy or home affairs, we Communists never fail to ask ourselves how and in what way a particular decision will affect the life and well-being of the Soviet people, the peaceful conditions for constructive labour in the name of Communism, and the consolidation of world peace.'

In the Soviet Union all economic, scientific, technical, and cultural achievements are designed to serve the working people and to ensure favourable conditions for the satisfaction of their material and spiritual needs and for the development of all their faculties. And this creates the unbreakable bond joining the Party with the people, with all Soviet citizens.

As a leader of Lenin's type, Brezhnev relies in his work on the collective experience of the masses. He is guided by the interests of the people in everything he does. 'As a result,' he says, 'I have become accustomed in all my work, and especially in the responsible offices entrusted to me by the Party, to approach all decisions from the angle of their significance for the working man, asking myself how they will affect his life, what they will yield him.' Indestructible faith in the boundless capacity of the people and ceaseless concern for its welfare, so typical of Brezhnev, have won him great respect and affection from the Soviet people.

Those who have met Brezhnev have been deeply impressed by his directness and sincerity, his sociability, and his modesty. Such qualities appeal not only to the Soviet public but to all people of good will elsewhere. He never fails to find the right words when chatting to the workers—and they are always words that come straight from the heart. He has the knack of getting on well with people of all occupations and age groups: they immediately sense that he, too, is a working man, that he is one of them. In all situations he is always himself—unpretentious, cordial, frank in expressing his feelings, and yet a man of principle as exacting with himself as with others.

Leonid Ilyich Brezhnev's personal qualities as a political leader have made for the smooth and fruitful functioning of the CPSU Central Committee and for the fact that the Leninist style and an atmosphere of creativity, trust, respect, and discipline—giving no room to subjectivism and uncritical complacency—have become established in the

Party's leadership. In Lenin's words, Brezhnev has the gift of 'ensuring efficient and close-knit effort by large numbers of people.'

The Leninist approach to vital matters of domestic and foreign policy; skill in assigning cadres according to their ability, thereby ensuring the maximum efficiency—a truly Leninist spirit of innovation; the role of the CPSU and the Soviet state in world affairs, now greatly enlarged; and consistent and meaningful Soviet foreign policy actions directed to social progress and to furthering world peace—all this has been secured by the activity of the Central Committee, its Politburo, and the General Secretary.

Brezhnev's inexhaustible energy and initiative, his theoretical, political, and organizational work, and his concern for the working people and for world peace are recognized and appreciated by the Communists, by the whole Soviet people, and by all decent people everywhere.

For his exceptional services to Party and state in building communism, enhancing the country's defences, and in the war against the Nazi invaders, the country has conferred on Brezhnev the title Hero of the Soviet Union. For his outstanding contribution to the development of rocketry and the success of the Soviet space programmes he is a Hero of Socialist Labour. He has been decorated with many orders and medals of the Soviet Union, with high awards of the fraternal socialist countries, and with the F. Joliot-Curie Gold Medal for Peace. He also holds the international Lenin Peace Prize. These are tokens of recognition conferred on Brezhnev for his services to the homeland and to all progressive mankind.

He was made Marshal of the Soviet Union in May 1976. This acknowledgement of his part in the defeat of fascism and the consolidation of the Soviet Union's defence potential, and also of the work he has done in furthering world peace and security, won approval not only from the Soviet people but from all progressive forces.

On 19 December 1976 Leonid Brezhnev celebrated his seventieth birthday. The Central Committee, the Presidium of the USSR Supreme Soviet, and the Council of Ministers together with the entire Party membership and the Soviet people warmly congratulated Brezhnev, a loyal son of the Soviet people, an outstanding leader of the Party, the Soviet state and the international communist movement, a fervent champion of peace and social progress and a consistent Marxist-Leninist. In the words of the message of greeting: 'For all your comrades, for all workers for the triumph of communism, you provide a shining example of what a real Communist and Leninist should be. Your entire activity is imbued with implicit faith in the creative potential of Party and people, with closeness to and respect for the working man'.

By decision of the Presidium of the USSR Supreme Soviet and to mark his birthday, Leonid Brezhnev was awarded the Order of Lenin and a second Gold Star of Hero of the Soviet Union in recognition of his outstanding services to Party and state in the course of building communism, of his active and fruitful work in the cause of peace and security of nations, of his substantial personal contribution to the Soviet Union's victory in the war against Nazi Germany and to strengthening her economic and defence potential. Leonid Brezhnev was also presented with a sword of honour with the Soviet Union's coat-of-arms embossed in gold on the hilt, in recognition of his outstanding services in building up the country's defence capability and armed forces.

Further recognition of the importance and effectiveness of the policy followed by the Party, its Central Committee and by Brezhnev personally, a policy aimed at strengthening the fraternal friendship of the peoples of socialist countries and the unity and cohesion of communist and workers' parties, at securing durable world peace and good-neighbourly co-operation among the nations of the world, came with the award to Brezhnev of top decorations of many different countries.

On the occasion of Leonid Brezhnev's seventieth birthday the CPSU Central Committee received tens of thousands of messages of greetings and congratulations addressed to Leonid Brezhnev and containing warm wishes. These were sent in by Party, Soviet, Trade Union, Komsomol and economic management bodies and organizations, by the workers of industrial enterprises, construction projects, collective and state farms, by the officers and men of the Soviet army and navy, by the staff of scientific and educational establishments, by members of the artistic community and public organizations, and by private individuals from every corner of the Soviet Union and around the world. These messages of greeting and congratulations expressed deep respect, love, affection and gratitude to Leonid Brezhnev and paid tribute to his titanic activity in the name of the welfare of the Soviet people and in the name of world peace and the triumph of communism. A Lenin-type politician and communist leader could wish for no greater, no more valued reward.

In his speech of reply after the presentation to him of the Order of Lenin and a second Gold Star of the Hero of the Soviet Union, Leonid Brezhnev said: 'If, occupying the position which the Party has now entrusted to me, I receive recognition from my country (recognition which is evidenced not only by the top award I have just received but by the thousands of letters from Soviet people expressing endorsement of the work of our Party and state and of my personal contribution to it), then this means that the policy which we, comrades, have been following in fulfilment of the decisions adopted by successive Party congresses—a policy aimed at enhancing the country's power, at raising living and cultural standards of the people, a policy of proletarian socialist internationalism and unflagging struggle for a durable peace—this means that the policy is correct. And we shall hold to this policy in the future.'

Leonid Brezhnev's seventieth birthday came as a major event in the Soviet Union's public life. Its celebration developed into a graphic demonstration of the unanimous approval and support by the Soviet people of the domestic and foreign policies and the entire fruitful activities of the Central Committee of the Party and its Politburo headed by the General Secretary. The people of the Soviet Union rallied closer round the Communist Party founded by Lenin, the Party that has always been the architect and driving spirit of all our victories.

Together with the Central Committee and the whole Party, Brezhnev is always intent on doing the greatest possible good for the communist cause, social progress, and peace.

The Communist Party is effectively and efficiently implementing its Leninist course in home and foreign policy with truly Leninist wisdom. It is worthily fulfilling its historical mission as outlined by the great Lenin—to direct and organize a new system, be teacher, guide, and leader of all working people, and lead the people to communism. The monolithic unity of Party and people is the source of the invincible might of Soviet society. There is nothing the CPSU places higher or cherishes more than the people's trust. It strengthens its ties with the masses in every way.

Soviet Communists in serving their people with utter devotion are leading them in their steady advance towards communism. Soviet Communists are placing their intellect, drive and enthusiasm at the service of the great struggle for the triumph of the cause of the October Revolution.

At his desk.

As Leonid Brezhnev has put it: 'The highest reward for every one of us, for every Communist of the Lenin type, is the fact that the Soviet people have come to associate all their achievements and victories with the leadership of the Communist Party. This is understandable, for our Party has always been one with the people. The best representatives of the country's working class, collective-farm peasantry and the intellectual community are among its members. The Party enjoys the people's total confidence and support.

'But we have to remember, comrades, that the people's confidence and trust in us imposes great responsibilities. That is why any decision taken by the Party, every move it makes in the political field, in its organizational, ideological and educational work, must be of a kind that strengthens the unity of Party and people, that ensures that the people's confidence and trust in the Party are never shaken.

'Our Party has everything it needs to measure up to the historic responsibility resting upon it. We are inspired by our supreme goal of ensuring the welfare of the people. We have at our command a wealth of experience of building a new life, an experience spanning several decades. Marxism-Leninism, the science which has absorbed the best achievements of the genius of man, is our guide to action. And we are confident of our powers.'

All Soviet people are legitimately proud of their Party for its powerful and lucid collective reason and because it acts in all situations as Lenin himself would. The Soviet people dedicate their hearts, thoughts, and deeds to their Party. They pay a tribute of deep respect and gratitude to its operational headquarters—the Central Committee headed by LEONID ILYICH BREZHNEV, that faithful and unshakable Leninist and devoted fighter for peace and Communism.

The Soviet people see the Communist Party of the Soviet Union as their tried and tested leader, their guide, and the organizer of all their victories. They have learned from experience (and every day brings further confirmation) that the Party's policy is truly Leninist and that the CPSU is leading the Soviet people firmly along the one correct course—the Leninist course—to Communism.

GENERAL EDITOR'S NOTE

L.I. Brezhnev was for fifteen years Chairman of the Constitutional Commission which was responsible for drafting the new Fundamental Law of the USSR. One of his main achievements, affecting every Soviet citizen, the new Constitution was unanimously approved and adopted by the Supreme Soviet on 7 October 1977.

I have thought it appropriate to include in this volume the official English text.

CONSTITUTION
(FUNDAMENTAL LAW)
OF THE UNION OF SOVIET SOCIALIST REPUBLICS

Adopted at the Seventh (Special) Session of the Supreme Soviet of the USSR, Ninth Convocation, on October 7, 1977

CONTENTS

Constitution (Fundamental Law) of the Union of Soviet Socialist Republics

The Great October Socialist Revolution, made by the workers and peasants of Russia under the leadership of the Communist Party headed by Lenin, overthrew capitalist and landowner rule, broke the fetters of oppression, established the dictatorship of the proletariat, and created the Soviet state, a new type of state, the basic instrument for defending the gains of the revolution and for building socialism and communism. Humanity thereby began the epoch-making turn from capitalism to socialism.

After achieving victory in the Civil War and repulsing imperialist intervention, the Soviet government carried through far-reaching social and economic transformations, and put an end once and for all to exploitation of man by man, antagonisms between classes, and strife between nationalities. The unification of the Soviet Republics in the Union of Soviet Socialist Republics multiplied the forces and opportunities of the peoples of the country in the building of socialism. Social ownership of the means of production and genuine democracy for the working masses were established. For the first time in the history of mankind a socialist society was created.

The strength of socialism was vividly demonstrated by the immortal feat of the Soviet people and their Armed Forces in achieving their historic victory in the Great Patriotic War. This victory consolidated the influence and international standing of the Soviet Union and created new opportunities for growth of the forces of socialism, national liberation, democracy, and peace throughout the world.

Continuing their creative endeavours, the working people of the Soviet Union have ensured rapid, all-round development of the country and steady improvement of the socialist system. They have consolidated the alliance of the working class, collective-farm peasantry, and people's intelligentsia, and friendship of the nations and nationalities of the USSR. Socio-political and ideological unity of Soviet society, in which the working class is the leading force, has been achieved. The aims of the dictatorship of the proletariat having been fulfilled, the Soviet state has become a state of the whole people. The leading role of the Communist Party, the vanguard of all the people, has grown.

In the USSR a developed socialist society has been built. At this stage, when socialism is developing on its own foundations, the creative forces of the new system and the advantages of the socialist way of life are becoming increasingly evident, and the working people are more and more widely enjoying the fruits of their great revolutionary gains.

It is a society in which powerful productive forces and progressive science and culture have been created, in which the well-being of the people is constantly rising, and more and more favourable conditions are being provided for the all-round development of the individual.

It is a society of mature socialist social relations, in which, on the basis of the drawing together of all classes and social strata and of the juridical and factual equality of all its nations and nationalities and their fraternal co-operation, a new historical community of people has been formed—the Soviet people.

It is a society of high organisational capacity, ideological commitment, and consciousness of the working people, who are patriots and internationalists.

It is a society in which the law of life is concern of all for the good of each and concern of each for the good of all.

It is a society of true democracy, the political system of which ensures effective management of all public affairs, ever more active participation of the working people in running the state, and the combining of citizens' real rights and freedoms with their obligations and responsibility to society.

Developed socialist society is a natural, logical stage on the road to communism.

The supreme goal of the Soviet state is the building of a classless communist society in which there will be public, communist self-government. The main aims of the people's socialist state are: to lay the material and technical foundation of communism, to perfect socialist social relations and transform them into relations, to mould the citizen of communist society, to raise the people's living and cultural standards, to safeguard the country's security, and to further the consolidation of peace and development of international co-operation.

The Soviet people,

guided by the ideas of scientific communism and true to their revolutionary traditions,

relying on the great social, economic, and political gains of socialism,

striving for the further development of socialist democracy,

taking into account the international position of the USSR as part of the world system of socialism, and conscious of their internationalist responsibility,

preserving continuity of the ideas and principles of the first Soviet Constitution of 1918, the 1924 Constitution of the USSR and the 1936 Constitution of the USSR,

hereby affirm the principles of the social structure and policy of the USSR, and define the rights, freedoms and obligations of citizens, and the principles of the organisation of the socialist state of the whole people, and its aims, and proclaim these in this Constitution.

Chapter 1

THE POLITICAL SYSTEM

Article 1. The Union of Soviet Socialist Republics is a socialist state of the whole people, expressing the will and interests of the workers, peasants, and intelligentsia, the working people of all the nations and nationalities of the country.

Article 2. All power in the USSR belongs to the people.

The people exercise state power through Soviets of People's Deputies, which constitute the political foundation of the USSR.

All other state bodies are under the control of, and accountable to, the Soviets of People's Deputies.

Article 3. The Soviet state is organised and functions on the principle of democratic centralism, namely the electiveness of all bodies of state authority from the lowest to the highest, their accountability to the people, and the obligation of lower bodies to observe the decisions of higher ones. Democratic centralism combines central leadership with local initiative and creative activity and with the responsibility of each state body and official for the work entrusted to them.

Article 4. The Soviet state and all its bodies function on the basis of socialist law, ensure the maintenance of law and order, and safeguard the interests of society and the rights and freedoms of citizens.

State organisations, public organisations and officials shall observe the Constitution of the USSR and Soviet laws.

Article 5. Major matters of state shall be submitted to nationwide discussion and put to a popular vote (referendum).

Article 6. The leading and guiding force of Soviet society and the nucleus of its political system, of all state organisations and public organisations, is the Communist Party of the Soviet Union. The CPSU exists for the people and serves the people.

The Communist Party, armed with Marxism-Leninism, determines the general perspectives of the development of society and the course of the home and foreign policy of the USSR, directs the great constructive work of the Soviet people, and imparts a planned, systematic and theoretically substantiated character to their struggle for the victory of communism.

All party organisations shall function within the framework of the Constitution of the USSR.

Article 7. Trade unions, the All-Union Leninist Young Communist League, co-operatives, and other public organisations, participate, in accordance with the aims laid down in their rules, in managing state and public affairs, and in deciding political, economic, and social and cultural matters.

Article 8. Work collectives take part in discussing and deciding state and public affairs, in planning production and social development, in training and placing personnel, and in discussing and deciding matters pertaining to the management of enterprises and institutions, the improvement of working and living conditions, and the use of funds allocated both for developing production and for social and cultural purposes and financial incentives.

Work collectives promote socialist emulation, the spread of progressive methods of work, and the strengthening of production discipline, educate their members in the spirit of communist morality, and strive to enhance their political consciousness and raise their cultural level and skills and qualifications.

Article 9. The principal direction in the development of the political system of Soviet society is the extension of socialist democracy, namely ever broader participation of citizens in managing the affairs of society and the state, continuous improvement of the machinery of state, heightening of the activity of public organisations, strengthening of the system of people's control, consolidation of the legal foundations of the functioning of the state and of public life, greater openness and publicity, and constant responsiveness to public opinion.

Chapter 2

THE ECONOMIC SYSTEM

Article 10. The foundation of the economic system of the USSR is socialist ownership of the means of production in the form of state property (belonging to all the people), and collective farm-and-co-operative property.

Socialist ownership also embraces the property of trade unions and other public organisations which they require to carry out their purposes under their rules.

The state protects socialist property and provides conditions for its growth.

No one has the right to use socialist property for personal gain or other selfish ends.

Article 11. State property, i.e. the common property of the Soviet people, is the principal form of socialist property.

The land, its minerals, waters, and forests are the exclusive property of the state. The state owns the basic means of production in industry, construction, and agriculture; means of transport and communication; the banks; the property of state-run trade organisations and public utilities, and other state-run undertakings; most urban housing; and other property necessary for state purposes.

Article 12. The property of collective farms and other co-operative organisations, and of their joint undertakings, comprises the means of production and other assets which they require for the purposes laid down in their rules.

The land held by collective farms is secured to them for their free use in perpetuity.

The state promotes development of collective farm-and-co-operative property and its approximation to state property.

Collective farms, like other land users are obliged to make effective and thrifty use of the land and to increase its fertility.

Article 13. Earned income forms the basis of the personal property of Soviet citizens. The personal property of citizens of the USSR may include articles of everyday use, personal consumption and convenience, the implements and other objects of a small-holding, a house, and earned savings. The personal property of citizens and the right to inherit it are protected by the state.

Citizens may be granted the use of plots of land, in the manner prescribed by law, for a subsidiary small-holding (including the keeping of livestock and poultry), for fruit and vegetable growing or for building an individual dwelling. Citizens are required to make rational use of the land allotted to them. The state, and collective farms provide assistance to citizens in working their small-holdings.

Property owned or used by citizens shall not serve as a means of deriving unearned income or be employed to the detriment of the interests of society.

Article 14. The source of the growth of social wealth and of the well-being of the people, and of each individual, is the labour, free from exploitation, of Soviet people.

The state exercises control over the measure of labour and of consumption in accordance with the principle of socialism: "From each according to his ability, to each according to his work." It fixes the rate of taxation on taxable income.

Socially useful work and its results determine a person's status in society. By combining material and moral incentives and encouraging innovation and a creative attitude to work, the state helps transform labour into the prime vital need of every Soviet citizen.

Article 15. The supreme goal of social production under socialism is the fullest possible satisfaction of the people's growing material, and cultural and intellectual requirements.

Relying on the creative initiative of the working people, socialist emulation, and scientific and technological progress, and by improving the forms and methods of economic management, the state ensures growth of the productivity of labour, raising of the efficiency of production and of the quality of work, and dynamic, planned, proportionate development of the economy.

Article 16. The economy of the USSR is an integral economic complex comprising all the elements of social production, distribution, and exchange on its territory.

The economy is managed on the basis of state plans for economic and social development, with due account of the sectoral and territorial principles, and by combining centralised direction with the managerial independence and initiative of individual and amalgamated enterprises and other organisations, for which active use is made of management accounting, profit, cost, and other economic levers and incentives.

Article 17. In the USSR, the law permits individual labour in handicrafts, farming, the provision of services for the public, and other forms of activity based exclusively on the personal work of individual citizens and members of their families. The state makes regulations for such work to ensure that it serves the interests of society.

Article 18. In the interests of the present and future generations, the necessary steps are taken in the USSR to protect and make scientific, rational use of the land and its mineral and water resources, and the plant and animal kingdoms, to preserve the purity of air and water, ensure reproduction of natural wealth, and improve the human environment.

Chapter 3

SOCIAL DEVELOPMENT AND CULTURE

Article 19. The social basis of the USSR is the unbreakable alliance of the workers, peasants, and intelligentsia.

The state helps enhance the social homogeneity of society, namely the elimination of class differences and of the essential distinctions between town and country and between mental and physical labour, and the all-round development and drawing together of all the nations and nationalities of the USSR.

Article 20. In accordance with the communist ideal—"The free development of each is the condition of the free development of all"—the state pursues the aim of giving citizens more and more real opportunities to apply their creative energies, abilities, and talents, and to develop their personalities in every way.

Article 21. The state concerns itself with improving working conditions, safety and labour protection and the scientific organisation of work, and with reducing and ultimately eliminating all arduous physical labour through comprehensive mechanisation and automation of production processes in all branches of the economy.

Article 22. A programme is being consistently implemented in the USSR to convert agricultural work into a variety of industrial work, to extend the network of educational, cultural and medical institutions, and of trade, public catering, service and public utility facilities in rural localities, and transform hamlets and villages into well-planned and well-appointed settlements.

Article 23. The state pursues a steady policy of raising people's pay levels and real incomes through increase in productivity.

In order to satisfy the needs of Soviet people more fully social consumption funds are created. The state, with the broad participation of public organisations and work collectives, ensures the growth and just distribution of these funds.

Article 24. In the USSR, state systems of health protection, social security, trade and public catering, communal services and amenities, and public utilities, operate and are being extended.

The state encourages co-operatives and other public organisations to provide all types of services for the population. It encourages the development of mass physical culture and sport.

Article 25. In the USSR there is a uniform system of public education, which is being constantly improved, that provides general education and vocational training for citizens, serves the communist education and intellectual and physical development of the youth, and trains them for work and social activity.

Article 26. In accordance with society's needs the state provides for planned development of science and the training of scientific personnel and organises introduction of the results of research in the economy and other spheres of life.

Article 27. The state concerns itself with protecting, augmenting and making extensive use of society's cultural wealth for the moral and aesthetic education of the Soviet people, for raising their cultural level.

In the USSR development of the professional, amateur and folk arts is encouraged in every way.

Chapter 4

FOREIGN POLICY

Article 28. The USSR steadfastly pursues a Leninist policy of peace and stands for strengthening of the security of nations and broad international co-operation.

The foreign policy of the USSR is aimed at ensuring international conditions favourable for building communism in the USSR, safeguarding the state interests of the Soviet Union, consolidating the positions of world socialism, supporting the struggle of peoples for national liberation and social progress, preventing wars of aggression, achieving universal and complete disarmament, and consistently implementing the principle of the peaceful coexistence of states with different social systems.

In the USSR war propaganda is banned.

Article 29. The USSR's relations with other states are based on observance of the following principles: sovereign equality; mutual renunciation of the use or threat of force; inviolability of frontiers; territorial integrity of states; peaceful settlement of disputes; non-intervention in internal affairs; respect for human rights and fundamental freedoms; the equal rights of peoples and their right to decide their own destiny; co-operation among states; and fulfilment in good faith of obligations arising from the generally recognised principles and rules of international law, and from the international treaties signed by the USSR.

Article 30. The USSR, as part of the world system of socialism and of the socialist community, promotes and strengthens friendship, co-operation, and comradely mutual assistance with other socialist countries on the basis of the principle of socialist internationalism, and takes an active part in socialist economic integration and the socialist international division of labour.

Chapter 5

DEFENCE OF THE SOCIALIST MOTHERLAND

Article 31. Defence of the Socialist Motherland is one of the most important functions of the state, and is the concern of the whole people.

In order to defend the gains of socialism, the peaceful labour of the Soviet people, and the sovereignty and territorial integrity of the state, the USSR maintains armed forces and has instituted universal military service.

The duty of the Armed Forces of the USSR to the people is to provide reliable defence of the Socialist Motherland and to be in constant combat readiness, guaranteeing that any aggressor is instantly repulsed.

Article 32. The state ensures the security and defence capability of the country, and supplies the Armed Forces of the USSR with everything necessary for that purpose.

The duties of state bodies, public organisations, officials, and citizens in regard to safeguarding the country's security and strengthening its defence capacity are defined by the legislation of the USSR.

Chapter 6

CITIZENSHIP OF THE USSR. EQUALITY OF CITIZENS' RIGHTS

Article 33. Uniform federal citizenship is established for the USSR. Every citizen of a Union Republic is a citizen of the USSR.

The grounds and procedure for acquiring or forfeiting Soviet citizenship are defined by the Law on Citizenship of the USSR.

When abroad, citizens of the USSR enjoy the protection and assistance of the Soviet state.

Article 34. Citizens of the USSR are equal before the law, without distinction of origin, social or property status, race or nationality, sex, education, language, attitude to religion, type and nature of occupation, domicile, or other status.

The equal rights of citizens of the USSR are guaranteed in all fields of economic, political, social, and cultural life.

Article 35. Women and men have equal rights in the USSR.

Exercise of these rights is ensured by according women equal access with men to education and vocational and professional training, equal opportunities in employment, remuneration, and promotion, and in social and political, and cultural activity, and by special labour and health protection measures for women; by providing conditions enabling mothers to work; by legal protection, and material and moral support for mothers and children, including paid leaves and other benefits for expectant mothers and mothers, and gradual reduction of working time for mothers with small children.

Article 36. Citizens of the USSR of different races and nationalities have equal rights.

Exercise of these rights is ensured by a policy of all-round development and drawing together of all the nations and nationalities of the USSR, by educating citizens in the spirit of Soviet patriotism and socialist internationalism, and by the possibility to use their native language and the languages of other peoples of the USSR.

Any direct or indirect limitation of the rights of citizens or establishment of direct or indirect privileges on grounds of race or nationality, and any advocacy of racial or national exclusiveness, hostility or contempt, are punishable by law.

Article 37. Citizens of other countries and stateless persons in the USSR are guaranteed the rights and freedoms provided by law, including the right to apply to a court and other state bodies for the protection of their personal property, family, and other rights.

Citizens of other countries and stateless persons, when in the USSR, are obliged to respect the Constitution of the USSR and observe Soviet laws.

Article 38. The USSR grants the right of asylum to foreigners persecuted for defending the interests of the working people and the cause of peace, or for participation in the revolutionary and national-liberation movement, or for progressive social and political, scientific or other creative activity.

Chapter 7

THE BASIC RIGHTS, FREEDOMS, AND DUTIES OF CITIZENS OF THE USSR

Article 39. Citizens of the USSR enjoy in full the social, economic, political and personal rights and freedoms proclaimed and guaranteed by the Constitution of the USSR and by Soviet laws. The socialist system ensures enlargement of the rights and freedoms of citizens and continuous improvement of their living standards as social, economic, and cultural development programmes are fulfilled.

Enjoyment by citizens of their rights and freedoms must not be to the detriment of the interests of society or the state, or infringe the rights of other citizens.

Article 40. Citizens of the USSR have the right to work (that is, to guaranteed employment and pay in accordance with the quantity and quality of their work, and not below the state-established minimum), including the right to choose their trade or profession, type of job and work in accordance with their inclinations, abilities, training and education, with due account of the needs of society.

This right is ensured by the socialist economic system, steady growth of the productive forces, free vocational and professional training, improvement of skills, training in new trades or professions, and development of the systems of vocational guidance and job placement.

Article 41. Citizens of the USSR have the right to rest and leisure.

This right is ensured by the establishment of a working week not exceeding 41 hours, for workers and other employees, a shorter working day in a number of trades and industries, and shorter hours for night work; by the provision of paid annual holidays, weekly days of rest, extension of the network of cultural, educational and health-building institutions, and the development on a mass scale of sport, physical culture, and camping and tourism; by the provision of neighbourhood recreational facilities, and of other opportunities for rational use of free time.

The length of collective farmers' working and leisure time is established by their collective farms.

Article 42. Citizens of the USSR have the right to health protection.

This right is ensured by free, qualified medical care provided by state health institutions; by extension of the network of therapeutic and health-building institutions; by the development and improvement of safety and hygiene in industry; by carrying out broad prophylactic measures; by measures to improve the environment; by special care for the health of the rising generation, including prohibition of child labour, excluding the work done by children as part of the school curriculum; and by developing research to prevent and reduce the incidence of disease and ensure citizens a long and active life.

Article 43. Citizens of the USSR have the right to maintenance in old age, in sickness, and in the event of complete or partial disability or loss of the breadwinner.

This right is guaranteed by social insurance of workers and other employees and collective farmers; by allowances for temporary disability; by the provision by the state or by collective farms of retirement pensions, disability pensions, and pensions for loss of the breadwinner; by providing employment for the partially disabled; by care for the elderly and the disabled; and by other forms of social security.

Article 44. Citizens of the USSR have the right to housing.

This right is ensured by the development and upkeep of state and socially-owned housing; by assistance for co-operative and individual house building; by fair distribution, under public control, of the housing that becomes available through fulfilment of the programme of building well-appointed dwellings, and by low rents and low charges for utility services. Citizens of the USSR shall take good care of the housing allocated to them.

Article 45. Citizens of the USSR have the right to education.

This right is ensured by free provision of all forms of education, by the institution of universal, compulsory secondary education, and broad development of vocational, specialised secondary, and higher education, in which instruction is oriented toward practical activity and production; by the development of extramural, correspondence and evening courses; by the provision of state scholarships and grants and privileges for students; by the free issue of school textbooks; by the opportunity to attend a school where teaching is in the native language; and by the provision of facilities for self-education.

Article 46. Citizens of the USSR have the right to enjoy cultural benefits.

This right is ensured by broad access to the cultural treasures of their own land and of the world that are preserved in state and other public collections; by the development and fair distribution of cultural and educational institutions throughout the country; by developing television and radio broadcasting and the publishing of books, newspapers and periodicals, and by extending the free library service; and by expanding cultural exchanges with other countries.

Article 47. Citizens of the USSR, in accordance with the aims of building communism, are guaranteed freedom of scientific, technical, and artistic work. This freedom is ensured by broadening scientific research, encouraging invention and innovation, and developing literature and the arts. The state provides the necessary material conditions for this and support for voluntary societies and unions of workers in the arts, organises introduction of inventions and innovations in production and other spheres of activity.

The rights of authors, inventors and innovators are protected by the state.

Article 48. Citizens of the USSR have the right to take part in the management and administration of state and public affairs and in the discussion and adoption of laws and measures of All-Union and local significance.

This right is ensured by the opportunity to vote and to be elected to Soviets of People's Deputies and other elective state bodies, to take part in nationwide discussions and referendums, in people's control, in the work of state bodies, public organisations, and local community groups, and in meetings at places of work or residence.

Article 49. Every citizen of the USSR has the right to submit proposals to state bodies and public organisations for improving their activity, and to criticise shortcomings in their work.

Officials are obliged, within established time-limits, to examine citizens' proposals and requests, to reply to them, and to take appropriate action.

Persecution for criticism is prohibited. Persons guilty of such persecution shall be called to account.

Article 50. In accordance with the interests of the people and in order to strengthen and develop the socialist system, citizens of the USSR are guaranteed freedom of speech, of the press, and of assembly, meetings, street processions and demonstrations.

Exercise of these political freedoms is ensured by putting public buildings, streets and squares at the disposal of the working people and their organisations, by broad dissemination of information, and by the opportunity to use the press, television, and radio.

Article 51. In accordance with the aims of building communism, citizens of the USSR have the right to associate in public organisations that promote their political activity and initiative and satisfaction of their various interests.

Public organisations are guaranteed conditions for successfully performing the functions defined in their rules.

Article 52. Citizens of the USSR are guaranteed freedom of conscience, that is, the right to profess or not to profess any religion, and to conduct religious worship or atheistic propaganda. Incitement of hostility or hatred on religious grounds is prohibited.

In the USSR, the church is separated from the state, and the school from the church.

Article 53. The family enjoys the protection of the state.

Marriage is based on the free consent of the woman and the man; the spouses are completely equal in their family relations.

The state helps the family by providing and developing a broad system of childcare institutions, by organising and improving communal services and public catering, by paying grants on the birth of a child, by providing children's allowances and benefits for large families, and other forms of family allowances and assistance.

Article 54. Citizens of the USSR are guaranteed inviolability of the person. No one may be arrested except by a court decision or on the warrant of a procurator.

Article 55. Citizens of the USSR are guaranteed inviolability of the home. No one may, without lawful grounds, enter a home against the will of those residing in it.

Article 56. The privacy of citizens, and of their correspondence, telephone conversations, and telegraphic communications is protected by law.

Article 57. Respect for the individual and protection of the rights and freedoms of citizens are the duty of all state bodies, public organisations, and officials.

Citizens of the USSR have the right to protection by the courts against encroachments on their honour and reputation, life and health, and personal freedom and property.

Article 58. Citizens of the USSR have the right to lodge a complaint against the actions of officials, state bodies and public bodies. Complaints shall be examined according to the procedure and within the time-limit established by law.

Actions by officials that contravene the law or their powers, and infringe the rights of citizens, may be appealed against in a court in the manner prescribed by law.

Citizens of the USSR have the right to compensation for damage resulting from unlawful actions by state organisations and public organisations, or by officials in the performance of their duties.

Article 59. Citizens' exercise of their rights and freedoms is inseparable from the performance of their duties and obligations.

Citizens of the USSR are obliged to observe the Constitution of the USSR and Soviet laws, comply with the standards of socialist conduct, and uphold the honour and dignity of Soviet citizenship.

Article 60. It is the duty of, and a matter of honour for, every able-bodied citizen of the USSR to work conscientiously in his chosen, socially useful occupation, and strictly to observe labour discipline. Evasion of socially useful work is incompatible with the principles of socialist society.

Article 61. Citizens of the USSR are obliged to preserve and protect socialist property. It is the duty of a citizen of the USSR to combat misappropriation and squandering of state and socially-owned property and to make thrifty use of the people's wealth.

Persons encroaching in any way on socialist property shall be punished according to the law.

Article 62. Citizens of the USSR are obliged to safeguard the interests of the Soviet state, and to enhance its power and prestige.

Defence of the Socialist Motherland is the sacred duty of every citizen of the USSR.

Betrayal of the Motherland is the gravest of crimes against the people.

Article 63. Military service in the ranks of the Armed Forces of the USSR is an honourable duty of Soviet citizens.

Article 64. It is the duty of every citizen of the USSR to respect the national dignity of other citizens, and to strengthen friendship of the nations and nationalities of the multinational Soviet state.

Article 65. A citizen of the USSR is obliged to respect the rights and lawful interests of other persons, to be uncompromising toward anti-social behaviour, and to help maintain public order.

Article 66. Citizens of the USSR are obliged to concern themselves with the upbringing of children, to train them for socially useful work, and to raise them as worthy members of socialist society. Children are obliged to care for their parents and help them.

Article 67. Citizens of the USSR are obliged to protect nature and conserve its riches.

Article 68. Concern for the preservation of historical monuments and other cultural values is a duty and obligation of citizens of the USSR.

Article 69. It is the internationalist duty of citizens of the USSR to promote friendship and co-operation with peoples of other lands and help maintain and strengthen world peace.

Chapter 8

THE USSR—A FEDERAL STATE

Article 70. The Union of Soviet Socialist Republics is an integral, federal, multinational state formed on the principle of socialist federalism as a result of the free self-determination of nations and the voluntary association of equal Soviet Socialist Republics.

The USSR embodies the state unity of the Soviet people and draws all its nations and nationalities together for the purpose of jointly building communism.

Article 71. The Union of Soviet Socialist Republics unites:
the Russian Soviet Federative Socialist Republic,
the Ukrainian Soviet Socialist Republic,
the Byelorussian Soviet Socialist Republic,
the Uzbek Soviet Socialist Republic,
the Kazakh Soviet Socialist Republic,
the Georgian Soviet Socialist Republic,
the Azerbaijan Soviet Socialist Republic,
the Lithuanian Soviet Socialist Republic,
the Moldavian Soviet Socialist Republic,
the Latvian Soviet Socialist Republic,
the Kirghiz Soviet Socialist Republic,
the Tajik Soviet Socialist Republic,
the Armenian Soviet Socialist Republic,
the Turkmen Soviet Socialist Republic,
the Estonian Soviet Socialist Republic.

Article 72. Each Union Republic shall retain the right freely to secede from the USSR.

Article 73. The jurisdiction of the Union of Soviet Socialist Republics as represented by its highest bodies of state authority and administration, shall cover:

1. the admission of new republics to the USSR; endorsement of the formation of new autonomous republics and autonomous regions within Union Republics;

2. determination of the state boundaries of the USSR and approval of changes in the boundaries between Union Republics;

3. establishment of the general principles for the organisation and functioning of republican and local bodies of state authority and administration;

4. the ensurance of uniformity of legislative norms throughout the USSR and establishment of the fundamentals of the legislation of the Union of Soviet Socialist Republics and Union Republics;

5. pursuance of a uniform social and economic policy; direction of the country's economy; determination of the main lines of scientific and technological progress and the general measures for rational exploitation and conservation of natural resources; the drafting and approval of state plans for the economic and social development of the USSR, and endorsement of reports on their fulfilment;

6. the drafting and approval of the consolidated Budget of the USSR, and endorsement of the report on its execution; management of a single monetary and credit system; determination of the taxes and revenues forming the Budget of the USSR; and the formulation of prices and wages policy;

7. direction of the sectors of the economy, and of enterprises and amalgamations under Union jurisdiction, and general direction of industries under Union-Republican jurisdiction;

8. issues of war and peace, defence of the sovereignty of the USSR and safeguarding of its frontiers and territory, and organisation of defence; direction of the Armed Forces of the USSR;

9. state security;

10. representation of the USSR in international relations; the USSR's relations with other states and with international organisations; establishment of the general procedure for, and co-ordination of, the relations of Union Republics with other states and with international organisations; foreign trade and other forms of external economic activity on the basis of state monopoly;

11. control over observance of the Constitution of the USSR, and ensurance of conformity of the Constitutions of Union Republics to the Constitution of the USSR;

12. and settlement of other matters of All-Union importance.

Article 74. The laws of the USSR shall have the same force in all Union Republics. In the event of a discrepancy between a Union Republic law and an All-Union law, the law of the USSR shall prevail.

Article 75. The territory of the Union of Soviet Socialist Republics is a single entity and comprises the territories of the Union Republics.

The sovereignty of the USSR extends throughout its territory.

Chapter 9

THE UNION SOVIET SOCIALIST REPUBLIC

Article 76. A Union Republic is a sovereign Soviet socialist state that has united with other Soviet Republics in the Union of Soviet Socialist Republics.

Outside the spheres listed in Article 73 of the Constitution of the USSR, a Union Republic exercises independent authority on its territory.

A Union Republic shall have its own Constitution conforming to the Constitution of the USSR with the specific features of the Republic being taken into account.

Article 77. Union Republics take part in decision-making in the Supreme Soviet of the USSR, the Presidium of the Supreme Soviet of the USSR, the Government of the USSR, and other bodies of the Union of Soviet Socialist Republics in matters that come within the jurisdiction of the Union of Soviet Socialist Republics.

A Union Republic shall ensure comprehensive economic and social development on its territory, facilitate exercise of the powers of the USSR on its territory, and implement the decisions of the highest bodies of state authority and administration of the USSR.

In matters that come within its jurisdiction, a Union Republic shall co-ordinate and control the activity of enterprises, institutions, and organisations subordinate to the Union.

Article 78. The territory of a Union Republic may not be altered without its consent. The boundaries between Union Republics may be altered by mutual agreement of the Republics concerned, subject to ratification by the Union of Soviet Socialist Republics.

Article 79. A Union Republic shall determine its division into territories, regions, areas, and districts, and decide other matters relating to its administrative and territorial structure.

Article 80. A Union Republic has the right to enter into relations with other states, conclude treaties with them, exchange diplomatic and consular representatives, and take part in the work of international organisations.

Article 81. The sovereign rights of Union Republics shall be safeguarded by the USSR.

Chapter 10

THE AUTONOMOUS SOVIET SOCIALIST REPUBLIC

Article 82. An Autonomous Republic is a constituent part of a Union Republic.

In spheres not within the jurisdiction of the Union of Soviet Socialist Republics and the Union Republic, an Autonomous Republic shall deal independently with matters within its jurisdiction.

An Autonomous Republic shall have its own Constitution conforming to the Constitutions of the USSR and the Union Republic with the specific features of the Autonomous Republic being taken into account.

Article 83. An Autonomous Republic takes part in decision-making through the highest bodies of state authority and administration of the USSR and of the Union Republic respectively, in matters that come within the jurisdiction of the USSR and the Union Republic.

An Autonomous Republic shall ensure comprehensive economic and social development on its territory, facilitate exercise of the powers of the USSR and the Union Republic on its territory, and implement decisions of the highest bodies of state authority and administration of the USSR and the Union Republic.

In matters within its jurisdiction, an Autonomous Republic shall coordinate and control the activity of enterprises, institutions, and organisations subordinate to the Union or the Union Republic.

Article 84. The territory of an Autonomous Republic may not be altered without its consent.

Article 85. The Russian Soviet Federative Socialist Republic includes the Bashkir, Buryat, Daghestan, Kabardin-Balkar, Kalmyk, Karelian, Komi, Mari, Mordovian, North Ossetian, Tatar, Tuva, Udmurt, Chechen-Ingush, Chuvash, and Yakut Autonomous Soviet Socialist Republics.

The Uzbek Soviet Socialist Republic includes the Kara-Kalpak Autonomous Soviet Socialist Republic.

The Georgian Soviet Socialist Republic includes the Abkhasian and Adzhar Autonomous Soviet Socialist Republics.

The Azerbaijan Soviet Socialist Republic includes the Nakhichevan Autonomous Soviet Socialist Republic.

Chapter 11

THE AUTONOMOUS REGION AND AUTONOMOUS AREA

Article 86. An Autonomous Region is a constituent part of a Union Republic or Territory. The Law on an Autonomous Region, upon submission by the Soviet of People's Deputies of the Autonomous Region concerned, shall be adopted by the Supreme Soviet of the Union Republic.

Article 87. The Russian Soviet Federative Socialist Republic includes the Adygei, Gorno-Altai, Jewish, Karachai-Circassian, and Khakass Autonomous Regions.

The Georgian Soviet Socialist Republic includes the South Ossetian Autonomous Region.

The Azerbaijan Soviet Socialist Republic includes the Nagorno-Karabakh Autonomous Region.

The Tajik Soviet Socialist Republic includes the Gorno-Badakhshan Autonomous Region.

Article 88. An Autonomous Area is a constituent part of a Territory or Region. The Law on an Autonomous Area shall be adopted by the Supreme Soviet of the Union Republic concerned.

Chapter 12

THE SYSTEM OF SOVIETS OF PEOPLE'S DEPUTIES AND THE PRINCIPLES OF THEIR WORK

Article 89. The Soviets of People's Deputies, i.e. the Supreme Soviet of the USSR, the Supreme Soviets of Union Republics, the Supreme Soviets of Autonomous Republics, the Soviets of People's Deputies of Territories and Regions, the Soviets of People's Deputies of Autonomous Regions and Autonomous Areas, and the Soviets of People's Deputies of districts, cities, city districts, settlements and villages shall constitute a single system of bodies of state authority.

Article 90. The term of the Supreme Soviet of the USSR, the Supreme Soviets of Union Republics, and the Supreme Soviets of Autonomous Republics shall be five years.

The term of local Soviets of People's Deputies shall be two and a half years.

Elections to Soviets of People's Deputies shall be called not later than two months before the expiry of the term of the Soviet concerned.

Article 91. The most important matters within the jurisdiction of the respective Soviets of People's Deputies shall be considered and settled at their sessions.

Soviets of People's Deputies shall elect standing commissions and form executive-administrative, and other bodies accountable to them.

Article 92. Soviets of People's Deputies shall form people's control bodies combining state control with control by the working people at enterprises, collective farms, institutions, and organisations.

People's control bodies shall check on the fulfilment of state plans and assignments, combat breaches of state discipline, localistic tendencies, narrow departmental attitudes, mismanagement, extravagance and waste, red tape and bureaucracy, and help improve the working of the state machinery.

Article 93. Soviets of People's Deputies shall direct all sectors of state, economic, and social and cultural development, either directly or through bodies instituted by them, take decisions and ensure their execution, and verify their implementation.

Article 94. Soviets of People's Deputies shall function publicly on the basis of collective, free, constructive discussion and decision-making, of systematic reporting back to them and the people by their executive-administrative and other bodies, and of involving citizens on a broad scale in their work.

Soviets of People's Deputies and the bodies set up by them shall systematically inform the public about their work and the decisions taken by them.

Chapter 13

THE ELECTORAL SYSTEM

Article 95. Deputies to all Soviets shall be elected on the basis of universal, equal, and direct suffrage by secret ballot.

Article 96. Elections shall be universal: all citizens of the USSR who have reached the age of 18 shall have the right to vote and to be elected, with the exception of persons who have been legally certified insane.

To be eligible for election to the Supreme Soviet of the USSR a citizen of the USSR must have reached the age of 21.

Article 97. Elections shall be equal: each citizen shall have one vote; all voters shall exercise the franchise on an equal footing.

Article 98. Elections shall be direct: deputies to all Soviets of People's Deputies shall be elected by citizens by direct vote.

Article 99. Voting at elections shall be secret: control over voters' exercise of the franchise is inadmissible.

Article 100. The following shall have the right to nominate candidates: branches and organisations of the Communist Party of the Soviet Union, trade unions, and the All-Union Leninist Young Communist League; co-operatives and other public organisations; work collectives, and meetings of servicemen in their military units.

Citizens of the USSR and public organisations are guaranteed the right to free and all-round discussion of the political and personal qualities and competence of candidates, and the right to campaign for them at meetings, in the press, and on television and radio.

The expenses involved in holding elections to Soviets of People's Deputies shall be met by the state.

Article 101. Deputies to Soviets of People's Deputies shall be elected by constituencies.

A citizen of the USSR may not, as a rule, be elected to more than two Soviets of People's Deputies.

Elections to the Soviets shall be conducted by electoral commissions consisting of representatives of public organisations and work collectives, and of meetings of servicemen in military units.

The procedure for holding elections to Soviets of People's Deputies shall be defined by the laws of the USSR, and of Union and Autonomous Republics.

Article 102. Electors give mandates to their Deputies.

The appropriate Soviets of People's Deputies shall examine electors' mandates, take them into account in drafting economic and social development plans and in drawing up the budget, organise implementation of the mandates, and inform citizens about it.

Chapter 14

PEOPLE'S DEPUTIES

Article 103. Deputies are the plenipotentiary representatives of the people in the Soviets of People's Deputies.

In the Soviets, Deputies deal with matters relating to state, economic, and social and cultural development, organise implementation of the decisions of the Soviets, and exercise control over the work of state bodies, enterprises, institutions and organisations.

Deputies shall be guided in their activities by the interests of the state, and shall take the needs of their constituents into account and work to implement their electors' mandates.

Article 104. Deputies shall exercise their powers without discontinuing their regular employment or duties.

During sessions of the Soviet, and so as to exercise their deputy's powers in other cases stipulated by law, Deputies shall be released from their regular employment or duties, with retention of their average earnings at their permanent place of work.

Article 105. A Deputy has the right to address inquiries to the appropriate state bodies and officials, who are obliged to reply to them at a session of the Soviet.

Deputies have the right to approach any state or public body, enterprise, institution, or organisation on matters arising from their work as Deputies and to take part in considering the questions raised by them. The heads of the state or public bodies, enterprises, institutions or organisations concerned are obliged to receive Deputies without delay and to consider their proposals within the time-limit established by law.

Article 106. Deputies shall be ensured conditions for the unhampered and effective exercise of their rights and duties.

The immunity of Deputies, and other guarantees of their activity as Deputies, are defined in the Law on the Status of Deputies and other legislative acts of the USSR and of Union and Autonomous Republics.

Article 107. Deputies shall report on their work and on that of the Soviet to their constituents, and to the work collectives and public organisations that nominated them.

Deputies who have not justified the confidence of their constituents may be recalled at any time by decision of a majority of the electors in accordance with the procedure established by law.

Chapter 15

THE SUPREME SOVIET OF THE USSR

Article 108. The highest body of state authority of the USSR shall be the Supreme Soviet of the USSR.

The Supreme Soviet of the USSR is empowered to deal with all matters within the jurisdiction of the Union of Soviet Socialist Republics, as defined by this Constitution.

The adoption and amendment of the Constitution of the USSR; admission of new Republics to the USSR; endorsement of the formation of new Autonomous Republics and Autonomous Regions; approval of the state plans for economic and social development, of the Budget of the USSR, and of reports on their execution; and the institution of bodies of the USSR accountable to it, are the exclusive prerogative of the Supreme Soviet of the USSR.

Laws of the USSR shall be enacted by the Supreme Soviet of the USSR or by a nationwide vote (referendum) held by decision of the Supreme Soviet of the USSR.

Article 109. The Supreme Soviet of the USSR shall consist of two chambers: the Soviet of the Union and the Soviet of Nationalities.

The two chambers of the Supreme Soviet of the USSR shall have equal rights.

Article 110. The Soviet of the Union and the Soviet of Nationalities shall have equal numbers of deputies.

The Soviet of the Union shall be elected by constituencies with equal populations.

The Soviet of Nationalities shall be elected on the basis of the following representation: 32 deputies from each Union Republic, 11 deputies from each Autonomous Republic, five deputies from each Autonomous Region, and one deputy from each Autonomous Area.

The Soviet of the Union and the Soviet of Nationalities, upon submission by the credentials commissions elected by them, shall decide on the validity of Deputies' credentials, and, in cases in which the election law has been violated, shall declare the election of the Deputies concerned null and void.

Article 111. Each chamber of the Supreme Soviet of the USSR shall elect a Chairman and four Vice-Chairmen.

The Chairmen of the Soviet of the Union and of the Soviet of Nationalities shall preside over the sittings of the respective chambers and conduct their affairs.

Joint sittings of the chambers of the Supreme Soviet of the USSR shall be presided over alternately by the Chairman of the Soviet of the Union and the Chairman of the Soviet of Nationalities.

Article 112. Sessions of the Supreme Soviet of the USSR shall be convened twice a year.

Special sessions shall be convened by the Presidium of the Supreme Soviet of the USSR at its discretion or on the proposal of a Union Republic, or of not less than one-third of the Deputies of one of the chambers.

A session of the Supreme Soviet of the USSR shall consist of separate and joint sittings of the chambers, and of meetings of the standing commissions of the chambers or commissions of the Supreme Soviet of the USSR held between the sittings of the chambers. A session may be opened and closed at either separate or joint sittings of the chambers.

Article 113. The right to initiate legislation in the Supreme Soviet of the USSR is vested in the Soviet of the Union and the Soviet of Nationalities, the Presidium of the Supreme Soviet of the USSR, the Council of Ministers of the USSR, Union Republics through their highest bodies of state authority, commissions of the Supreme Soviet of the USSR and standing commissions of its chambers, Deputies of the Supreme Soviet of the USSR, the Supreme Court of the USSR, and the Procurator-General of the USSR.

The right to initiate legislation is also vested in public organisations through their All-Union bodies.

Article 114. Bills and other matters submitted to the Supreme Soviet of the USSR shall be debated by its chambers at separate or joint sittings.

Where necessary, a bill or other matter may be referred to one or more commissions for preliminary or additional consideration.

A law of the USSR shall be deemed adopted when it has been passed in each chamber of the Supreme Soviet of the USSR by a majority of the total number of its Deputies. Decisions and other acts of the Supreme Soviet of the USSR are adopted by a majority of the total number of Deputies of the Supreme Soviet of the USSR.

Bills and other very important matters of state may be submitted for nationwide discussion by a decision of the Supreme Soviet of the USSR or its Presidium taken on their own initiative or on the proposal of a Union Republic.

Article 115. In the event of disagreement between the Soviet of the Union and the Soviet of Nationalities, the matter at issue shall be referred for settlement to a conciliation commission formed by the chambers on a parity basis, after which it shall be considered for a second time by the Soviet of the Union and the Soviet of Nationalities at a joint sitting. If agreement is again not reached, the matter shall be postponed for debate at the next session of the Supreme Soviet of the USSR or submitted by the Supreme Soviet to a nationwide vote (referendum).

Article 116. Laws of the USSR and decisions and other acts of the Supreme Soviet of the USSR shall be published in the languages of the Union Republics over the signatures of the Chairman and Secretary of the Presidium of the Supreme Soviet of the USSR.

Article 117. A Deputy of the Supreme Soviet of the USSR has the right to address inquiries to the Council of Ministers of the USSR, and to Ministers and the heads of other bodies formed by the Supreme Soviet of the USSR. The Council of Ministers of the USSR, or the official to whom the inquiry is addressed, is obliged to give a verbal or written reply within three days at the given session of the Supreme Soviet of the USSR.

Article 118. A Deputy of the Supreme Soviet of the USSR may not be prosecuted, or arrested, or incur a court-imposed penalty, without the sanction of the Supreme Soviet of the USSR or, between its sessions, of the Presidium of the Supreme Soviet of the USSR.

Article 119. The Supreme Soviet of the USSR, at a joint sitting of its chambers, shall elect a Presidium of the Supreme Soviet of the USSR, which shall be a standing body of the Supreme Soviet of the USSR, accountable to it for all its work and exercising the functions of the highest body of state authority of the USSR between sessions of the Supreme Soviet, within the limits prescribed by the Constitution.

Article 120. The Presidium of the Supreme Soviet of the USSR shall be elected from among the Deputies and shall consist of a Chairman, First Vice-Chairman, 15 Vice-Chairmen (one from each Union Republic), a Secretary, and 21 members.

Article 121. The Presidium of the Supreme Soviet of the USSR shall:

1. name the date of elections to the Supreme Soviet of the USSR;
2. convene sessions of the Supreme Soviet of the USSR;
3. co-ordinate the work of the standing commissions of the chambers of the Supreme Soviet of the USSR;
4. ensure observance of the Constitution of the USSR and conformity of the Constitutions and laws of Union Republics to the Constitution and laws of the USSR;
5. interpret the laws of the USSR;
6. ratify and denounce international treaties of the USSR;
7. revoke decisions and ordinances of the Council of Ministers of the USSR and of the Councils of Ministers of Union Republics should they fail to conform to the law;
8. institute military and diplomatic ranks and other special titles; and confer the highest military and diplomatic ranks and other special titles;
9. institute orders and medals of the USSR, and honorific titles of the USSR; award orders and medals of the USSR; and confer honorific titles of the USSR;
10. grant citizenship of the USSR, and rule on matters of the renunciation or deprivation of citizenship of the USSR and of granting asylum;
11. issue All-Union acts of amnesty and exercise the right of pardon;
12. appoint and recall diplomatic representatives of the USSR to other countries and to international organisations;
13. receive the letters of credence and recall of the diplomatic representatives of foreign states accredited to it;
14. form the Council of Defence of the USSR and confirm its com-

position; appoint and dismiss the high command of the Armed Forces of the USSR;

15. proclaim martial law in particular localities or throughout the country in the interests of defence of the USSR;

16. order general or partial mobilisation;

17. between sessions of the Supreme Soviet of the USSR, proclaim a state of war in the event of an armed attack on the USSR, or when it is necessary to meet international treaty obligations relating to mutual defence against aggression;

18. and exercise other powers vested in it by the Constitution and laws of the USSR.

Article 122. The Presidium of the Supreme Soviet of the USSR, between sessions of the Supreme Soviet of the USSR and subject to submission for its confirmation at the next session, shall:

1. amend existing legislative acts of the USSR when necessary;
2. approve changes in the boundaries between Union Republics;
3. form and abolish Ministries and State Committees of the USSR on the recommendation of the Council of Ministers of the USSR;
4. relieve individual members of the Council of Ministers of the USSR of their responsibilities and appoint persons to the Council of Ministers on the recommendation of the Chairman of the Council of Ministers of the USSR.

Article 123. The Presidium of the Supreme Soviet of the USSR promulgates decrees and adopts decisions.

Article 124. On expiry of the term of the Supreme Soviet of the USSR, the Presidium of the Supreme Soviet of the USSR shall retain its powers until the newly elected Supreme Soviet of the USSR has elected a new Presidium.

The newly elected Supreme Soviet of the USSR shall be convened by the outgoing Presidium of the Supreme Soviet of the USSR within two months of the elections.

Article 125. The Soviet of the Union and the Soviet of Nationalities shall elect standing commissions from among the Deputies to make a preliminary review of matters coming within the jurisdiction of the Supreme Soviet of the USSR, to promote execution of the laws of the

USSR and other acts of the Supreme Soviet of the USSR and its Presidium, and to check on the work of state bodies and organisations. The chambers of the Supreme Soviet of the USSR may also set up joint commissions on a parity basis.

When it deems it necessary, the Supreme Soviet of the USSR sets up commissions of inquiry and audit, and commissions on any other matter.

All state and public bodies, organisations and officials are obliged to meet the requests of the commissions of the Supreme Soviet of the USSR and of its chambers, and submit the requisite materials and documents to them.

The commissions' recommendations shall be subject to consideration by state and public bodies, institutions, and organisations. The commissions shall be informed, within the prescribed time-limit, of the results of such consideration or of the action taken.

Article 126. The Supreme Soviet of the USSR shall supervise the work of all state bodies accountable to it.

The Supreme Soviet of the USSR shall form a Committee of People's Control of the USSR to head the system of people's control.

The organisation and procedure of people's control bodies are defined by the Law on People's Control in the USSR.

Article 127. The procedure of the Supreme Soviet of the USSR and of its bodies shall be defined in the Rules and Regulations of the Supreme Soviet of the USSR and other laws of the USSR enacted on the basis of the Constitution of the USSR.

Chapter 16

THE COUNCIL OF MINISTERS OF THE USSR

Article 128. The Council of Ministers of the USSR, i.e. the Government of the USSR, is the highest executive and administrative body of state authority of the USSR.

Article 129. The Council of Ministers of the USSR shall be formed by the Supreme Soviet of the USSR at a joint sitting of the Soviet of the Union and the Soviet of Nationalities, and shall consist of the Chairman of the Council of Ministers of the USSR, First Vice-Chairmen and Vice-Chairmen, Ministers of the USSR, and Chairmen of State Committees of the USSR.

The Chairmen of the Councils of Ministers of Union Republics shall be *ex officio* members of the Council of Ministers of the USSR.

The Supreme Soviet of the USSR, on the recommendation of the Chairman of the Council of Ministers of the USSR, may include in the Government of the USSR the heads of other bodies and organisations of the USSR.

The Council of Ministers of the USSR shall tender its resignation to a newly-elected Supreme Soviet of the USSR at its first session.

Article 130. The Council of Ministers of the USSR shall be responsible and accountable to the Supreme Soviet of the USSR and, between sessions of the Supreme Soviet of the USSR, to the Presidium of the Supreme Soviet of the USSR.

The Council of Ministers of the USSR shall report regularly on its work to the Supreme Soviet of the USSR.

Article 131. The Council of Ministers of the USSR is empowered to deal with all matters of state administration within the jurisdiction of the Union of Soviet Socialist Republics insofar as, under the Constitution, they do not come within the competence of the Supreme Soviet of the USSR or the Presidium of the Supreme Soviet of the USSR.

Within its powers the Council of Ministers of the USSR shall:

1. ensure direction of economic, social, and cultural development; draft and implement measures to promote the well-being and cultural development of the people, to develop science and engineering, to ensure rational exploitation and conservation of natural resources, to consolidate the monetary and credit system, to pursue a uniform prices, wages, and social security policy, and to organise state insurance and a uniform system of accounting and statistics; and organise the management of industrial, constructional, and agricultural enterprises and amalgamations, transport and communications undertakings, banks, and other organisations and institutions of All-Union subordination;

2. draft current and long-term state plans for the economic and social development of the USSR and the Budget of the USSR, and submit them to the Supreme Soviet of the USSR; take measures to execute the state plans and Budget; and report to the Supreme Soviet of the USSR on the implementation of the plans and Budget;

3. implement measures to defend the interests of the state, protect socialist property and maintain public order, and guarantee and protect citizens' rights and freedoms;

4. take measures to ensure state security;

5. exercise general direction of the development of the Armed Forces of the USSR, and determine the annual contingent of citizens to be called up for active military service;

6. provide general direction in regard to relations with other states, foreign trade, and economic, scientific, technical, and cultural co-operation of the USSR with other countries; take measures to ensure fulfilment of the USSR's international treaties; and ratify and denounce intergovernmental international agreements;

7. and when necessary, form committees, central boards and other departments under the Council of Ministers of the USSR to deal with matters of economic, social and cultural development, and defence.

Article 132. A Presidium of the Council of Ministers of the USSR, consisting of the Chairman, the First Vice-Chairmen, and Vice-Chairmen of the Council of Ministers of the USSR, shall function as a standing body of the Council of Ministers of the USSR to deal with questions relating to guidance of the economy, and with other matters of state administration.

Article 133. The Council of Ministers of the USSR, on the basis of, and in pursuance of, the laws of the USSR and other decisions of the Supreme Soviet of the USSR and its Presidium, shall issue decisions and ordinances and verify their execution. The decisions and ordinances of the Council of Ministers of the USSR shall be binding throughout the USSR.

Article 134. The Council of Ministers of the USSR has the right, in matters within the jurisdiction of the Union of Soviet Socialist Republics, to suspend execution of decisions and ordinances of the Councils of

Ministers of Union Republics, and to rescind acts of ministries and state committees of the USSR, and of other bodies subordinate to it.

Article 135. The Council of Ministers of the USSR shall co-ordinate and direct the work of All-Union and Union-Republican ministries, state committees of the USSR, and other bodies subordinate to it.

All-Union ministries and state committees of the USSR shall direct the work of the branches of administration entrusted to them, or exercise inter-branch administration, throughout the territory of the USSR directly or through bodies set up by them.

Union-Republican ministries and state committees of the USSR direct the work of the branches of administration entrusted to them, or exercise inter-branch administration, as a rule, through the corresponding ministries and state committees, and other bodies of Union Republics, and directly administer individual enterprises and amalgamations of Union subordination. The procedure for transferring enterprises and amalgamations from Republic or local subordination to Union subordination shall be defined by the Presidium of the Supreme Soviet of the USSR.

Ministries and state committees of the USSR shall be responsible for the condition and development of the spheres of administration entrusted to them; within their competence, they issue orders and other acts on the basis of, and in execution of, the laws of thc USSR and other decisions of the Supreme Soviet of the USSR and its Presidium, and of decisions and ordinances of the Council of Ministers of the USSR, and organise and verify their implementation.

Article 136. The competence of the Council of Ministers of the USSR and its Presidium, the procedure for their work, relationships between the Council of Ministers and other state bodies, and the list of All-Union and Union-Republican ministries and state committees of the USSR are defined, on the basis of the Constitution, in the Law on the Council of Ministers of the USSR.

Chapter 17

HIGHER BODIES OF STATE AUTHORITY AND ADMINISTRATION OF A UNION REPUBLIC

Article 137. The highest body of state authority of a Union Republic shall be the Supreme Soviet of that Republic.

The Supreme Soviet of a Union Republic is empowered to deal with all matters within the jurisdiction of the Republic under the Constitutions of the USSR and the Republic.

Adoption and amendment of the Constitution of a Union Republic; endorsement of state plans for economic and social development, of the Republic's Budget, and of reports on their fulfilment; and the formation of bodies accountable to the Supreme Soviet of the Union Republic are the exclusive prerogative of that Supreme Soviet.

Laws of a Union Republic shall be enacted by the Supreme Soviet of the Union Republic or by a popular vote (referendum) held by decision of the Republic's Supreme Soviet.

Article 138. The Supreme Soviet of a Union Republic shall elect a Presidium, which is a standing body of that Supreme Soviet and accountable to it for all its work. The composition and powers of the Presidium of the Supreme Soviet of a Union Republic shall be defined in the Constitution of the Union Republic.

Article 139. The Supreme Soviet of a Union Republic shall form a Council of Ministers of the Union Republic, i.e. the Government of that Republic, which shall be the highest executive and administrative body of state authority in the Republic.

The Council of Ministers of a Union Republic shall be responsible and accountable to the Supreme Soviet of that Republic or, between sessions of the Supreme Soviet, to its Presidium.

Article 140. The Council of Ministers of a Union Republic issues decisions and ordinances on the basis of, and in pursuance of, the legislative acts of the USSR and of the Union Republic, and of decisions and ordinances of the Council of Ministers of the USSR, and shall organise and verify their execution.

Article 141. The Council of Ministers of a Union Republic has the right to suspend the execution of decisions and ordinances of the Councils of Ministers of Autonomous Republics, to rescind the decisions and orders of the Executive Committees of Soviets of People's Deputies of Territories, Regions, and cities (i.e. cities under Republic jurisdiction) and of Autonomous Regions, and in Union Republics not divided into regions, of the Executive Committees of district and corresponding city Soviets of People's Deputies.

Article 142. The Council of Ministers of a Union Republic shall coordinate and direct the work of the Union-Republican and Republican ministries and of state committees of the Union Republic, and other bodies under its jurisdiction.

The Union-Republican ministries and state committees of a Union Republic shall direct the branches of administration entrusted to them, or exercise inter-branch control, and shall be subordinate to both the Council of Ministers of the Union Republic and the corresponding Union-Republican ministry or state committee of the USSR.

Republican ministries and state committees shall direct the branches of administration entrusted to them, or exercise interbranch control and shall be subordinate to the Council of Ministers of the Union Republic.

Chapter 18

HIGHER BODIES OF STATE AUTHORITY AND ADMINISTRATION OF AN AUTONOMOUS REPUBLIC

Article 143. The highest body of state authority of an Autonomous Republic shall be the Supreme Soviet of that Republic.

Adoption and amendment of the Constitution of an Autonomous Republic; endorsement of state plans for economic and social development, and of the Republic's Budget; and the formation of bodies accountable to the Supreme Soviet of the Autonomous Republic are the exclusive prerogative of that Supreme Soviet.

Laws of an Autonomous Republic shall be enacted by the Supreme Soviet of the Autonomous Republic.

Article 144. The Supreme Soviet of an Autonomous Republic shall elect a Presidium of the Supreme Soviet of the Autonomous Republic and shall form a Council of Ministers of the Autonomous Republic, i.e. the Government of that Republic.

Chapter 19

LOCAL BODIES OF STATE AUTHORITY AND ADMINISTRATION

Article 145. The bodies of state authority in Territories, Regions, Autonomous Regions, Autonomous Areas, districts, cities, city districts, settlements, and rural communities shall be the corresponding Soviets of People's Deputies.

Article 146. Local Soviets of People's Deputies shall deal with all matters of local significance in accordance with the interests of the whole state and of the citizens residing in the area under their jurisdiction, implement decisions of higher bodies of state authority, guide the work of lower Soviets of People's Deputies, take part in the discussion of matters of Republican and All-Union significance, and submit their proposals concerning them.

Local Soviets of People's Deputies shall direct state, economic, social and cultural development within their territory; endorse plans of economic and social development and the local budget; exercise general guidance over state bodies, enterprises, institutions and organisations subordinate to them; ensure observance of the laws, maintenance of law and order, and protection of citizens' rights; and help strengthen the country's defence capacity.

Article 147. Within their powers, local Soviets of People's Deputies shall ensure the comprehensive, all-round economic and social development of their area; exercise control over the observance of legislation by enterprises, institutions and organisations subordinate to higher authorities and located in their area; and co-ordinate and supervise their activity as regards land use, nature conservation, building, employment of manpower, production of consumer goods, and social, cultural, communal and other services and amenities for the public.

Article 148. Local Soviets of People's Deputies shall decide matters within the powers accorded them by the legislation of the USSR and of the appropriate Union Republic and Autonomous Republic. Their decisions shall be binding on all enterprises, institutions, and organisations located in their area and on officials and citizens.

Article 149. The executive-administrative bodies of local Soviets shall be the Executive Committees elected by them from among their deputies.

Executive Committees shall report on their work at least once a year to the Soviets that elected them and to meetings of citizens at their places of work or residence.

Article 150. Executive Committees of local Soviets of People's Deputies shall be directly accountable both to the Soviet that elected them and to the higher executive and administrative body.

Chapter 20

COURTS AND ARBITRATION

Article 151. In the USSR justice is administered only by the courts.

In the USSR there are the following courts: the Supreme Court of the USSR, the Supreme Courts of Union Republics, the Supreme Courts of Autonomous Republics, Territorial, Regional, and city courts, courts of Autonomous Regions, courts of Autonomous Areas, district (city) people's courts, and military tribunals in the Armed Forces.

Article 152. All courts in the USSR shall be formed on the principle of the electiveness of judges and people's assessors.

People's judges of district (city) people's courts shall be elected for a term of five years by the citizens of the district (city) on the basis of universal, equal and direct suffrage by secret ballot. People's assessors of district (city) people's courts shall be elected for a term of two and a half years at meetings of citizens at their places of work or residence by a show of hands.

Higher courts shall be elected for a term of five years by the corresponding Soviet of People's Deputies.

The judges of military tribunals shall be elected for a term of five years by the Presidium of the Supreme Soviet of the USSR and people's assessors for a term of two and a half years by meetings of servicemen.

Judges and people's assessors are responsible and accountable to their electors or the bodies that elected them, shall report to them, and may be recalled by them in the manner prescribed by law.

Article 153. The Supreme Court of the USSR is the highest judicial body in the USSR and supervises the administration of justice by the courts of the USSR and Union Republics within the limits established by law.

The Supreme Court of the USSR shall be elected by the Supreme Soviet of the USSR and shall consist of a Chairman, Vice-Chairmen, members, and people's assessors. The Chairmen of the Supreme Courts of Union Republics are *ex officio* members of the Supreme Court of the USSR.

The organisation and procedure of the Supreme Court of the USSR are defined in the Law on the Supreme Court of the USSR.

Article 154. The hearing of civil and criminal cases in all courts is collegial; in courts of first instance cases are heard with the participation of people's assessors. In the administration of justice people's assessors have all the rights of a judge.

Article 155. Judges and people's assessors are independent and subject only to the law.

Article 156. Justice is administered in the USSR on the principle of the equality of citizens before the law and the court.

Article 157. Proceedings in all courts shall be open to the public. Hearings *in camera* are only allowed in cases provided for by law, with observance of all the rules of judicial procedure.

Article 158. A defendant in a criminal action is guaranteed the right to legal assistance.

Article 159. Judicial proceedings shall be conducted in the language of the Union Republic, Autonomous Republic, Autonomous Region, or Autonomous Area, or in the language spoken by the majority of the people in the locality. Persons participating in court proceedings, who do not know the language in which they are being conducted, shall be ensured the right to become fully acquainted with the materials in the case; the services of an interpreter during the proceedings; and the right to address the court in their own language.

Article 160. No one may be adjudged guilty of a crime and subjected to punishment as a criminal except by the sentence of a court and in conformity with the law.

Article 161. Colleges of advocates are available to give legal assistance to citizens and organisations. In cases provided for by legislation citizens shall be given legal assistance free of charge.

The organisation and procedure of the bar are determined by legislation of the USSR and Union Republics.

Article 162. Representatives of public organisations and of work collectives may take part in civil and criminal proceedings.

Article 163. Economic disputes between enterprises, institutions, and organisations are settled by state arbitration bodies within the limits of their jurisdiction.

The organisation and manner of functioning of state arbitration bodies are defined in the Law on State Arbitration in the USSR.

Chapter 21

THE PROCURATOR'S OFFICE

Article 164. Supreme power of supervision over the strict and uniform observance of laws by all ministries, state committees and departments, enterprises, institutions and organisations, executive-administrative bodies of local Soviets of People's Deputies, collective farms, co-operatives and other public organisations, officials and citizens is vested in the Procurator-General of the USSR and procurators subordinate to him.

Article 165. The Procurator-General of the USSR is appointed by the Supreme Soviet of the USSR and is responsible and accountable to it and, between sessions of the Supreme Soviet, to the Presidium of the Supreme Soviet of the USSR.

Article 166. The procurators of Union Republics, Autonomous Republics, Territories, Regions and Autonomous Regions are appointed by the Procurator-General of the USSR. The procurators of Autonomous Areas and district and city procurators are appointed by the Procurators of Union Republics, subject to confirmation by the Procurator-General of the USSR.

Article 167. The term of office of the Procurator-General of the USSR and all lower-ranking procurators shall be five years.

Article 168. The agencies of the Procurator's Office exercise their powers independently of any local bodies whatsoever, and are subordinate solely to the Procurator-General of the USSR.

The organisation and procedure of the agencies of the Procurator's Office are defined in the Law on the Procurator's Office of the USSR.

THE EMBLEM, FLAG, ANTHEM, AND CAPITAL OF THE USSR

Article 169. The State Emblem of the Union of Soviet Socialist Republics is a hammer and sickle on a globe depicted in the rays of the sun and framed by ears of wheat, with the inscription "Workers of All Countries, Unite!" in the languages of the Union Republics. At the top of the Emblem is a five-pointed star.

Article 170. The State Flag of the Union of Soviet Socialist Republics is a rectangle of red cloth with a hammer and sickle depicted in gold in the upper corner next to the staff and with a five-pointed red star edged in gold above them. The ratio of the width of the flag to its length is 1:2.

Article 171. The State Anthem of the Union of Soviet Socialist Republics is confirmed by the Presidium of the Supreme Soviet of the USSR.

Article 172. The Capital of the Union of Soviet Socialist Republics is the city of Moscow.

THE LEGAL FORCE OF THE CONSTITUTION OF THE USSR AND PROCEDURE FOR AMENDING THE CONSTITUTION

Article 173. The Constitution of the USSR shall have supreme legal force. All laws and other acts of state bodies shall be promulgated on the basis of and in conformity with it.

Article 174. The Constitution of the USSR may be amended by a decision of the Supreme Soviet of the USSR adopted by a majority of not less than two-thirds of the total number of Deputies of each of its chambers.